Your Guide to

PHOTOGRAPHY

*the text of this book is printed
on 100% recycled paper*

EVERYDAY HANDBOOKS

Your Guide to

PHOTOGRAPHY

HELEN FINN BRUCE

BARNES & NOBLE BOOKS

A DIVISION OF HARPER & ROW, PUBLISHERS

New York, Evanston, San Francisco, London

FOREWORD

Although it is apparent to anyone connected with photography that changes in methods and equipment are too fast and frequent for any individual to keep track of, there are many basic photographic principles which continue to hold true. Yet too many amateurs, in a rush toward quick results, bypass these fundamentals from which they could benefit with even a little study.

Your Guide to Photography is a welcome find which makes an excellent basis for such study. By combining a knowledge of photography with professional writing experience the author has provided, in clear layman's language, a well organized compilation of photographic information which neither skimps on technical explanations nor dwells on complicated techniques. This book should prove a practical teaching aid and casual reference text, as well as a general introduction to the subject, for anyone interested in a better understanding of photography.

FRANK F. ERICSON
Member of the
Professional Photographers of America, Inc.

PREFACE

A decade ago it was possible to ask someone "who knows about photography" a simple question or two and obtain some clear-cut answers. Now the acceleration of photographic products and relevant data has developed "specialists" rather than "family doctors"; and seldom do the opinions or even the "facts" of the experts agree. Nor should they: for one who is glibly certain he has all the answers has ceased to look at the questions. This text, consequently, represents not an unarguable consensus but my understanding of the information it includes, reinforced wherever practicable by first-hand trials and errors.

This guidebook is intended for beginners, or even more proficient photographers, who are interested in learning or reviewing some of the principles and basic techniques that underlie the taking and making of photographs; it is not a course in professional photography, nor is it addressed to those advanced "amateurs" who are so often more "expert" than many professionals. Recently I had occasion to show a young student how a handful of snapshots could be improved by handling the camera thus and so. A few minutes later he turned to me with a gratifying smile and said, "You know, you explained that so well, I'm never going to forget how to do it." I hope I have done as well with the explanations in these pages.

My foremost indebtedness is to George L. Cantzlaar (author of the Barnes & Noble Everyday Handbook *Your Guide to the Weather*) not only for his helpful starter suggestions about organizing the material but most of all for the illustrations. Since they are such an important part of this book, and since he is responsible for obtaining all of the illustrations and permission for their inclusion, I consider him a kind of "co-author." My personal thanks go with his to Miss Betty Wolcott of Eastman Kodak's editorial service for her invaluable assistance in supplying so many excellent prints on a wide variety of subjects, most of them derived from prize-winning photographs in national competitions. Our special gratitude is due also to Wayne Waters, head of the Training Publications Branch, Bureau of Naval Personnel, for the use of numerous technical illustrations; and to the Pictorial Branch, Office of Information, Department of the Air Force, for supplying additional art work.

I am appreciative, too, of the time and talent shared with amateurs generally by more camera-club judges and lecturers than I can name here. And I would like to thank William J. Daly of Sekonic for being one of my most obliging informants. Finally, I wish especially to thank Frank Ericson, not only for his high opinion of this book but also for his unstinting contribution of time and experience on behalf of amateurs; particularly in his training classes for the Volunteer Service Photographers, it is pleasantly apparent that, after twenty years as a successful professional, he has not forgotten how it feels to be a beginner.

H. F. B.

TABLE OF CONTENTS

1

A Look at Photography

IN THE rapidly expanding world of photography it is easy for a newcomer, or even a relatively old hand, to be so overwhelmed by complex techniques and confounding technology as to forget that picture taking can be fun. There is a nonstop parade of new developments in camera designs and accessories, in film emulsions and processing procedures. And who would want a lively art to be static? But that does not mean you must absorb every detail or master the whole realm of optics or of film manufacture and the scientific jargon of the laboratory unless you choose to. You need consider only the data relating to your camera, your goal, and your own personal interests. You may wish to study all of this text or just parts of it; or you may be satisfied with a casual reading. Only you know what interests you.

GENERAL CONSIDERATIONS

Photographic Incentives. What starts people taking pictures? Photographers themselves often don't know. It may be a new baby on the premises or a playful pet. It may be a rare visit from friends or relatives living far away. It may be spectacular scenery or some pier-sitting seagulls. It may be the unforgettable beauty of a brilliant summer day or the winter wonder of a brook carving a course through banks of snow. Travel frequently triggers the camera urge, and sometimes a business need sets one to taking pictures. Photography can be contagious, too: you might catch the "bug" from fellow vacationers or from your neighbors.

Owning a camera has long been a fundamental impulse, for the wish to preserve precious moments is universal. Photography is one way to retain and relive the big and little events that mark a personal

1

progression through life. Pictures of such events might be classified as "record" shots, but they can also be interesting photographs in their own right.

You CAN Take It with You. Another common-denominator reason for the popularity of photography is that it provides a ready outlet for creative energy—with no palette to scrape or brushes to clean. Photography is certainly no substitute for painting, but it does have its own physical as well as creative advantages: a camera can be transported more conveniently than a sketchbox and easel; and, unlike a painting, which requires a certain "showcase," a photograph can be looked at anywhere—it can be held in the hand, hung on a wall, projected on a screen, or carried in a wallet.

In addition to being a communicative and sociable hobby in itself, photography complements other hobbies or studies. The sports fan or coin collector, the fisherman or flower fancier, the standing bird watcher or speeding boatnik adds an extra thrill to his favorite projects by taking pictures and sharing his interest with others.

About the word *take:* The phrase "to take pictures" is more than idiomatic; it is significantly accurate. When you focus your lens on a group of friends or a cathedral or an orchid, you are actually *taking* something from the subject. And the subject is giving something to you. The give-and-take connotation applies further: The more study, imagination, and practice you give to photography, the more rewards you are likely to *take* from it in better pictures.

Pictures Are Everywhere. Developing the ability to see picture possibilities is often what makes photography an art as well as a pastime. One of the deep delights of exploring with your camera is the discovery of new patterns, waiting to be noticed, in familiar surroundings. As you become interested in the creation of your own pictures, you will find fresh material, original viewpoints, and new photographic opportunities all around you. And one of the great advantages of modern lenses and faster films is freedom from the whims of weather. Direct sunlight, once a must for acceptable exposures, is now not only unnecessary but frequently quite undesirable. Pictures can be taken in rain or shine, day or night, indoors or out, on trips or at home.

So learn to look with discernment and master your equipment, whether you have an inexpensive box camera or a costly miniature. A camera can be as individual as a pet: it needs to belong to someone who understands it, cares for it properly, and makes a close friend of it.

SOME FUNDAMENTAL RULES

There can be no hard and fast rules for taking pictures; rules are general guides to which the photographer must bring observation and judgment. All the points mentioned here will come up in later chapters dealing with different kinds of pictures. However, they are so basic that they should become part of your photographic thinking from the very beginning.

Closing In. First of all, as you get on closer terms with your camera, learn to get close to your pictures, too. When a photograph seems to lack interest, it is quite probable that the photographer was too far from his subject and that too much distracting background (or foreground) got into the act. An expressive face with a plain background will make a better picture than a figure competing with trees, houses, and clouds for attention. A kitten arranging a ball of yarn on a minimum of carpet will be much more interesting than a lot of carpet and chair legs with a minimum of kitty.

Guide Lines. Your outdoor scenes can have various curves and angles, but it is important to keep the horizon line straight; otherwise the whole picture will be off balance. In architectural shots, such as buildings and monuments, learn to align some straight perpendicular line of the subject with the vertical edge of your viewfinder —unless you are after a deliberate angle shot or a Leaning Tower. Avoid a too even distribution of the elements of your picture, either horizontally or vertically, as this will seem to cut the picture in two and destroy its unity; for example, try to keep at least two-thirds of a landscape view below the horizon line, or two-thirds of a sky scene above the horizon line. Also, endeavor to keep your main subject, your center of interest, out of dead center, as this usually results in a weak composition.

Framing. A photograph, like any other picture, can be greatly enhanced by its frame, by an impression that your subject is contained within appropriate boundaries. Experiment with ways to frame your pictures and give them depth; sometimes a foreground figure will do it, sometimes a doorway, a shadow, or an overhead branch. Then see that you fill the frame—not with unrelated elements but by an avoidance of blank areas.

Most still cameras can be held to take horizontal or vertical views, so don't get into the habit of holding yours only one way. For example, a reclining figure generally belongs in a horizontal frame and a tall standing figure in a vertical frame.

Haste Makes Waste. Some pictures must be snapped in a hurry or missed completely. On the whole, however, you will find it worthwhile to take time to study your pictures before you click the shutter —and afterwards. Have a really good look at what you see in your viewfinder, from several angles, before you decide where you and your camera should be positioned. Then, equally important, study your finished photographs, both good and bad; mistakes frequently furnish the most persuasive instruction.

Basic Precepts. Make it a habit also to analyze photographs in newspapers and magazines; try to discover why it is that some of them capture and hold your attention more than others. You will find that most of the interesting ones follow these three rules:

> *Keep it simple.* A direct, uncomplicated statement is, visually as well as orally, the most effective.
>
> *Use contrast backgrounds.* Keep a light object against a dark background, or a dark object against a light background, so that you can tell readily what it is.
>
> *Give it a personal viewpoint.* Your pictures express you as surely as your speech or your handwriting. Try to convey your interest in what you see.

Practice does not necessarily make perfect. Experienced camera fans as well as beginners find that photography, like life, is full of ups and downs, trials and errors, elation and consternation. An "expert" may appear to produce only good pictures, but this may be so because he shows only the ones that make him look good. He has taken many that you never see and has wisely learned to discard more than he keeps. So don't envy him: go ahead and take your own pictures. And remember that pictures—like paintings, music, and words—have different meanings for different people; seldom are two opinions identical. If a picture really pleases you, you are entitled to consider it a good picture.

2

```
┌─────────────────────────────────────────┐
│   Cameras: Selection and Handling        │
└─────────────────────────────────────────┘
```

"WHICH CAMERA should I get"? is undoubtedly the number one question asked by newcomers to this country's number one hobby, and it can and does produce a baffling multitude of answers. Even the basic camera classifications are subject to change—as a comparison of the annual buying guides of photography magazines from one year to another attests.

PRELIMINARY QUESTIONS

If you already own a camera and wish to replace or supplement it, you probably know what features are most important to you. But if you are buying your first camera, you should start by assessing your photographic intentions. Until you know more or less what your goals and preferences are, you cannot ask questions and get answers that might help guide your choice. Even with some appropriate questions, you may find that every "expert" will have a different recommendation. As a first step, try asking yourself the following questions:

> Do I expect to take pictures just for pleasure or more for business?
> Do I plan to photograph mostly outdoors or indoors?
> Am I interested primarily in color?
> If so, do I want color slides for projection or color prints for an album?
> Do I plan to take extremely close close-ups?
> Am I likely to shoot a lot of very fast action?
> Will I be taking many pictures of buildings and other architectural subjects?
> Do I intend to become a darkroom do-it-yourselfer?

Will I want many accessories? Extra lenses?

Is my photographic economy based on a strict-budget, a shoot-the-works, or an in-between plan?

Just how much time and study am I prepared to give to photography?

Add more questions of your own to the list and see how your answers shape up. Sometimes answers and useful suggestions can be found in camera clubs, which are generally cordial to newcomers and visitors. Senior members of such groups are glad to try to help beginners; moreover, a clubber's opinion may be less biased than that of a dealer who is in the business of selling photographic equipment. Another source of information is the annual "buying guide" in year-end issues of monthly magazines like *Popular Photography* and *Modern Photography*. They provide extensive data about cameras and other items, information that can answer some questions but cannot tell you which camera you should have. That decision must be yours. One of the important points to remember in making it is that, whether you spend five dollars or five hundred dollars, there there is no one camera that is best for every kind of photography.

Some of the great and gone camera models that are still in use and available in stores which carry used cameras may also be detailed in some special issue of a photography magazine. Sometimes this used-camera listing includes dates, specifications, the going price bracket, and other information that is helpful if you are considering buying a secondhand camera from a store or from an individual.

CAMERA CATEGORIES AND VARIATIONS

Despite endless variations all cameras have a few fundamentals in common. Every camera starts out as a lighttight compartment for housing a lens, shutter, and diaphragm at the front and a support to carry film at the back. Every camera can take black-and-white or color pictures. Every camera has some sort of winder to advance the film and a counter to tell you how many pictures you have taken. But from there on, individualism reigns, with cameras falling generally into two broad categories: preset and adjustable. The former term refers to cameras having a fixed focus and few adjustable controls, the latter to cameras whose controls can be set by the operator. Not many years ago cameras fitted readily into fairly rigid categories such as box types, folding cameras, miniatures, twin-lens reflexes, and press cameras. Now the classifications overlap and shift to an extent that defies any permanent pigeonholing. Favorites disappear, and sometimes return. New types appear, to dazzle briefly or to win long-term favor. And quite often the esoteric nomenclature of individual manufacturers contributes to the confusion.

Many of today's cameras are "automatic" types, which usually means that the lens aperture adjusts automatically to the existing light and signals in the viewfinder if the light is inadequate. These are also called "electric eye" or "EE" cameras; they are not a separate group but may be preset or adjustable, and of various sizes. Many cameras are classified according to the film size they use, such as 35mm or rollfilm cameras; but, as you will see from the descriptions to follow, this covers a lot of territory. Some small cameras have built-in flash units; some have built-in exposure meters.

Other variations are in shutter speeds, from a fixed speed of about 1/50 second to an adjustable 1/1000 second; in shutter types and viewfinders (see Chapter 4); in the additional lenses and other accessories that a camera accepts; and in the aperture, shutter speed, and distance markings. Before discussing the camera types in more detail, it might be practical to have a brief look at the wide categories and a few of the variations to be encountered within them:

> *Preset Cameras* include "box" or "simple" types with minimum adjustments or none at all. They are sometimes classified as "rollfilm" cameras to encompass simple reflex and other modifications of the basic cameras.
>
> *Twin-lens Reflex Cameras* are also referred to as "rollfilm" cameras, but more often as "2¼ reflex" cameras. "Twin-lens" usually refers to a camera that has two lenses in vertical alignment and a waist-level groundglass viewfinder, and that takes rollfilm pictures 2¼ x 2¼ inches.
>
> *35mm Cameras* are sometimes still called by their original "miniature" designation. However, their subdivisions of "rangefinder" and "single-lens reflex" have become more usual, especially with the advent of more subminiatures, half-frames, and other sub-35mm types.
>
> *Smaller Cameras* include cameras using 35mm film but producing twice as many half-frame pictures as a standard 35mm camera; subminiatures using 8mm, 16mm, or in-between film sizes; and odd sizes like the Kodak Instamatics.
>
> *Professional Cameras,* which refer to groups of larger-than-

35mm cameras, include costly 2¼ x 2¼ single-lens reflexes (sometimes disconcertingly called "rollfilm reflex" cameras); press and view cameras; and a handful of cameras for very specialized uses.

Other Cameras include Polaroid Land cameras, stereo cameras, and home-movie cameras. "Folding" cameras, once a sizable category, are no longer being manufactured.

Some popular cameras representative of these different categories are illustrated in Figures 1 through 9.

Preset Cameras. Cameras known as the box type are the easiest to operate and the most inexpensive and rugged. From time to time they offer various improvements, and they are usually fitted with a flash connection. The variations may be quite superficial since the manufacturers, in presetting the equipment, leave a minimum of decision-making to the operator. Fully preset box cameras are designed for normally bright days outdoors or flash shots indoors. The focus is fixed at a distance of about fifteen feet which, at a small aperture, keeps everything in a picture reasonably sharp from approximately eight feet to infinity. Usually there is one shutter speed, about 1/50 of a second (it may be a trifle faster on some new models and slower on old models which were intended for slower films), and one aperture around $f/11$ or $f/16$.

Some so-called simple cameras are preset for one or two variables but not for all three. For example, a camera may have a limited range of f/stops although its shutter speed and focus are fixed. Close-ups are not in the province of preset cameras. The near-point

Fig. 1.—Box camera.

Fig. 2.—Instamatic camera.

limit varies with different models, but you should not attempt to get closer than five or six feet with any box camera; all simple cameras perform better if your subject is somewhat farther away than the near limit.

There is a good choice of roll films for box cameras but, since films are subject to almost as much change as cameras, you should ascertain what size a specific camera takes and what kinds of film are available in that size. Color negative films for color prints (e.g., Kodacolor), as well as popular black-and-white makes, fit box cameras; and some models provide for making color slides in a super size which is larger than 35mm but fits standard 2-inch cardboard mounts. The definition that good enlargements require should not be expected from a box camera.

Twin-lens Reflex Cameras. This type is identified by its two lenses in vertical alignment and its pop-up hood which protects a square, groundglass focusing screen. You look down into this viewfinder to see the subject as it will appear in the photograph except that the image is reversed from right to left; when the image in the groundglass looks sharp, the subject is in focus. Since the $2\frac{1}{4}$ picture is square, there is no decision to make about holding the camera horizontally or vertically.

Fig. 3.—Twin-lens camera.

Twin-lens reflexes have a *finding* lens and a *taking* lens, which are not always identical: the top lens is the finder and may not be quite as well corrected as the bottom lens which takes the picture. The aperture of the finder lens is wide open to give as bright an image as possible on the groundglass, and both lenses are focus-controlled simultaneously. Because the two lenses are on different levels, parallax can be a problem. (*Parallax* refers to the disconcerting habit some cameras have of chopping off the top of a subject's head. See page 58.) Obviously if the taking lens is below the finding lens, it will see a small fraction less at the top of the picture than the finding lens sees. Some models have parallax-correction indicators and, if so, this is specifically stated; otherwise the photographer must learn through practice to make his own correction with a slight upward tilt of the camera.

Films for the twin-lens and other rollfilm cameras have a protective paper backing with vital statistics like the ASA index number (film speed) printed on it at the start of the roll. Standard roll films have 12 exposures and are removed from the camera without rewinding. The $2\frac{1}{4}$ x $2\frac{1}{4}$ picture is a satisfactory viewing size in contact prints, and much easier to crop than the 35mm size; it is often possible to enlarge one portion of a negative to obtain a print with a closeup effect from a not-so-close shot. Color slides in the $2\frac{1}{4}$ x $2\frac{1}{4}$ size are generally more brilliant and dramatic than 35mm slides but their cost per slide is greater and they do not fit all projectors.

The very adaptable twin-lens camera is popular with many amateurs and some professionals, particularly for journalism and illustration work. The approximately waist-level position at which it is held is especially advantageous in photographing children because it allows you to talk to them without hiding part of your face while focusing. The advantages of the twin-lens reflex balance the disadvantages of parallax and the fact that its two lenses and normal 75mm focal length make it somewhat bulkier than 35mm types.

35mm Cameras. The introduction of a "candid camera" in the years just prior to 1930 attracted hundreds of fans who were intrigued by the novelty of being able to snap unsuspecting subjects with an inconspicuous yet precise instrument. These first miniatures (made in Europe by Leitz) had well-corrected lenses (previously found in large cameras with greater focal lengths). They used short strips of 35mm film (previously used only in motion-picture cameras). Hand held, they could take pictures under adverse light conditions (previously the province of careful time exposures). Furthermore, they could utilize many fascinating extra gadgets. In fact, it was not uncommon in the early days of amateur photography to see an eager fan so intent on his satchel-load of accessories that his camera was no longer "miniature" nor his snapshots very "candid."

Catching subjects off guard ceased to be a factor in the miniature's popularity as more and more of the original "accessories" were built into bulkier and bulkier cameras, but the introduction of color to 35mm film supplied even greater momentum. The original Eastman Kodachrome remained *the* amateur color film for many years and has only recently given way to its faster successors. Because of their top popularity, 35mm cameras have the widest choice of film speeds and types in color or black-and-white and the most widespread availability of generally dependable processing.

Rewind feature: A unique characteristic of the true miniature, besides the lightproof metal cassettes in which the film comes, is the wind-and-rewind mechanism. The exposed 35mm film must be wound back from the takeup spool into its original container before the camera is opened to remove the film. Although this might seem a slight disadvantage to someone in a big hurry, the extra step has the advantage of making it possible to remove a partly exposed film from a 35mm camera and reinsert it later (see page 22).

35mm variations: Because it is the favorite amateur size, the 35mm camera has probably more variations than any other type—many of them applying to rangefinder or single-lens reflex cameras although the two kinds are generally classified separately. A 35mm camera can have a lens speed for catching faster action than the average amateur has any use for, or a moderate speed which may seem poky by comparison but is more than adequate for most purposes. Furthermore, with today's stepped-up film speeds, a relatively slow lens plus a fast film can use the same light conditions as a fast lens plus a slower film—so one can have a "fast" camera either way. Shutter speeds can be up to 1/1000 of a second, though 1/500 or less is usual. For more about types of shutters and apertures, see Chapter 4.

Many 35mm cameras accept separate lenses, such as wide-angle and telephoto, as well as a host of optional accessories. If lens interchangeability, or any additional supplementary equipment, is important to you, ask about it before deciding on your camera.

RANGEFINDER CAMERAS. This designation refers, often rather loosely, to most 35mm cameras without the prism-mirror mechanism characteristic of the single-lens reflex camera which may also have a rangefinder. A so-called rangefinder camera may have a single-window range-viewfinder or separate windows or a built-in optical viewfinder. Because this type of 35mm camera has a viewing and a taking lens, parallax must be considered. Some models have parallax-correction devices, which are usually frameline markings on the viewfinder, while others have none. Many have between-the-lens shutters; some have focal-plane shutters or behind-the-lens shutters, either of which permits lens interchangeability.

Most 35mm cameras have rapid-wind levers which advance the film and cock the shutter simultaneously. This prevents unintentional double exposures, but in some cases it also interferes with intentional multiple exposures, so this is a point to check when you choose a camera. Shutter speeds vary, as do *f*/stop markings and individual features. In general, these cameras are more compact than other adjustable types, but there is no limit to their variety—probably because they are the most numerous category and the most in demand. Their prices have a greater spread than other types, too, from well under fifty dollars to—well, to a Leica.

SINGLE-LENS REFLEX (SLR) CAMERAS. Because focusing is through the camera's one lens, all single-lens reflexes are parallax-proof: you see exactly what you will get, including depth-of-field changes as the lens is stopped down or opened up. The eye-level prism finder of an SLR lets you look straight ahead at a right-side-up, normal left-to-right image—the way you would view a subject with other eye-level viewers. But instead of seeing it beyond the camera, you view a mirror image reflected from a groundglass focusing screen within the camera. When you are all set to click the shutter, the mirror that relays the picture preview must quickly fly out of the way so that the lens will take the actual scene and not the reflected image.

A problem of early SLR models was blackout, or the case of the vanishing image: when the mirror flew up, it stayed up until the shutter was wound for the next exposure—leaving the operator sans mirror, sans image, during the interim. Most single-lens reflexes have an instantaneous mirror-return mechanism which sends the mirror up for the brief instant of exposure, then promptly drops it back into viewing position. Another basic feature is the fully automatic diaphragm: this means that the lens opens to maximum aperture after each exposure to provide a bright image during focusing, then automatically closes down to the selected *f*/stop when the shutter is released.

Its great versatility has made the single-lens reflex first choice

Fig. 4.—35mm Leica rangefinder.

Fig. 5.—Single-lens reflex camera.

Fig. 6.—Subminiature camera.

of a majority of serious amateurs. It lends itself to the closer-than-normal trend in photos and is often used with closeup accessories—supplementary lenses, extension tubes or bellows—which enable it to get within a few inches of a small subject while maintaining adequate depth of field. It is especially well adapted to nature studies, such as close-ups of flowers and insects, and to still-life compositions. Versatility is increased by the fact that most modern SLR cameras accept interchangeable lenses and a wealth of other photographic tools. As always, variety is rampant, so ask about the specific designs in which you may be interested.

Smaller Cameras. The main subdivisions of this arbitrary category are the 35mm types currently referred to as "half-frame" and the subminiatures using 16mm or narrower film.

HALF-FRAME 35MM CAMERAS. The relatively recent appearance of several models of this type probably indicates a reaction to the gradually increased size of regular 35mm cameras, a desire for more compactness in a camera that still uses 35mm film. Actually, back in those early "candid" days, there were cameras that took the size picture presently described as half-frame; then it was called single-frame and for quite a while today's standard 35mm picture was called double-frame.

The lenses of the new half-frame cameras have a 28-30mm focal length; the 35mm wording of the camera-type designation refers to their use of 35mm film. But instead of the standard 20 or 36 exposures, these cameras get 40 or 72 per roll. The contact prints are pretty tiny, of course, but the half-frame 35mm camera offers an economical way to take a lot of snapshots with a view to having jumbo or postcard-size prints made of just a few good ones. Other modern features are similar to standard 35mm cameras but shutter speeds generally are not as fast.

SUBMINIATURES. If this type had appeared along with the early "candids," it probably would have been dubbed just plain miniature without the "sub." These cameras, also known as "ultraminiatures," can be really inconspicuous, and many people get surprisingly good results with them. Focusing must be accurate, camera movement avoided, and processing controlled precisely—for it is not exactly easy to achieve sharpness in even a jumbo print from such a tiny negative.

Subminiatures have lenses of short focal lengths, but the variations make it difficult to say what is "average" either in lens size or in adjustable and automatic features. Nor have films and cartridges the standardization and interchangeability of other camera categories, though this may come in time. A majority of subminiatures use 16mm film, some use smaller film, and the number of frames per roll varies also. The films come in a double cartridge, called a *film load,* which is dropped into position in the camera and requires no rewind prior to removal of the exposed film.

Because these drop-in double cartridges are designed for a particular camera, they do not have the widespread availability of 35mm and roll films; therefore, it is a good idea to check on whether a shop in your locality stocks them before buying your camera. The shop may handle processing, too, and may be able to tell you what processor specializes in that work so you can mail your films direct. The best-known subminiatures are of foreign craftsmanship.

First to be adopted to any extent by amateur photographers was the Minox, originally designed as an undercover instrument. Balancing the actual and potential drawbacks of the subminiature is the convenience of a fairly fast camera that fits in the palm of your hand.

Professional Cameras. This category, not intended for amateurs in general, should be of academic interest at least to any novices who may be considering photography as a career.

SINGLE-LENS REFLEXES FOR ROLL AND SHEET FILMS. The combined advantages of the single-lens reflex and the twin-lens reflex to provide parallax-free focusing on a waist-level groundglass, and negative sizes $2\frac{1}{4}$ x $2\frac{1}{4}$ or larger, are to be found in a few expensive cameras such as the Hasselblad. These are the elite and are usually referred to by their individual names rather than by a general name. Their impressive capabilities are not found in any of the types used by most amateurs; they are more akin to those of press cameras. The cameras in this group are much less bulky than press types and, on the average, cost more.

PRESS AND VIEW CAMERAS. A few amateurs elect to work with professional cameras, usually of the press classification. One advantage is that such cameras allow the making of one or two pictures without concern about rolls of film. Another is that the 4 x 5 negative produces a contact print of useful size and enlargements that retain sharpness. The chief disadvantage is that, compared with 35mm cameras, press cameras are heavy and cumbersome.

Press cameras are essentially stripped-down view cameras and are intended for portability. Their prototype was the single-lens Graflex

Fig. 7.—Graphic press camera.

Fig. 8.—Polaroid Land camera.

camera and even today its Graphic successors are practically synonymous with press cameras, although they are often used outside the sphere of journalism. The 4 x 5 format is standard for press or view cameras but other sizes are available. View cameras, which are designed for mounting on a very sturdy and rigid tripod, are bulkier and slower to operate than press types. They have numerous swings, slides, rises, and tilts similar to those of large studio cameras.

Other Cameras. In this final group are three camera types, each of which is a distinct classification in itself.

POLAROID LAND CAMERAS. In a solo category are Polaroid Land cameras, which have undergone many changes since the combination of processing chemicals with negative and positive films introduced the novelty of "a picture in a minute." The earliest models, in which development took place inside the camera, were only for black-and-white prints; the prints were one-of-a-kind and required prompt coating with a prescribed liquid to protect them from scratches.

Newer models became speedier and more versatile, and additional improvements keep appearing. The time for a black-and-white picture was reduced to ten seconds, and a color picture was produced in fifty seconds. Now special film packs are used and development takes place outside the camera so that one picture can be taken right after another. For models such as the Polaroid Automatic 100 Land Camera, the standard picture size at the present writing is $3\frac{1}{4}$ x $4\frac{1}{4}$ inches. For users of 4 x 5 press and view cameras there is a special Polaroid Land Film Holder and a film pack that produces both print and negative.

STEREO CAMERAS. Three-dimensional realism is the aim of stereo photography; so, quite naturally, a stereo camera has two identical lenses in horizontal alignment, like a pair of eyes. Also, like average eyes, stereo lenses are about two-and-a-half inches apart, center to center, and they take two pictures simultaneously on the same film; one picture corresponds to what your left eye sees with the right eye closed, the other vice versa. Stereo cameras use 35mm film in standard cartridges, and the end product is a twin color-transparency for either hand viewing or projection.

The first rule for handling a stereo camera is to keep it level as well as steady. It is all right to tilt it up at a high building, or down at a canyon, but not sideways; that would result in some weird effects—as if one eye looked up while the other looked down. An unwanted tilt could be corrected by do-it-yourself mounting, but standard mounts do not tilt.

Stereo hand viewers are lineal descendants of the stereoscopic slide holder from great-grandmother's parlor and similar to modern one-at-a-time viewers except that they have two viewing lenses and a double-length slot for the twin-slide cardboard mount. Hand viewers are reasonably satisfactory for looking at pictures that take in about six feet to infinity, but not for close-ups. A stereo projector is desirable for an audience of more than one, and so is a different mount. There are different types, to be placed between glass and used for closeup, medium, or far-

ther viewing. If you have ever attended a 3-D movie, you know that you wear polarizing "glasses" and that sections toward the front and center of the seating area offer the best view, as they do in stereo projection.

HOME-MOVIE CAMERAS. While home movies and still photographs seem to remain on opposite sides of a very high fence, the two types of photography have much in com-

Fig. 9.—8mm movie camera.

mon. Cameras and the subject of home movies generally are discussed in Chapter 21.

LEARNING TO USE A CAMERA

Camera Parts. Once you have decided on your camera, get to know it intimately. The instruction manual or booklet that comes with a camera is vital to its correct and trouble-free use since camera makes vary so much. Study the camera and the booklet together to determine what each letter, each number, each arrow, each lever, each knob stands for and how it operates. Consult your camera dealer if necessary and *keep the booklet* even when you think you no longer need to refer to it. If the booklet for your camera has been lost, write the manufacturer for a duplicate; and get into the habit of keeping it where you keep your camera and accessories.

Study your camera systematically, part by part, either from front to back or in the order in which the parts are listed in the booklet. Figure 10 indicates most of the parts on one 35mm camera which, although typical, may be quite different from the design of your camera; also, some of the features may be called by other names in

A Film exposure counter
B Shutter release
C Shutter-speed dial
D Film advance lever
E Prism/Mirror housing (SLR only)
F Diaphragm ring (f/stops)
G Depth-of-field scale
H Distance scale
I Focusing ring
J Lens
K Rewind knob
L Type-of-film reminder
M Flash terminals
N Back lock

O Viewfinder
P Focal plane shutter
Q Film cassette chamber
R Tripod head attached to tripod socket
S Film pressure plate
T Film perforation sprockets
U Film takeup spool
V Film-rewind release button

Fig. 10.—Partial identification of typical 35mm camera parts. (Front and back views of Pentax courtesy of Honeywell Photographic Products) other cameras. Handle the camera as you study it, and give it several dry runs before you put in any film. Aim it at different subjects to see how steady you can hold it and what you can see in the viewfinder from different angles. Click away as if you were taking pictures so that you will lessen the risk of losing pictures by fumbling later.

Common Errors in Camera Handling. Besides the parallax already mentioned, blur is a most common photographic error. When a picture turns out blurred all over, it is usually because the camera moved during exposure; a partial blur is generally the result of motion by the subject. One way to improve camera steadiness is to keep your arms in close to your body and to hold a deep breath while you click. If you have an eye-level viewfinder, try pressing the camera against your cheek. If glasses interfere, try pressing your thumb against the back of the camera and against the side of your nose. If you have a waist-level viewfinder, hold the camera close but not pressed against the body and pull down slightly on the neck strap. Always press the shutter release gently. A point frequently overlooked is that the photographer's stance is as important to steadiness as his hands. If you place one foot well ahead of the other, like a bipod, you not only have a tripod-like firmness but you can bend easily at the knees to lower and raise the camera position.

Unintentional double exposures from forgetting to advance the film after each picture are less common than formerly because many cameras are designed to prevent this particular error. Still a common error, however, is the blackout caused by forgetting to remove the lens cap, or a partial blackout caused by allowing a thumb or camera case to get in front of the lens during exposure.

LOADING AND REMOVING FILM

Since specific instructions for your camera should be followed, only a few general ones are included here. First, open the camera according to directions and find out where the film is supposed to go and how it should move inside the camera before trying to install it. Look for helpful little arrows, but *never force anything* that does not turn or move easily. If something doesn't move, there is a reason. Look again and refer to the instruction booklet. Whether you are loading roll film or 35mm, be sure to *get the film in straight* or it will almost certainly cause trouble later. Note also that any film should be inserted or removed in subdued light.

Loading Rollfilm Cameras. Box and twin-lens reflex types of cameras have a removable spool near the winding knob. The films have a protective paper backing and a paper leader to guide them onto the spool. Roll films generally are not packaged with separate information leaflets but have the ASA index and exposure-count numbers printed compactly on the paper leader. It is a good idea to jot down the type and index of the film you are loading and to either slip the notation inside the leather carrying case or attach it to the back of the camera with a bit of masking tape until the roll is removed. After you have noted the printed information, insert the leader into a slot of the takeup spool, keeping a finger lightly on the film so that it will not unroll. A method that usually works efficiently with a twin-lens or similar type is to hold the camera in your lap, with the open back away from you. Try to use a smooth, almost continuous motion in turning the winding knob. Printed arrows on the paper backing indicate when the film locks in place. Then shut the case and wind the film-advance knob until number "1" appears in the little counter window to tell you that the film is in position for the first picture.

Unless you want to surprise yourself with some modernistic effects, always remember to advance the film after each exposure. After the last exposure, wind until more arrows signal that the film has been taken up on the spool. Open the case and remove film for processing.

Loading and Removing 35mm Film. Cameras that use 35mm film have a wind-and-rewind mechanism and, near the film-advance lever, a fixed takeup spool. The rewind knob is usually marked by an "R" and arrow. The film has no protective backing but comes in light-proof little cartridges called *cassettes*. Very useful and informative leaflets are packaged with the film and it is a good habit to look at them regularly, not only to familiarize yourself with the recommendations but to note any unexpected changes in them. Another good habit is to slip the folded leaflet between the camera and its case as a reminder; it is very easy to forget whether you have loaded your camera with a color film rated ASA 25 or a black-and-white film rated ASA 400 if the film is not used up right away.

To load, open the camera back and insert the film leader into the slot of the takeup spool. See that the mechanism is set for "A" (advance), and be sure that the sprockets of the little wheels next to the spool engage the perforations at the edges of the film as you wind it onto the spool. When the film is correctly anchored, close the camera and advance two blank frames to get any lightstruck film out of the way. Set the counter for your first picture; some count from "1" up to the last exposure, some count from 36 or 20 down to "1." Advance the film after each exposure; but if your camera has a single-stroke lever that simultaneously advances the film and cocks the shutter, see that the shutter is not left in the wound-up position for an indefinite length of time.

To remove 35mm film, set the mechanism at "R" and rewind the film into its original cassette. Turn the rewind knob gently, learning to look, feel, and listen. There will probably be a revolving dot to watch as you turn; also there will be a little click and a slight tug when the film goes off the takeup spool. If the entire film has been exposed, wind (or push) the leader all the way into the cassette so that it cannot be mistaken for a new film and reloaded into the camera.

However, if you wish to remove a partly exposed film in mid-reel, stop winding when you get the little click and the slight tug in order to leave the leader outside the cassette for reloading. Note at what number you removed the film, and wrap a notation of the number of frames already exposed around the cassette before putting it aside. When reloading the partly used film it is not necessary to use a darkroom but it is important to keep the lens covered, either by a lens cap or holding it face down on a dark surface such as a table or a book while you advance the previously exposed film. Allow a loss of at least one frame (two to be on the safe side) in the transfer, and see that the counter is reset for the number of frames still to be exposed.

A word about buying film: what might perhaps be listed as an additional common error is carelessness about ordering film for your camera. Films are discussed at length in Chapter 6 but, as an elementary step, you should ascertain what size your camera accepts and what types are available in that size. Know whether you want a slow or a fast film, for example, whether you want color film for slides or prints, whether your film comes in a choice of 20 or 36 exposures (as 35mm films do) or just in 12 exposures (as 120 roll films do). Then ask clearly and correctly for the film you want.

3

```
┌─────────────────────────────────────────────┐
│         Theory and Behavior of Light         │
└─────────────────────────────────────────────┘
```

THE FIRST fundamental requirement for a photograph is light. Obvious, you may say, yet such a simple basic fact is sometimes overlooked. It is true that with the fascinating and fast-growing complex of photographic wonders nowadays, less and less light is needed to make a good picture. But even our miracle-making scientists have not yet foreseen the time when they will be able to take photographs in total darkness. And anyway, who wants to?

So, just what *is* this all-important light? For centuries physicists have been striving to determine its exact nature and to reconcile such famous and contradictory findings of the late seventeenth century as Newton's theory that a beam of light consists of a stream of infinitely minute particles with Huygens' theory that all space is occupied by a substance he called *ether*, through which light travels in small waves.

NATURE OF LIGHT

Quantum Theory. At the beginning of this century the scientist Max Planck discovered that, under certain circumstances, light can knock electrons off various substances, transferring its energy to the electrons in measurable amounts. Assuming that light energy traveled in infinitesimal particle-like packages, Planck named them *quanta;* hence the quantum theory. This was corroborated by Einstein who demonstrated, with mathematical equations, not only that quanta (or photons) have a frequency comparable to waves but also that they are actually particles of energy. Today all radiation, including light, is generally considered to be composed of electromagnetic particles with definite wave properties; and when absorbed or emitted by an atom of material, the energy is measurable.

Light Wavelengths. Light radiates from its point of origin in waves that go out in all directions until they come into contact with some substance. To visualize such radial waves, imagine dropping a pebble into a pool of still water: now watch the resulting waves move out from the pebble-point to all the various edges of the pool. Next think of several straight lines drawn from the pebble-center (or from an actual light source) to the different points on the curved lines of the waves. These imaginary straight lines indicate light rays and the *direction* of the light movement. The form of radiant energy that reaches our eyes as light can travel from the sun or from a distant star or from the glow of a small candle a few feet away.

Radio transmission works in much the same way: vibrations in the air produce waves that reach our ears as *sound,* or audio impulses.

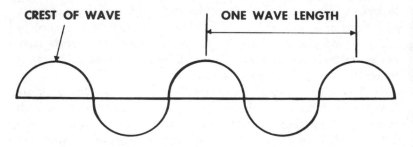

CREST OF WAVE   **ONE WAVE LENGTH**

Fig. 11.—Measurement of wavelength.

But light and sound waves have very different wavelengths. Waves that produce sound are long, but waves that produce light are extremely short. If shown in magnified lines, light waves would somewhat resemble hairpin loops. As illustrated in Figure 11, wavelengths are measured from the crest of one wave, or loop, to the crest of the next. To avoid decimals of unwieldy smallness, these measurements are usually stated in millimicrons. A meter is slightly more than three feet (39.37 inches), a millimeter is one-thousandth of a meter, and a micron is one-thousandth of a millimeter. A millimicron, therefore, is one-millionth of a millimeter. Light wavelengths vary from about 400 to 700 millimicrons, the average being about one fifty-thousandth of an inch.

The Visible Spectrum. Of the entire electromagnetic spectrum, a relatively small part is occupied by visible light, as illustrated in Figure 12. The reason for this is that neither comparatively long nor short light waves are visible to the human eye. As the wavelength shortens, the eyes gradually perceive the deepest reds at one end of the visible spectrum. As the wavelength decreases further, the eyes perceive the orange, yellow, green, blue, and violet rays. Then the wavelengths become so short that they are again invisible.

These six colors are based on the classic Newtonian spectrum from which most of our conceptions of color derive. ("Indigo," a seventh color between blue and violet, is sometimes included in illustrations referring to the visible spectrum.) Each wavelength of light has its

Fig. 12.—Electromagnetic spectrum.

own typical color; but nearly every color that we see and call by an accepted color name is a combination of various wavelengths.

White Light and Primary Colors. Our most important light source, of course, is the sun. Sunlight is termed *white light* and is an ideal or equal blending of all the wavelengths of the visible spectrum. If any of these wavelengths are missing, even in part, we have another color instead of white light.

The primary colors of the visible spectrum, which add up to white light, are not the same as pigment primaries used in mixing paints. This is frequently a source of vast confusion since most people learn the pigment primaries at nursery-school level. As a photographer, you should know that the *primary colors of photographic light* are Red, Green, and Blue. (These fundamental colors and their complementaries are discussed in detail in Chapter 9.)

Natural and Artificial Light. In general, photography makes use of two kinds of light: natural and artificial. It has become standard practice to refer to these two broad classifications, for convenience, as *daylight* and *tungsten*. Daylight actually is a combination of whatever direct sunlight is present plus sky light. Tungsten takes its name from the filaments of an ordinary electric light bulb; photograpically speaking, though, it includes all artificial light.

TRANSMISSION, REFLECTION, AND ABSORPTION

When light rays traveling in straight lines encounter any substance, they are either transmitted through it, reflected from it, or absorbed by it. What happens is dependent to a considerable degree on whether the medium is transparent, translucent, or opaque—as shown in Figure 13.

Fig. 13.—Effect of media on light rays.

Transmission. Light can be transmitted, or passed through, transparent and translucent substances. A clear window glass through which an object can be seen distinctly is an example of a *transparent* medium; it permits maximum transmission of light. A frosted glass pane, through which light is visible but through which objects are seen indistinctly, is an example of a *translucent* medium; it transmits diffused light. A wood door or a brick wall is an *opaque* medium and transmits no light.

Reflection. Reflected light describes rays that are bounced back from the surface of the object encountered instead of being transmitted or absorbed by it. Light rays that strike the surface of an object are termed *incident* (literally: falling upon) rays, and their point of contact is called the *point of incidence*. Reflected light falls into two categories: specular and diffused.

Specular light travels in one direction. When the incident light strikes a perfectly smooth surface, it rebounds from the point of impact at exactly the same angle as the incident ray. Figure 14 illustrates this cherished principle of Physics I: the angle of incidence equals the angle of reflection.

Fig. 14.—Reflected light.

Diffused light travels in more than one direction. If a light ray strikes an uneven surface, the light obviously cannot be reflected at an even angle; the incident rays will be tossed back at various angles, making the light diffused. Once again look at Figure 14. Since absolutely smooth, polished surfaces are rather a rarity in ordinary encounters, most of the light you will use in photography will be diffused.

Absorption. Light is absorbed by different substances much as water is taken up by a sponge. There is always some degree of absorption whenever light rays encounter any surface. Furthermore, the way in which a given object absorbs incident light determines its color to a great extent. Dull-finish black fabrics and deep woodlands, for example, absorb far more light than a white cloth or a snowy landscape. The colors we think of as neutral—like black, white, and some grays—absorb the primary colors of the light rays in almost equal amounts. It is the difference in the reflective properties of these so-called neutrals that affects our perception of their colors. A totally black surface refuses to reflect any appreciable amount of light and can be filmed only by contrast with other colors. White is just the opposite in its highly reflective character and needs the contrast of darker tones to be recorded properly in a photograph.

When you see red—in something such as a dress or tie—the reason is that the object is absorbing the blue and green rays of the incident white light and reflecting the red rays. In the same way, grass looks green because it tends to absorb all the red and blue rays, sending back to your eyes mostly the green rays. Because different objects absorb different kinds and amounts of incident light, you can use filters to exercise considerable control over the color values of your pictures, especially over the gray tones of your black-and-whites. (The subject of filters is covered in Chapter 10.)

REFRACTION

The rays of light striking the clear glass head-on in Figure 13 are so-called normal rays. Their air-travel speed of 186,000 miles per second is reduced when they go through the glass, which has a greater density than that of air, but they are being transmitted straight through the heavier substance in a line perpendicular to the surface.

Law of Refraction. When light rays strike the glass at an angle, however, you have a more interesting phenomenon. The glass then bends the rays of light, forcing on them a change in direction. When light obliquely enters a transparent substance of different density from the one in which it is traveling, the resultant change in direction is known as *refraction.* Knowledge of the effects of refraction underlies the design and manufacture of optical and photographic lenses. Refraction follows a fixed law: *when a ray of light obliquely enters a medium of greater density, refraction is toward the normal; when a ray of light obliquely enters a medium of lesser density, refraction is away from the normal.* This rule is shown diagrammatically in Figure 15.

Fig. 15.—Law of refraction.

Index of Refraction. The speeds at which light travels through substances of varying degrees of transparency are measurable and determine the light-bending capacity of the substance. The measure of this ability, a sort of local speed limit, is termed the *index of refraction*. If light travels one-and-a-half times as fast in air as in a specific piece of glass, for instance, the refractive index of that glass is 1.5. By shaping the surfaces of a piece of glass, as in making a prism, it is possible to control the *degree* to which the light will be bent.

OTHER CHARACTERISTICS OF LIGHT

Besides refraction and the other properties already described, light has several interesting habits and abilities affecting the design and use of lenses. Sometimes these properties are a big help; sometimes one or another of them can be a big headache. A brief look at three common characteristics follows.

Dispersion. The component colors of white light do not all refract equally; this is because of their different wavelengths. When a ray of light enters a prism, its colors disperse according to length. As you know from the illustration of the electromagnetic spectrum earlier in this chapter, red has the longest (700 millimicrons) and violet the shortest (400 millimicrons) light wavelength. To repeat, the shorter the wavelength, the greater will be its refraction—i.e., its deviation from the normal. The longest wavelength will be bent least. This separation of white-light components is known as *dispersion,* illustrated in Figure 16. You can imagine that if you were trying to persuade a lens to bend many visible color rays to one precise point, dispersion could be quite a tricky problem.

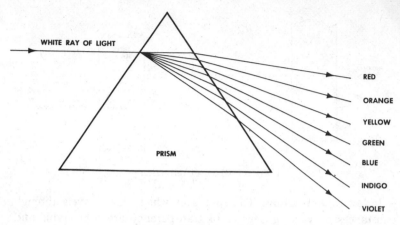

Fig. 16.—Dispersion of light.

Diffraction. When light strikes the edge of an opaque medium, it has a tendency to scatter slightly. As the rays go past some opaque object, such as a ball, a deep shadow forms, ringed by a lighter area with a blurred edge. The outermost rim of the lighter blurry edge darkens toward the inner part and merges with the black center, thus evidencing that some light has scattered into the shadow. This scattering of light is called *diffraction*.

Diffraction is readily discernible in a pinhole type of camera. With this primitive photographic instrument, images are pretty much in focus without being sharply defined. The sharpness of definition, or lack of it, depends on the pinhole size: too small an opening will

Fig. 17.—Diffraction of light.

scatter some light, while too large an opening will admit more than one ray from the same object point. Light scattering can result from various causes in any camera, as you will note in the chapter on lenses.

Polarization. In ordinary light waves the vibrations are supposed to be in all possible directions perpendicular to the ray. *Polarization* is a process of affecting the light so that the vibrations assume a definite direction, such as straight lines, circles, or ellipses.

Filters or screens designed to polarize light are very useful in certain kinds of photography, especially when it is necessary to

Fig. 18.—Light plane polarized by reflection.

minimize glare. Light-wave vibrations can be restricted to one plane, as shown in Figure 18. This diagram indicates how ordinary light, reflected in one (specular) direction from a nonmetallic object at an angle of 30 to 35 degrees, is polarized so that the vibrations are parallel to the reflecting surface. Other angles can also effect some polarization, but not at zero or 90-degree extremes.

THE PINHOLE PRINCIPLE

You can't put an image on film without light, but you can produce a picture without a lens. The *camera obscura,* Latin for *dark chamber,* preceded our modern photographic mechanisms by several centuries; and even now you will sometimes hear a simple preset camera fondly referred to as "the little black box." A dark box or a dark room—any lighttight compartment—can be used to form an image on film placed inside the box at the wall opposite a small hole which admits a beam of light. There is no focusing problem, no reshaping of the object as sometimes occurs with corrected lenses, and you can have as large an image as your box size allows.

But while such an image will be more or less "in focus," you should not expect it to be really sharp. If the pinhole is very tiny, light rays will strike the edges, causing diffraction and a fuzzily edged image. If the hole is too large, it will admit multiple rays and make the entire image blurred. If the pinhole manages to be exactly the right size for the box and object, the image will be reasonably sharp. This is illustrated by the three diagrams in Figure 19.

Fig. 19.—Characteristics of images formed by different size pinholes: (A) pinhole too small; (B) pinhole too large; (C) pinhole correct size.

Inverted Image. Another pinhole illustration, Figure 20, shows why images on film are always upside-down, whether they are formed by pinholes or by a modern camera lens. Notice that the line representing a ray of light from the top of the tree slants downward to the pinhole. As it enters the opening, the ray continues in the same direction, thus putting the top of the tree on the bottom of the film or of the box wall. The ray from the base of the tree travels upward through the pinhole to the top of the image area. Hence the *inverted image* that is characteristic of photography.

Suppose we see what happens if the dark box acquires more than

Fig. 20.—Inverted image.

one pinhole. Assume that it has two holes. Two images would appear. Right? If the twin images could be superimposed, of course, the resulting image would have a double portion of light and so would be twice as bright as either separate image. Now apply the refraction principle (page 28) and place a precisely angled prismatic glass at each pinhole. Imagine here that both beams of light are refracted to the same point and imprismed, as it were, in a single image. All right, how about trying four pinholes with four prisms around the original center pinhole? If the holes are the correct size and the

Fig. 21.—Multiple pinhole images made to coincide.

surfaces of the refracting prisms at the correct angles, the result should be one image five times as bright as the single-pinhole tree we started with. This hypothetical tree is illustrated in Figure 21.

The foregoing facts about prisms and control of *direction* of light and about apertures and control of *amount* of light bring us directly to the subject of lenses.

4

$$\boxed{\text{Lenses}}$$

THE LENS element is the camera's eye, recording the image it sees on a light-sensitive film which remembers the image and repeats it in print or on a slide. A camera is, in fact, merely a light-gathering mechanism whose parts correspond quite remarkably to those of the human eye: *lens* = pupil, *diaphragm* = iris, *shutter* = eyelid, and *film* = retina.

To understand more clearly how a photographic lens works, recall the law of refraction explained in the preceding chapter. This fundamental law of physics concerns the change in direction of light rays: in passing from one transparent medium into a more dense one, refraction is toward the normal; into a less dense one, refraction is away from the normal. Because light travels faster or slower in different substances, it can be controlled by varying the substance, such as optical glass, and imparting to it a high or low refractive index. X rays, although of the same nature as light rays, are extremely short and travel right through a substance; they allow no control of their direction, which is why they make shadow patterns instead of photographs.

POSITIVE AND NEGATIVE LENSES

Positive, convergent lenses act essentially like base-to-base prisms. Figure 22 shows triangular prisms having only four refracting surfaces. You will observe that although the refracted light rays intersect, they do not do so at a single point. Now imagine the prisms with their surfaces rounded into convex curves possessing many more refracting possibilities. The *biconvex* shape will be thickest at the center and thin out toward the edges. These curvatures will form an image by pulling light rays to a definite point of convergence, the top half of

Fig. 22.—Above: Convergent refraction of light rays by two base-to-base prisms.

Fig. 23.—Below: Refraction of parallel light rays by a positive lens.

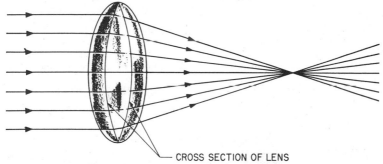

CROSS SECTION OF LENS

the convex lens bending incident rays downward and the bottom half of the lens bending the rays upward, as shown in Figure 23.

Simple positive lenses can have other shapes than the biconvex. One is a half-convex, as if a double-convex lens had been cut down the center to give it one flat plane opposite a convex curve—like half a football. The third most common simple lens shape is a concave-convex curve—like a quarter moon—which is known most often as the *positive meniscus.*

The meniscus is a single piece of glass tapering from center thickness to thin edges and is frequently used alone in low-cost cameras of simple construction. Such a lens, like a box camera, can perform quite satisfactorily within its limitations which usually restrict the feasible apertures to $f/11$, or smaller, and limit the color of light in which really sharp images can be obtained on modern panchromatic films. A simple meniscus lens, not corrected for chromatic aberration, will

Fig. 24—Above: Divergent refraction of light rays by two apex-to-apex prisms.

Fig. 25.—Below: Refraction of parallel light rays by a negative lens.

CROSS SECTION OF LENS

focus images of light rays from different zones of the spectrum on different planes, thus decreasing the potential sharpness of the photograph.

Negative, divergent lenses are concave in shape, as if two prisms were joined apex to apex (Figure 24). A negative lens cannot focus light rays passing through it but causes them to diverge from the center, as illustrated in Figure 25. This type of lens is thickest at its edges, thinning toward its center. A negative lens can also be half of the biconcave shape with one flat plane opposite a concave curve; or it can be a convex-concave curve. The three shapes are just the reverse of the most common positive lens shapes.

Simple negative lenses are never used alone but are combined with positive lenses to counteract specific aberrations and so help to produce more accurate images.

FACTORS IN LENS SELECTION

The lens with which a camera is equipped depends largely on the performance expected of that camera, much as an engine may be designed for a jet plane or a small car or something in-between. Once you have decided on your kind of camera, there are certain lens characteristics to look for, which may be grouped generally as follows: (1) focal length, (2) aperture, (3) lens quality, and (4) mechanical features. First, a preview of these factors; later in this chapter they are discussed in greater detail.

Focal length is a fixed factor of lens design and cannot be varied by the camera user. Focal length represents the distance between the lens and the plane on which the image comes to a sharp focus when the subject is at infinity. The focal length, therefore, is going to determine what size image appears on the film, a longer focal length producing a larger image in less area and a shorter focal length producing a relatively smaller image with greater depth of field. All this, in turn, influences perspective by affecting the distance required to fill the picture area.

The average focal length of a lens is approximately the diagonal of the film size. For example, the popular 35mm type of camera has a 24 x 36mm (about 1 x 1½″) film size and generally has a 50mm, or two-inch, focal length. However, its lens may have a focal length as short as a 44mm or as long as 58mm. Look for this information on the lens mount.

The *aperture* is the lens opening, and the *speed* of a lens is determined by the size of its largest possible opening, known as the "maximum effective aperture." A series of f/numbers shown on the lens mount designate the different amounts of light the lens is capable of transmitting at a given setting. The lowest number, such as $f/2$, indicates the largest opening and, therefore, the speed of the lens.

This may appear as $f/2$ or f-2 or 1:2. A typical series may range from $f/2$, the largest aperture, to $f/22$, the smallest aperture.

The "f" symbol is actually an abbreviation of "focal length" and the "$/$" after it denotes a fraction; the number after the slant line completes the fraction. Thus an $f/4$ lens is one whose maximum effective aperture has a diameter equal to $\frac{1}{4}$ of its focal length. If you will remind yourself occasionally that $\frac{1}{2}$ is a larger fraction than $\frac{1}{4}$, and $\frac{1}{4}$ is considerably larger than $\frac{1}{16}$, it is easy to remember which f/numbers mean larger openings and more light and which mean smaller openings and less light.

The *quality* of a lens is judged by the sharpness of the picture it is capable of producing. This depends on the quality of the optical glass, the number of elements, and the extent to which the aberrations, or defects, of the lens components have been reduced or eliminated. The *aberrations* which an uncorrected lens may contain are (1) chromatic aberration, (2) spherical aberration, (3) coma, (4) astigmatism, (5) curvature of field, (6) distortion, and (7) flare. All of these are explained in the following pages.

By designing one component of a lens specifically to create opposing and equal aberrations that will offset those in another component, camera makers endeavor to cancel out these aberrations. The degree of correction is greater in the lenses of better cameras, and because these refinements are costly, they are reflected in the camera price. Price alone should never be the criterion of lens quality but, given the same speed and focal length, a more expensive lens can generally produce better photographic results.

After focal length, aperture, and lens quality, the final consideration in selecting a lens is the inclusion of any *mechanical extras* which may be important for your particular purpose.

Lens interchangeability and type of shutter, flash synchronization and equipment are among the points you might be concerned with. Focusing adjustments vary, as do the markings of f/stops and shutter speeds. (These various features are discussed in the different sections of this book where they are more directly relevant.)

Focal Length. The distance between the optical center of a lens and the plane where parallel light rays from an object at infinity come to a sharp focus has been termed the *focal length* of the lens. *Infinity* is defined as the distant point at which parallel lines seem to converge, as in the vanishing end of a section of railroad tracks; with most small cameras it refers to distances over fifty feet.

Since focal length is controlled by the surface curvatures and thickness of the lens, an understanding of the basic principle of lens action can sometimes be helpful to the photographer in analyzing certain problems as they are encountered.

The *principal plane* of a compound lens is its vertical axis at the joining of the two flat lens planes, indicated by the dotted line through the center of the biconvex "football" in Figure 26. The broken line cutting horizontally through the center of the football, and normal to both surfaces, is the *optical axis*. The point at which these two lines cross is the *optical center* of the lens. Since the purpose of the lens

Fig. 26.—Cross-section of convergent lens showing positions of principal plane, optical axis, and optical center.

design is to bend light rays up and down to a single focal point, it should be apparent from the diagram that only the rays traveling along the true optical axis can pass through the lens without bending.

Any light ray at an angle to the optical axis will be refracted at each lens surface in passing through the optical center. When these refractions are equal and in opposite directions—as in corrected lenses—the result will be as if the ray had gone through in a straight line. Look at Figure 27: the broken line represents the path of a

Fig. 27.—Light ray passing through optical center at an angle.

light ray through a biconvex lens, and the solid line shows how the ray starts and ends at the same points as the straight line.

When a lens is focused on an object at infinity, it is one focal length from the principal plane. At this position only, the principal plane is the same as the focal plane where film records the image. When a lens is focused on an object at any distance nearer than infinity, the movable focal plane on which the film is placed occupies a position separate from the principal plane. When a lens is focused on the nearest distance at which it can bring an object into sharp focus, the parallel rays of light converge at the "point of principal focus." (The basic technique of focusing is explained in detail in the next chapter.)

Aperture. The size of the lens aperture and the length of time it is opened determine how much light reaches the film during any one exposure. The *diaphragm,* or partition, of a camera is the mechanical device that controls the amount of light passing through the lens; it is usually referred to as the *f*/stops, collectively, and is part of every

Fig. 28.—Iris of eye and the iris diaphragm.

lens assembly. Most often this light-controlling mechanism is a series of overlapping thin metal leaves. One end of each leaf is attached to a mount inside the lens barrel and the other end to a movable circular ring on which the *f*/stops are marked. Rotating the ring moves the center of each leaf toward or away from the optical center of the lens.

Because of its close resemblance to the mechanics of the human eye, this part of the camera lens has been further labeled the *iris diaphragm,* as illustrated in Figure 28. When you turn the control ring so that it enlarges the aperture, you are "opening up" the lens. When you turn the control ring in the opposite direction to reduce the size of the opening (the way the pupil of your eye contracts within the iris to shut out excessive light in bright sunshine), you are "stopping down" the lens.

RELATIVE APERTURE RATIO. To get the best results from your lens it is important to have some understanding of the relationship between its aperture and its focal length. This relationship, or *relative aperture,* governs the brightness intensity at the focal plane where the image is recorded. The relative-aperture ratio can be written as a simple formula:

$$f/\text{number} = \frac{F \text{ (focal length of lens)}}{D \text{ (diameter of effective aperture)}}$$

This same relationship can be stated mathematically by the *inverse square law:* the intensity of light varies inversely with the square of the distance from the light source. The diagram in Figure 29, with its accompanying explanation, visualizes clearly how this applies to photography.

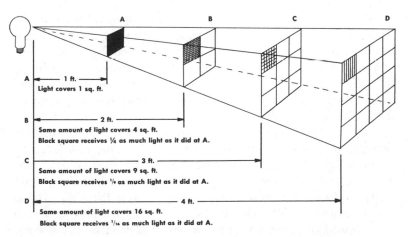

Fig. 29.—Inverse square law. Example: If you place a card one foot from a light source, the light striking the card is of a certain intensity. If the card is moved two feet away, the intensity of the light decreases with the square of the distance (2^2 or 4 times) and is $\frac{1}{4}$ as bright. If the card is moved three feet away, the decrease is 3^2 or the light is 1/9 as intense. If the card is moved four feet away, the light is 1/16 as intense.

Applying this law to the f/number formula: if the focal length of a given lens is 8 inches and the diameter of the maximum effective aperture is 2 inches, the lens has a relative aperture of 4. The same f/4 rating would apply to a lens with a 4-inch focal length and a 1-inch aperture, or to a 6-inch focal length and a $1\frac{1}{2}$-inch aperture. If the focal length is 8 inches but the effective aperture has a diameter of 4 inches, the lens has an f/2 rating. (Since inches are easier to visualize than millimeters, the foregoing examples are stated in focal lengths of large-camera lenses.)

From this you can see that if D (diameter of lens opening) is decreased, the ratio (f/numbers) will be increased. As the f/numbers increase, the relative apertures decrease. For example, an f/22 stop on a lens will be one of the smallest openings with relatively less light-transmitting capacity. The lowest f/number on the lens will admit the greatest amount of light.

THE f/VALUE SYSTEM. The system of f/numbers used to calibrate diaphragm openings was devised to standardize the markings on a wide variety of cameras. It is found on most cameras today, although a comparatively new calibration, known as the *Exposure Value System* (EVS), is being used on some cameras with cross-coupled lens and shutter dials. (EVS is discussed in Chapter 7.) Cameras with EV numbers usually have the f/markings also.

Being a ratio of the lens' focal length and opening diameter, the same f/number can be expected to transmit the same amount of light on any camera, whatever its focal length, provided that other factors remain constant. Since the shutter speed determines the length of time the light will be in contact with the film, f/stops and shutter speeds are generally lined up in a series of equivalent exposures on the lens scale.

Standard Full Stops. The f/values on a scale of full stops are arranged so that each f/number, going up the scale, transmits half as much light as the next. Or looking at it from right to left, going down the scale, you will find that each opening doubles the amount of light. (Remember those fractions—$\frac{1}{4}$ is larger than $\frac{1}{16}$! If you are not mathematically minded, the figures may not *look* as if each represented half as much light as the next, but don't worry—it does; the scale has been figured out by experts.) The STANDARD FULL STOPS are:

f/1 f/1.4 f/2 f/2.8 f/4 f/5.6 f/8 f/11 f/16 f/22 f/32 f/45 f/64

On most lenses, and on all American lenses, the lowest f/number represents the *correct value for the maximum aperture* and often does not correspond to a full stop. For example, many popular good cameras have an f/3.5 lens, with the next marking at f/4. Some cameras have markings for other intermediate or half-stops, such as f/4.5 and f/6.3. The aperture can be set anywhere between full stops whether marked or not. Most cameras do not go higher than f/22 on the scale. When a half-stop is the largest aperture, the half-as-much-light principle begins at the next f/number on that lens' scale.

These arbitrarily devised numbers do not indicate nth-degree exactitude but are sufficiently precise for all practical photographic purposes. It is a good idea to memorize the full stops on the standard f/scale; in fact, their repeated use makes memorizing almost inevitable.

T-Stops. The *transmission stop system*, rarely employed in amateur photography, is based on the f/system. But instead of using only the focal length and effective diameter of the lens, the T-system takes into account the results of the scattering, absorption, and reflection of light, and the different effects of coated and uncoated lenses. By utilizing a photoelectric cell to measure light transmission, T-stops provide more precise calibration where extreme accuracy is required, principally in professional movie cameras. For T-stops to have any appreciable advantage over f/stops, other factors affecting exposure must have equally precise control.

Lens Quality. It is a recognized fact that there are no absolutely perfect lenses, although designers and technicians are making them better and better. Nevertheless, a moderately well-corrected lens of high-quality optical glass serves most photographic requirements very well indeed.

There are two general classifications of optical glass—crown and flint—and each can vary considerably. By combining different varieties of alkali-lime crown for low-dispersion characteristics with different types of heavier, more brilliant flint glass for high dispersion in different types of single lenses, it is possible to meet the specifications of almost any design in refractive and dispersive power.

Lens designs follow a variety of formulas, usually based on previous models, and may combine one to seven elements in various ways. Besides the types of optical glass for each element and the myriad surface curvatures, other considerations in the complicated process of designing a lens include the placement of the aperture, the posi-

Fig. 30.—Lens designs vary in number of elements and other details.

tioning of the elements in relation to each other, and the air spaces. Before a new compound lens is manufactured in quantity, a prototype is first subjected to a barrage of bench tests to ascertain how successfully the aberrations inherent in simple denses have been corrected.

LENS TEST. The best test of a camera lens is to put it through a trial run of comparative picture-making yourself. One way to make a lens test is to photograph some printed matter—a page from a magazine or newspaper—at the different apertures. With the camera firmly fixed on a tripod and squarely level to a wall, take shots of the printed page tacked to the wall. Insure against camera motion by using a cable release and short exposure, and be sure to focus very accurately. Don't blame the lens for anything that could be your fault! Then start at the largest opening and go up through the range of f/stops to the smallest opening. After the negatives have been carefully developed, make a few 11 x 14 enlargements. With a good lens the printed letters will be generally sharp. With a very fast lens—say $f/2$—on a small camera, the desired sharpness should be obtained from at least $f/2.8$ on through to the smaller openings—say $f/16$ or less—where there may quite normally be some decrease in sharpness. At its largest aperture a high-speed lens on a small camera may also produce less sharpness at the edges of the negative than in the center area.

LENS ABERRATIONS. As previously noted, there are seven types of aberration which an uncorrected lens may contain. Correction of these defects during the course of lens design and manufacture is essentially a matter of good balance, since total elimination of all errors all of the time is not possible. Learning something about the different aberrations can prove useful by helping you to identify them and possibly to compensate for them yourself to some extent. Such compensation must be by trial and error since the causes and effects of the aberrations described are too varied for rules regarding supplementary "correction" in individual cameras.

Chromatic Aberration. The failure of a lens to bring light rays of different lengths, or colors, to a focus on one plane is called *chromatic aberration.* The rays that make up white light will separate into their different wavelengths when passed through a prism, or a single lens, as shown in Figure 31.

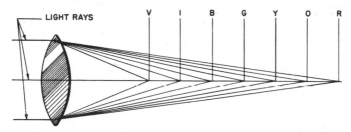

Fig. 31.—Chromatic aberration in a convergent lens.

A negative lens placed in optical contact with a simple positive lens causes sharper refraction of the longer wavelengths and less sharp refraction of the shorter wavelengths, thus pulling all of the colors nearer a common plane. A smaller aperture in the design of a compound lens can further reduce the problem.

Spherical Aberration. The inability of a lens to focus parallel central and marginal light rays at the same plane along the optical axis is termed *spherical aberration.* This is a normal defect of a simple lens with curved surfaces and makes for lack of sharp definition:

Fig. 32.—Spherical aberration in a convergent lens.

either the central area of the image will be sharp with softness in the edge areas, or vice versa, depending on the location of the focal plane.

Spherical aberration, illustrated in Figure 32, is inherent in divergent (negative) lenses also, but their concave surfaces will spread the rays up and down from the optical axis—just the opposite of the direction shown in the figure. A compound lens system equalizes these spherical errors by combining positive and negative lenses.

The design of a compound lens and its effectiveness must be looked at as a whole, however; it is not feasible to correct spherical aberration completely since that would adversely affect the chromatic correction. Additional reduction of spherical errors can be achieved by decreasing the aperture size of the lens, but this reduces image brightness as well.

Coma. The aberration labeled *coma* has a slight resemblance to a comet. It is produced by strong light rays passing through the lens edges at an angle and falling in much the same plane but at different distances from the optical axis. Because they are not accurately superimposed, such rays do not come to a true circular point but to a pear-shaped image, as illustrated in Figure 33.

Image point is in the form of a coma

Fig. 33.—Coma.

Coma is an error not generally observable by itself but is rather an aspect of spherical aberration (sometimes it is called a *lateral spherical error*) and of flare. Coma is corrected to some degree in the same manner as spherical aberration, but neither error is entirely absent from a lens.

Astigmatism. This aberration is the inability of a lens to project a sharp image of lines running at angles to each other—almost as if the lens had one focal length for horizontal and another for vertical projection. If you will look at Figure 34, you will observe that when

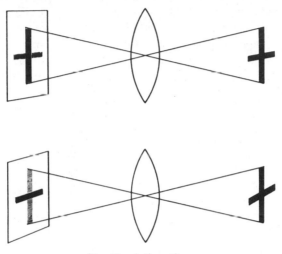

Fig. 34.—Astigmatism.

the horizontal line of the cross is in sharp focus, the vertical line is anything but sharp. By adjusting the focal plane to a greater distance from the lens, the vertical line can be focused sharply but the horizontal will be blurry. The most acceptable image of the cross will be formed by a midway focus between the horizontal and vertical focuses. Both lines will then be slightly and more evenly blurred.

A lens corrected for minimum separation between the horizontal and vertical focuses is termed *anastigmat*. These lenses are extremely complex and infinitely varied, sometimes possessing as many as ten elements. Because they are capable of producing sharp lines on a single flat plane, they are especially important when any measurements are wanted from the finished photograph. As in other aberrations, astigmatism can be lessened by using a smaller opening so that the image is projected by only the center area of the lens—in the same way that the eye records its sharpest image at the center of the retina.

An anastigmat lens may be tagged *apochromat process,* indicating a higher degree of color correction; such a lens is used for commercial color work.

Curvature of Field. When a flat-plane image comes out slightly curved, like a saucer, the aberration is referred to as *curvature of field,* illustrated in Figure 35. Because it is not possible for a simple lens with a curved image field to focus sharply at both center and edges simultaneously, one area will be blurred when the other is sharp. Here again a compromise is the standard solution: a focus between the two points of sharpness and a relatively small aperture.

Complex types of positive and negative lenses are incorporated in a compound lens system to produce sharp images on a flat focal plane. This correction imparts a flat field to the lens. As you might

OBJECT LENS IMAGE

Fig. 35.—Curvature of field.

expect, a lens with a wide angle of view will have a more apparent curvature of field than a corrected normal-angle lens. However, even very good modern lenses, if used at wide openings, will manifest some curvature of field.

Fig. 36.—Curvilinear distortion: barrel (top), pincushion (below).

Distortion. This rather general label refers to a particular kind of distortion: curvilinear. *Curvilinear distortion* is an aberration that causes the lens to render straight lines in the subject as curved lines in the image. There are two types: (1) When the image lines curve out toward the picture edges, the error is *barrel distortion* and is caused by placing the diaphragm in front of the lens. (2) When the image lines pinch inward like a wasp waist, the error is *pincushion distortion* and is caused by placing the diaphragm behind the lens. Both types are illustrated in Figure 36.

Curvilinear distortion is usually corrected in a compound lens by placing the diaphragm (control of the *f*/stops) near the center of the lens combination. In the case of a single lens, or elements cemented into a single unit, the diaphragm placement is generally in front of the lens because barrel distortion is considered the less objectionable of the two types.

Flare. This aberration can be defined generally as stray or scattered light not controlled by the lens. It can have a variety of aspects, the two most prevalent being optical flare and mechanical flare.

Optical flare is common to every lens and, paradoxically, is caused to a considerable degree by corrections. In overcoming the six aberrations just explained, a good expensive lens acquires innumerable reflecting surfaces which result in internal reflections and double images. Sometimes a kind of mist seems to cover the main image of semicircular sections of it. Or flare may take the pear shape called coma. When this twice-reflected light forms a definite secondary image, whether out-of-focus or sharp, it is termed a *ghost image*. The amount of stray light under average conditions is negligible for most photographic purposes. Optical flare becomes a problem, however, when some very bright object within the lens field—from a wrongly placed lamp, or a window reflection—throws an intense light spot into the lens, causing a troublesome flare in your subject image.

Coatings on modern lenses are effective in subduing optical flare. Like many another invention, this one originated in a casual discovery—that old lenses with a blue tarnish had less flare and transmitted more light than untarnished lenses. Early tries at duplicating this result did not succeed too well; the synthetic tarnishes were so soft that they either became scratched or wiped off easily. But the newer coatings are tougher and more satisfactory; furthermore, the continuing improvement in overall lens design, while not routing ghosts completely, is reducing the haunting power of optical flare to a minimum.

Mechanical flare is reflection from a bright spot close to the lens. It can come from within the camera or the lens mounting and can be caused by parts of the diaphragm, shutter, or mount that have worn shiny. This is an infrequent kind of flare, fairly controllable, and not responsible for ghost images. Mechanical flare is generally prevented by blackening inner surfaces thoroughly and—once more—by using a smaller aperture.

Mechanical Features. These have to do mainly with shutter types, lens interchangeability, variations in viewfinder and focusing mechanisms.

SPECIAL LENSES. Accessory lenses and lenses for specialized professional work are available in amazing variety. Their focal lengths may range from 21mm to 1000mm, and their angles of view vary proportionately. Because a lens of shorter focal length is closer to the film than one of normal length, it records a wider view of a given scene; a lens of longer focal length, being farther from the film, records a smaller portion of the same scene. Quite a few types, not in the extreme focal lengths, are designed for miniature cameras; and good ones, like all quality lenses, are expensive. When interchangeable lenses or other accessories fit a particular camera model, or series of models, they are said to be part of a camera system—for example, the "Leica system" or Eastman's "Retina system."

The most-used extra lenses for amateur photography are wide-angle and telephoto lenses. The angle of view of medium or normal lenses is usually between 45 and 55 degrees, whereas wide-angle lenses have angles of view about 60 degrees and sometimes much greater. On the other side of the normal line, telephoto lenses have much narrower angles of view, ranging down to less than 10 degrees in professional equipment.

Wide-angle lenses are used mainly for working in limited space. They permit inclusion of a broader and higher area in places where it is not possible to move the camera farther back from the scene; they can let you take in a larger portion of a room interior, for instance, or of a cathedral or other building in a narrow street. Instead of an average focal length of approximately the diagonal of the film size, a true wide-angle lens generally has a short focal length of about half the film's diagonal. Therefore, if you use a wide-angle lens to include all of a children's ball game or a panoramic view, as in Figure 37, remember that a shorter focal length tends to exaggerate distances and distort close objects. Because of their cramped mounting space, wide-angle lenses are apt to have no shutters; however, the lens cap usually serves adequately as a shutter.

Fig. 37.—Above: A wide-angle lens can include relatively broad views. (Courtesy of Scholastic High School Photo Awards)

Fig. 38.—Below: Telephoto shot of lioness awaiting feeding time. (Courtesy of the Newspaper National Snapshot Awards)

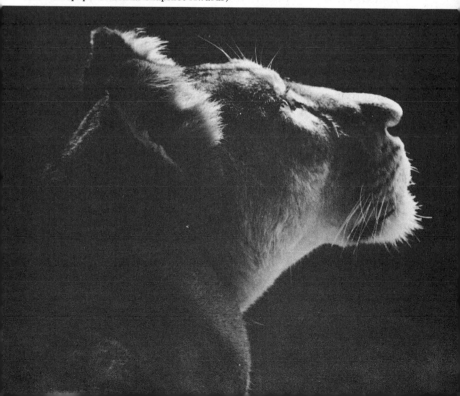

Telephoto lenses for amateur use with standard cameras are designed for a long-focal and narrow-angle effect. A camera lens of very long focal length requires an extra-long bellows extension and, consequently, rather bulky equipment. But the condensed construction of separate telephoto lenses makes them usable on small cameras that feature interchangeability. Their purpose is to get a smaller portion of distant subjects, thus producing larger, frame-filling images than a normal-angle lens is capable of except in a clumsily large camera. For example, you might want a closeup effect when photographing a coy zebra on the far side of a zoo cage or the wide-eyed wonder of a child absorbed with a new toy. (See Figure 38.)

SHUTTERS. The shutter of a lens is the mechanical device governing the length of time that light is in contact with the film. After the diaphragm has been set to the f/stop desired and the shutter-speed pointer set for $\frac{1}{125}$ of a second or $\frac{1}{60}$ or whatever, the shutter is first cocked by a lever which puts it at-the-ready, then tripped by a release lever to admit light for the set period. *The amount of light for any exposure, therefore, is controlled by the diameter of the diaphragm opening and the length of time it remains in open position.*

Although it is good practice to set the lens aperture anywhere you choose between full stops on the f/scale, it is not advisable to set the shutter between speeds indicated on the lens mount. In the first place, most shutters will not work at an in-between timing but will trip at whichever time the indicator is nearer. In the second place, there is the possibility of damaging the shutter, which no doubt gets confused trying to determine whether you want $\frac{1}{60}$ or $\frac{1}{125}$. Furthermore, don't leave the shutter cocked for long periods. It is not good for the shutter, and you will probably trip it unintentionally and waste one picture anyway. And don't change your mind about what speed you want after cocking the shutter, as resetting the shutter while it is in cocked position puts undue strain on the mechanism.

There are at present three types of lens shutters, each with its particular advantage for different photographic aims: between-the-lens, focal-plane, and the less familiar behind-the-lens.

Between-the-lens Shutters. This most frequently used type is placed just where its name indicates: with the iris diaphragm between the front and rear elements of a compound lens. It consists of overlapping metal leaves which spring open when the shutter release is pressed, allow the light to pass through for the time specified, then spring shut. The midway placement is especially effective in correcting distortion, as explained above in the section about aberrations.

Between-the-lens shutters (also referred to as "leaf shutters") usually have timings up to $\frac{1}{500}$ of a second, although a few boast higher speeds. One advantage is that at any speed these shutters can be synchronized with flash much more easily than focal-plane types.

Interchangeable lenses cannot be used in most cameras with between-the-lens shutters. The camera must have a lens mount especially designed for interchangeability, and each lens must have its own shutter. This equipment runs into quite an expenditure, and it is considered more practical to use a focal-plane type or the rarer behind-the-lens type when interchangeability is a prime consideration.

Focal-plane Shutters. These are lightproof curtains, usually of rubberized black cloth but sometimes of extremely thin and flexible metal, mounted on spring-tension rollers; they move just in front of the film to admit a slit of light when the shutter is released. In 35mm cameras a focal-plane shutter consists of two curtains on opposite rollers: the curtains overlap at the center and may move horizontally or vertically as they open to admit a strip of light and quickly close. In larger cameras a standard single curtain has slits of varying widths which traverse the film plane.

The advantages of these shutters are that their position back at the focal plane permits easy interchangeability of lenses and that they have high speeds, usually to $\frac{1}{1000}$ of a second. Their versatility and speed make them preferred for action photographs, especially in press cameras. However, they cannot be used with electronic flash at the highest shutter speeds. Also, the location and speed of focal-plane shutters do contribute to positional distortions which placement of the shutter between lens elements helps to avoid. These distortions are quite apparent with press cameras when the curtain slits admit light in successive strips; a fast-moving car, for instance, can take on a stretched, forward-straining appearance because the image was not recorded all at once. Other distortions depend on the direction in which the slit moves in relation to the image.

All focal-plane shutters have less distortion when the lens is stopped down, and in 35mm cameras the distortion is generally negligible. When you are photographing action, distortion will be minimized if the movement of the shutter curtains corresponds to the movement of the action. If you know the action of your own shutter, you can hold the camera horizontally or vertically to match the shutter movement to the subject movement.

Behind-the-lens Shutters. Developed primarily for lens interchangeability, this type of shutter has overlapping blades and operates the same as between-the-lens shutters, with similar speeds, but it is placed at the back of the lens mount instead of in the lens itself. Behind-the-lens shutters provide easy interchangeability but, of course, they offer less distortion correction.

Shutter Markings. Some cameras have shutter speeds that include $\frac{1}{25}$, $\frac{1}{50}$, $\frac{1}{100}$, and so on, in their markings. Corresponding markings on other cameras are $\frac{1}{30}$, $\frac{1}{60}$, $\frac{1}{125}$. The newer system of markings is 1 second, $\frac{1}{2}$, $\frac{1}{4}$, $\frac{1}{8}$, $\frac{1}{15}$, $\frac{1}{30}$, $\frac{1}{60}$, $\frac{1}{125}$, $\frac{1}{250}$, $\frac{1}{500}$, designed to permit a more nearly exact doubling of shutter speeds. However, for all practical purposes the exposure values are the same for either series.

LENS CARE

As with any valued delicate instrument, proper care is primarily common-sense care. Treat your lens with respect and appreciation, and a good lens will serve willingly and well. If a lens is in need of doctoring, take it to an expert for diagnosis and prescription.

Your lens should be protected from bumps and falls, from extremes of temperature and dampness, from fumes and salt spray, from dust and fingermarks. You may sometimes prefer to use your camera without a case, but the leather protection does cushion a camera against minor encounters with the outside world.

Always store your camera carefully. Where you keep it when it's not in use depends, of course, on climatic conditions and available facilities. But if you live in a hot and humid area—or are traveling through a steamy jungle—try to find a dry cabinet or locker in which a moderate temperature can be maintained. If you do not have a case for it, keep the camera in a plastic bag.

Among *the worst storage spots* (for camera or film) are the temptingly convenient glove compartment of a car and the ledge inside the car's rear window. Almost as bad is a casual windowsill at home, since any lengthy exposure to the elements, especially direct sunlight, can weaken the lens structure as well as necessitate cleaning. By keeping the camera in its case or using a protective lens cap whenever you are not taking pictures, by handling it carefully and storing it sensibly, you can avoid most of the dust and fingermarks which might cause lens damage and beclouded images.

It should rarely be necessary to clean camera lenses if you abide by the simple rules of good camera care. But when obvious fingermarks, dust particles, and moisture call for cleaning, do it *gently*.

First, use a very fine camelhair or sable brush on the surface. If light brushing does the trick, go no further. But if smudges seem to cling, wipe the surface very gently with a soft lens tissue or fresh lintfree linen handkerchief. Ordinary paper tissues or silicone materials should not be used as they affect the porous lens coatings. If the surface has any greasiness, as might come from fingermarks, you may need to moisten the tissue or linen slightly with a lens cleaner.

Never use acids, alcohol, or any other agents except a professionally recommended lens-cleaning fluid. Apply minimum pressure with a circular motion; and use the fluid very sparingly since even an approved cleaner can be harmful if it seeps into the lens mount.

If the condition of your lens calls for more than superficial cleaning, do not attempt to take the camera apart or otherwise tamper with it. Rather, take it to a reputable photographic dealer, preferably to the store where you bought it or to a licensed representative of the manufacturer. If this is not possible, write the manufacturer for advice about sending your camera to the company for reconditioning.

5

```
┌─────────────────────────┐
│   Focusing the Lens     │
└─────────────────────────┘
```

FOCUS in photography means just what it means outside photography. The eyes bring objects into focus by adjusting to different distances and to different degrees of darkness and light. Actually, the right eye sees a view slightly different from that seen by the left eye, but in normal eyesight the views converge simultaneously into a single distinct view.

The photographer focuses a lens on a given object at a given distance in order to control the light that reaches the focal plane and to assure the formation of a distinct image on the film. Some focusing aids, and the factors affecting sharpness of focus, are discussed in this chapter.

VIEWING SYSTEMS

Fundamentally, a rangefinder is an optical mechanism that measures the distance between your lens and the subject you are sorting out in the viewfinder. Thus the *viewfinder* delineates the area to be included in the picture and the *rangefinder* helps to bring a superimposed or split image into a sharp single focus. Nomenclature here, as in other photographic designations, occasionally gets a bit confused from overlapping: you may hear "viewfinders" and "viewers" and "rangefinders" and just plain "finders" used without very sharp dividing lines.

So-called rangefinder cameras do not have the mirror device that distinguishes the single-lens reflex. But an SLR may combine a mirror-prism groundglass and a split-image rangefinder. A few expensive cameras feature eye-level prism viewers that are interchangeable with waist-level viewers.

Since the viewfinder in which you compose your picture is one of the important points of camera differences, you should investigate various types to determine which best suits you. Convenience and efficiency are matters of individual preference, and one's eyesight often influences the choice. Eyeglasses, for instance, may interfere with getting a viewer window close enough to the eye to see the complete frame. Most twin-lens reflex cameras have a hinged magnifier that swings out above the groundglass, and certain costly cameras even offer custom viewers with prescription lenses. Be sure to try out the focusing knobs, too, as they are in different places on different cameras.

General Viewfinder Types. The great variety of viewfinders may be broadly classified as direct-vision and groundglass types. Direct-vision viewfinders, mounted on top of hand cameras, are held at eye level and show the subject you wish to photograph, but not necessarily whether it is in focus. Some contain lenses, some do not. "Through-the-lens viewing" refers to the SLR system of viewing through the taking lens, with the scene mirrored on a groundglass within the prism housing.

Groundglass viewfinders used below eye level, more or less at waist level, are characteristic of twin-lens and simple reflex types of cameras. Looking down at the groundglass gives you view and range since the composition you see is the same as the picture except that the image is reversed from right to left. If what you see in the groundglass is sharp, it is in focus, the degree of sharpness depending on the quality of the lens.

A camera may have an auxiliary viewer to give a rough outline of the picture area without blocking the view around it. It may be an open-frame viewer, simply a wire pullup at the front of the camera; or it may be a press-camera type of sportsfinder with an optical peepsight behind the wire frame.

Rangefinders. A rangefinder can be a separate accessory, although in most modern cameras it is coupled to the lens. Basically, a separate rangefinder is a small oblong case with a tiny mirror mounted at an angle and a prism which receives an indirect image. By looking through the eyepiece at some vertical line of the subject (a tree trunk or the edge of a building, for example) and turning the focusing dial until the direct mirror image of the vertical line fuses with the indirect prism image, you discover how many feet away the in-focus subject is by referring to the distance scale on the dial.

With a typical coupled rangefinder you look through the camera's eyepiece at a subject framed by a luminous outline, in the center of which is the rangefinder field of maximum brightness, usually cir-

OUT OF FOCUS

IN FOCUS

Fig. 39.—Rangefinder principle.

cular. Rotate the focusing knob until the split or superimposed lines of this circular field coincide, bringing the image into sharp focus. Groundglass viewing screens may have a center spot, with or without lines, to aid in judging the sharpness of the reflected image.

PARALLAX PROBLEMS

The apparent displacement of an object when seen from two different viewpoints is termed *parallax*. Photographically, it is not at all mysterious since what you see through a viewfinder is usually not exactly what the picture-taking lens sees. Suppose you stand near a window and look at a house across the street. Now sit down and look at the house. Not quite the same chimney, perhaps.

Except for single-lens reflex cameras, the camera lens is generally lower than the viewfinder, and this is where the minor discrepancy comes in. Since any lens records a picture subject upside down on the film (see *inverted image* explanation in Chapter 3), uncorrected parallax results most often in cut-off tops of picture subjects. At scenic distances parallax is negligible, but bringing the camera closer to a subject proportionately increases the lens-finder discrepancy. This is especially disconcerting, and rather frequent, in taking pictures of people that come out with the top of the head missing in the finished photograph. The golfer in Figure 40 has lost not only her head but also her club and golf ball because of the photog pher's

Fig. 40.—Closeup focus increases parallax problem.

Fig. 41.—Slight tilt toward viewfinder overcomes parallax.

eagerness for a closeup shot. Figure 41 shows how a more thoughtful camera position and a slight tilt have made it possible to obtain the intended picture.

Unless a camera description specifically states that the lens is corrected for parallax, you should make your own parallax correction by tilting the camera almost imperceptibly in the direction of the viewfinder: up for horizontal pictures and to the right for vertical ones. Make it a habit to remember this slight tilt, especially for close subjects, after you have composed your pictures in the finder. Practice and a comparative study of your prints are the best way to learn the correct little tilt for your particular camera.

FACTORS AFFECTING SHARPNESS

Circle of Confusion. In bending light rays to produce an image, the lens ideally projects cones of light to fine points on the focusing plane. But just as no lens is perfect, so the image points are not perfect points but actually infinitesimal circles of measurable light. Hence, *circle of confusion* refers to the diameter of an image point as formed by a given lens. A lens has its own fixed minimum circle of confusion; in high-grade lenses this is customarily less than 1/100 of an inch. If the circles of confusion are extremely small, they have the sharp effect of true points unless other factors are contributing to a blurred result.

The fact that a good lens can bend subject light rays into cones and bring them to sharp points at a specific distance poses the problem of what happens at other distances. Absolutely sharp focus is possible only for a subject at a known distance. When objects nearer or farther than the in-focus subject form cones of light that strike planes in front of or in back of the critical focal plane, you get small circles instead of points, as shown in the diagram in Figure 42. These circles are simply cross sections of coming or going cones of

Fig. 42.—Circle of confusion.

light. When an image is made up of millions of true or nearly true points, you get sharpness; but when an image is composed of millions of overlapping little circles, you get a dandy blur.

The *acceptable circle of confusion* is generally regarded as 1/100 of an inch or less in prints held at a normal viewing distance of ten or twelve inches. If this is a contact print and you want to enlarge the negative, the allowable circle of confusion decreases proportionately to the blowup size. For example, if the final print is to be enlarged ten times, the picture should be made with a lens corrected to produce a circle of confusion no larger than 1/1000 of an inch in order to assure the 1/100-inch acceptability in the finished enlargement.

The *resolving power,* or *definition,* of a lens is its ability to form sharply defined images. The same term is applied to film to indicate the capacity of the emulsion to reproduce fine detail in the image. The lens' minimum circle of confusion, which is dependent on the quality of the lens, controls the resolving power—that is, the maximum definition of which the lens is capable.

Critical Aperture. To obtain optimum definition from a fairly fast lens, most manufacturers advise closing down the aperture about two *f*/stops from the wide-open position. This is done because it is not possible to correct any lens uniformly from center to edges; so by stopping down a fine lens to bypass its edges and utilize mainly its central area, you can operate it at the aperture at which it works best. This optimum opening is termed the critical aperture of a particular lens.

Critical aperture concerns the subtle sharpness differences when the lens is focused *at one plane*. At that single plane all objects will be sharply defined. However, out of the possible acceptable openings for a given focus, *one* aperture will make them sharpest. Usually it is not a very noticeable sharpness difference, not to be compared with the sharpness variations of far and near objects when a lens is used at different openings. If the lens is still focused at one plane, a smaller opening than the critical aperture may actually result in a slight loss of definition due to diffraction of light rays as they bend out at the rim of the diaphragm. For subjects in more than one plane, the greater depth of field should cancel out any decrease in definition caused by a smaller-than-critical aperture.

Perspective. Normal human eyes see things in three dimensions: length, width, and depth. A photographic lens "sees" only the first two of these dimensions. A thoughtful photographer therefore helps the lens out on the missing third dimension with a suggestion of depth in the relative size and position of the different parts of the scene. This relationship of near and far objects as they appear to the eyes from a given viewpoint is termed *perspective*. Figure 43 is a classic example of perspective, with the receding lines of the landscape appearing as normally viewed.

The position of the camera and the focal length of its lens are

Fig. 43.—Perspective.

Fig. 44A. — Camera viewpoint at a distance (negative enlarged).

Fig. 44B. — Camera viewpoint up close.

important in controlling the apparent relation and position of objects in a picture. By a discerning selection of viewpoints the photographer can achieve a remarkable diversity of results, creating the illusion of space and distance in a flat two-dimensional plane.

Positioning the camera at a distance from the scene makes the background seem disproportionately large in relation to the foreground and makes the distance between foreground and background seem considerably less. Bringing the camera up close to the scene produces the opposite effect: an exaggerated size of the foreground in proportion to the background and an apparency of greater distance between the two. For an example, look at the illustrations in figures 44A and 44B.

A lens with a longer focal length has a narrower field than the area covered by one with a shorter focal length. These lengths are, you remember, relative to the diagonal of the film, normal focal length being one diagonal. However, you can obtain the same perspective with lenses of different focal lengths, although the effects will not be exactly alike. For example, if a negative from a lens of short focal length is enlarged and the view restricted to the narrower one made by a longer focal length, the perspective in both prints will seem about the same.

Size of image therefore is controlled by focal length, other factors remaining the same. Briefly again, a longer focal length will produce a larger image in less area and a shorter focal length will produce a smaller image in a larger area.

Hyperfocal Distance. The nearest distance at which a lens can be focused to produce a reasonably satisfactory sharpness in everything from half that distance to infinity is the *hyperfocal distance* of that lens. This varies with different lenses and with different apertures. Some manufacturers provide hyperfocal-distance tables (worked out from a mass of mathematical calculations based on the focal length, minimum circle of confusion, and the f/stop being used), but it is quite simple to get this information from a depth-of-field scale. Adjust the focusing mechanism so that the aperture you intend to use is opposite the scale's infinity mark and your lens will then be focused at its hyperfocal distance.

Depth of Field. The area between the nearest and farthest points in acceptably sharp focus is called the *depth of field*, illustrated in Figure 45. Depth of field is affected by (1) the distance of the point

Fig. 45.—Depth of field.

upon which the lens is focused and (2) the aperture at which the lens is set. Depth-of-field computations are based on all factors that make up the hyperfocal distance, just explained, including focal length of lens, circle of confusion, and f number being used.

Various depth-of-field indicators are found on many modern

cameras, and the individual instruction booklets should be consulted. Or you can consult a separate depth-of-field card on which you can dial the distance to be focused upon, then read the near and far distances within which your subject will be in focus at different apertures. As an example, if you have focused a 50mm lens at a distance of 10 feet, and wish to use an aperture of *f*/11, everything from just under 7 feet to approximately 20 feet will be in acceptably sharp focus. With an aperture of *f*/4.5 at the same 10 feet, your picture will be in focus from about 9 feet to 13 feet.

You will notice that *decreasing the lens aperture increases the depth of field* and that *lengthening the distance at which the lens is focused increases the depth of field*. Bringing your focus in to three or four feet for a close-up, with a wide aperture, will reduce the depth of field to a minimum. Figure 46 shows how opening up or closing down the lens affects depth of field. Observe now that the

Fig. 46.—Effect of aperture on depth of field.

lines in the diagram take cone shapes, like·the cones of light described under circles of confusion, a wide-open lens producing short wide cones and a small aperture producing long narrow cones.

When maximum depth within a given scene is desired, use your rangefinder (or estimate) to determine the distances to the far and near boundaries of the scene. Then refer to your depth-of-field scale for the most effective setting. Suppose you are using a popular minia-ture camera with an average 50mm lens and find that you want the area between 6 feet and 20 feet to be in focus: the depth-of-field scale will indicate a small *f*/16 opening and a distance setting of almost 10 feet as your best bet.

Zone Focusing. If you are photographing a children's game or a group of dancers or any activity confined to an approximate zone of predictable distances from your camera, focus on a distance about one-third into the area and check your depth-of-field scale. Suppose you estimate that the subject will move within a range of 8 to 20 feet. If you focus at 12 feet, you will find that a reasonably sharp image can be expected in the zone of 8 to 20 feet. Some simple cameras are preset for three focusing zones: a close area for a single subject, a medium zone for groups, and a distance zone for scenery. (Prefocusing is discussed further in Chapter 14.)

In considering depth of field and other aspects of photography, it is necessary to be aware that "sharpness" is a relative term. Quite obviously, a lens cannot focus exactly on different objects at different distances simultaneously. Some compromise is inevitable, a fact which explains why we use a qualifying adjective such as "reasonable" or "satisfactory" or "acceptable" when discussing sharpness.

For the same reason, the term *universal focus* is really a misnomer. It is understandably applied to the fixed focus of some preset cameras and to a similar setting on any adjustable camera. It means that with a medium aperture at a distance setting of about 15 feet for 35mm cameras and about 25 feet for twin-lens reflexes in a general landscape everything from 8 or 10 feet to infinity will be acceptably sharp—which is the nearest thing to true universal focus that a fallible human-made lens can achieve.

6

Structure and Types of Films

FILMS are the light-sensitive materials on which your camera lens records the pictures you elect to take. The term is no longer confined to the thin, transparent, emulsified medium that is used to register negative images and from which prints can be subsequently reproduced on positive material. *Film* is now the accepted designation for any negative-producing material, regardless of its flexibility or thickness and regardless of whether the negative is made on cellulose, glass, or paper. Most of us give little thought to a film's construction these days, nor is it necessary to do so: like the telephone and the jet airplane, it has become a taken-for-granted miracle.

The visible and invisible effects of light on everyday objects are all around you: a wall that darkens; a curtain that fades; substances that become insoluble under light; plants that absorb carbon and release oxygen by using the radiant energy of light. Photographic developing relies on the properties of compounds which are made to yield to specific reactions by exposing them to light. This principle applies photographically to metals, especially the halogen salts of silver.

STRUCTURE OF FILM

Light-sensitive materials comprise two main parts: an *emulsion* which records images and a *base,* or support, on which to spread the emulsion. This applies also to positive light-sensitive materials, or printing papers, which are discussed in Chapter 19, but in this chapter we are considering only *negative materials*.

Emulsions. Fundamentally, a photographic emulsion is chemically pure gelatin holding in suspension microscopically fine salts of light-sensitive silver bromide. Since the complex process itself is of no vital concern to you as a photographer, only a brief description covering information of fairly general interest is included in this text. What is important, of course, is a working knowledge of the characteristics and performance of the finished product.

To begin with, pure gelatin is water-soaked to a swollen state (much like dried legumes before cooking) and then gradually heated to dissolve it completely. To the gelatin solution is added a quantity of halogen salts; then silver nitrate, which is obtained by dissolving bars of silver in nitric acid, is added under darkroom conditions to produce light-sensitive crystals of silver bromide. The silver bromide grains, insoluble in water, are held dispersed and suspended by the gelatin and can be seen (sort of cream-colored) all through it. At this point the gelatin mixture becomes an emulsion instead of a solution.

The emulsion is then "ripened" by repeated heating and chilling to recrystallize the silver bromide and to fix the size-frequency of the particles. After the ripening process, when the emulsion is in a jellied state, it is slivered into small strips, washed to remove the excess soluble salts, and reheated to receive the addition of hardeners, preservatives, and other special-purpose agents.

At various phases of the procedure, technicians control the built-in qualities of the finished film. For example, the longer the "cooking" period, the larger will be the silver bromide particles and the greater the emulsion *speed;* the larger particles account for the relatively coarse grain of very fast films. When all the various substances have been incorporated, the emulsion is ready for application to the supporting base.

Bases. Supporting bases for light-sensitive emulsions vary according to their intended use. Generally, you will find all *negative* materials (which we are discussing here) on transparent bases and all *positive* materials (such as printing papers) on opaque or translucent bases. But like every other generalization this one has its exceptions: color transparencies, lantern slides, and movie "films" are positives on transparent bases.

Pioneer photographers rolled their own emulsions almost always onto glass plates—a procedure that required steady hands, stout hearts, and clumsy equipment. But glass was the only available material that was clear, inert chemically, and would not swell or shrink in solutions. Glass plates are still in limited use as emulsion supports but, needless to say, photographers do not have to construct their own. They are preferred for some portrait and commercial work, for some types of photogrammetry, for lantern slides, and for special situations where rigidity with no expansion-contraction is sufficiently important to outweigh the disadvantges of bulk and breakage.

Transparent film bases for light-sensitive emulsions have come a long way from the early post-glass products and are being continually improved through persistent research. The first flexible transparent bases to prove satisfactory on many counts were so highly flammable that they constituted a storage danger as well as a handling hazard; and if ignited, their fumes were not only disagreeable but toxic.

It was not easy to find new materials to fill these rather exacting specifications: chemically they had to be stable, moisture resistant, and capable of furnishing good adherence without reacting on the emulsion. Physically they had to be light but tough, stiff but flexible, hard but not brittle, resistant to curling and tearing. Optically, of course, they had to be perfectly and colorlessly transparent. The fact that they should also possess dimensional stability so they would not buckle when the edges become shorter than the center, or flute when the edges become longer than the center, made (and still makes) certain compromises inevitable.

Safety bases of cellulose acetate have been replacing cellulose nitrate films for more than a decade. Because of their greatly reduced flammability, these modern products are called *safety films*. Although acetate will burn while in direct contact with a flame, it is easily discouraged and quits when the flame is withdrawn. And while you would never mistake its fumes for a rose garden, the rather acidy odor is nontoxic. To make these bases, cellulose or cotton derivatives are dissolved into a gooey solution to which the textile term "dope" has been applied. (When your acetate or rayon shirt is "dope-dyed," its color has been added to the synthetic fiber solution, or dope.) The volatile dope for film is fed onto enormous polished-metal drums where heat drives off the excess solvents until the solution acquires sufficient body to be removed to other machines for drying and winding. The thickness—or thinness, if you prefer—of the safety bases depends on the kind of film. Roll films and film packs have very thin, flexible bases. Those for miniature and movie films are a bit thicker; sheet films usually have still more body.

So, EMULSION + BASE = FILM. But manufacturers give you a few extras in the precise process of putting these two major components together. Between base and emulsion there is a special adhesive sub-coating of cellulose and gelatin which assures better adhesion than the cellulose base alone provides. On top of the emulsion there is usually a very thin antiabrasion overcoating of clear gelatin to counteract scratches and friction before the film gets to the developing stage. Underneath all this, sometimes incorporated in an anticurl coating, is an antihalation backing to keep the halo of secondary light around a particularly bright object, like a street lamp, from spreading through the film. It is hard to believe that so many elements, so much scientific accomplishment, can be contained in the wonderful, almost weightless bit of material you insert so casually into your camera.

BLACK–AND–WHITE FILMS

If you read the following explanation of black-and-white film characteristics thoughtfully, you will realize that much of it applies also to color film. A basic difference is that color film has three layers of emulsion while black-and-white has only one. A black-and-white film structure is layered like this:

> Protective overcoating
> Emulsion
> Adhesive subcoating
> Supporting base
> Antihalation backing

Some films are engineered to meet very precise requirements, while others can be expected to serve multiple photographic purposes very satisfactorily. There are several qualities to consider in choosing film and, as always, experience will prove to be the most effective guide later on. A study of the following points should help you decide which black-and-white film will give you best results under certain conditions and will best fill your individual needs.

Film Characteristics. The most important characteristics to consider in choosing your film are: (1) color sensitivity, (2) speed, (3) contrast, (4) latitude, (5) grain, and (6) resolving power. In addition, one must consider the available packaging—whether a particular kind of film comes in a size to fit your camera.

Color Sensitivity. Although negative emulsions fall into four categories of color response, rendered in black and white as brightness differences, only panchromatic emulsions are of much interest to the average amateur photographer because of their great versatility, pleasingly normal values, and adaptability to a longer range of daylight hours. The different types of black-and-white film, in order of sensitivity to color, are: monochromatic, orthochromatic, panchromatic, and infrared.

Monochromatic, sometimes termed "blue-sensitive" or "colorblind," has a basic sensitivity only to the blue-violet end of the spectrum; all other colors reproduce as unlighted darks. These emulsions are mainly for specialized commercial uses, particularly photocopying.

Orthochromatic emulsions respond to the blue-violet range and also to the green-yellow areas of the visible spectrum, with reds showing only as darks. Ortho film, once the old reliable of photo fans, has given way to panchromatic films with few exceptions: it is still available in commercial sheet film, mostly for portraiture, and a small minority of amateur processors appreciate its insensitivity to red as well as its greater exposure latitude.

Panchromatic emulsions, as the name implies, are sensitive to all colors of the visible spectrum, including red, and offer a wide variety of speeds and tone ranges. In general, their sensitivity parallels that of the human eye, which makes these emulsions the most popular black-and-white film choice at present.

Infrared emulsions are highly sensitive to red rays beyond the humanly visible spectrum. They also have an ultraviolet-blue sensitivity band, with very little yellow-green sensitivity. Infrared films are used a great deal for aerial photography, particularly by the armed services; in medical and other scientific areas; and sometimes just for dramatic pictorial effects.

SPEED. The emulsion speed, or rating, is quite likely to be an amateur's first concern in choosing film. A film's built-in sensitivity to light has a direct bearing on the exposure required for correct negative density and a resulting satisfactory image. Ratings are assigned by the manufacturers according to a specific procedure set up in 1947 by the ASA (American Standards Association). In Europe it is usually the DIN (Deutsche Industrie Norm) rating of Germany.

Film speeds have increased by leaps and bounds in recent years, which is another way of saying that films need less and less light for satisfactory exposure. Films of high speeds—both black-and-white and color—offer new freedom to photographers, making an $f/3.5$ or an $f/4.5$ lens as versatile as a much faster lens with a slow film. Seldom is it necessary nowadays to pass up a good shot for the old "not enough light" reason, and the opportunity to utilize higher shutter speeds permits action to be caught more sharply. This gain cannot be all one-sided, to be sure; something has to be sacrificed, such as grain and contrast.

Do not, therefore, let film speed run away with your judgment. Consider what pictures you are going to take and where and why before you decide what film to use. What will be the probable brightness range of the scenes? Will there be any fast action? Will you want enlargements? What is the maximum lens opening and shutter speed your camera permits? Trying out different films and carefully comparing the results should provide the wisest answers.

Since a safety margin for protection against underexposure is included in the ASA standard, it is possible to expose black-and-white film at a higher rating, sometimes twice the published one, and obtain sharper results with special processing. This is because the exposure nearest the correct minimum generally produces the best negative, whereas overexposure produces too much density for really good printability. Re-rated films must be sent to a custom lab (or handled in your own darkroom) and the lab should be instructed to process the entire roll at your arbitrary index.

CONTRAST. The degree to which a film is capable of recording closely related tones in gradations of black and white is termed *contrast*. The darkest and densest areas on a negative are reverse images of the scene's brightest objects, which affect the greatest number of silver bromide particles and transform them into metallic silver. Conversely, the lightest parts of the negative correspond to the deepest shadows in the picture.

Thus the term *density* indicates the amount of metallic silver in different areas of the negative. If your negative is "too dense" you have probably overexposed it, allowing too much brightness to affect too many grains of the emulsion. Inexperienced photographers generally tend to overexpose film. A relatively "thin" negative can be expected to produce a better print, although to an unpracticed eye it may seem distressingly underexposed.

Contrast is another basic quality which is incorporated during the manufacture of film—and also of the sensitized emulsions of printing papers. A film of *average contrast* will reproduce highlights, halftones, and shadows with a full range of densities; the highlights will reveal their dark areas and the shadows will show whatever brightness they encompass. A *high-contrast* film will record only highlights and shadows, giving you mostly blacks and whites without the in-between grays. A *low-contrast* film records little differentiation in negative densities, resulting in softer tones. Portraits and general snapshots, for instance, benefit from the softer effects of medium- or low-contrast films. High-contrast films are especially useful in copying line drawings, documents, and other printed matter.

Finally, remember that no one of these qualities operates alone. The contrast built into a film is affected by the other qualities of the film and to a considerable degree by the exposure and development of the film.

LATITUDE. Latitude is the film characteristic most closely related to contrast and may be defined as the film's ability to record differences in brightness as differences in negative densities.

The range of brightness differences can extend from 1 to 128; that is, it is possible, with most general panchromatic films, for a highlight to be reproduced as much as 128 times as bright as a shadow without loss of tone gradations. An average scene has about one-fourth of that extreme range, thus utilizing only one-fourth of the emulsion capacity under normal conditions. Therefore minor exposure variations above or below normal need not detract from the print quality of a negative. If a film is described as having "little latitude" it can produce a relatively shorter range of brightness differences.

There is seldom a single correct exposure; usually there is a short range of acceptable exposures referred to as the *exposure latitude*. Black-and-white films have considerably more exposure latitude than color films. A point to bear in mind, however, is that latitude decreases when the brightness range of a scene increases. Also, the density of a negative will be increased by longer exposures.

GRAIN. The film characteristic most likely to be affected adversely by any appreciable increase in emulsion speed is the grain structure. The faster the film, the larger will be the silver bromide grains of the emulsion and the metallic silver particles into which they are developed. These are what compose the latent photographic image; so the size and distribution of the grains have a direct relation to the sharpness of the picture and to the capacity of the negative to impart fine detail. Since all the film characteristics are interdependent, there are a few ifs to consider.

If a very fine-grain emulsion is coated thinly on the film base, it will increase the potential sharpness of the picture over that of a thicker application. The reason for this is that, with a thin emulsion, there is less chance for the light to bounce about and scatter during the printing process. If the film base is comparatively thin, the diffusion will be cut down still further.

If a negative of coarser grain has good contrast quality, the finer details of a picture can sometimes be brought out more sharply than those of a fine-grain negative with insufficient contrast. How the negative is developed, as well as the kind of emulsion, affects the visible graininess of a finished picture.

Where grain assumes the greatest importance is in *enlargements,* especially in those blown up to more than seven or eight times the original size. Grain is rarely discernible in standard small prints such as those returned with your processed black-and-white film, regardless of the type of film. But it is possible for an individual grain to be magnified in reproduction from 2,500 to 25,000 times; an extra-large blowup of a negative can, therefore, really put spots before your eyes. An enlargement can come out as smooth as a glass floor or as mottled as a weatherbeaten sidewalk, and grain is a major factor in the result.

One cause of the granular look is the inclination of the grains to join groups during development. Actually the exposed emulsion particles develop as individual grains; however, when grains are close or touching, one grain can touch off development in its neighbors and induce them to cluster. A fine-grain developer, as well as a fine-grain emulsion, will lessen this togetherness tendency. The price of thus disciplining the grain structure is usually a slight loss in contrast and speed, but there is a gain on the side of a good enlargement.

RESOLVING POWER. This term refers to the capacity of the film to resolve, or reproduce, distinctly fine lines for sharpness of detail. The lines, which are an integral part of the photographic image, are etched on the film by light and are affected by the proneness of a given emulsion to scatter the light. The less opportunity a film offers the light to spread, the sharper the lines will be. This is somewhat comparable to differences in pen-and-ink lines: on some hard-surface papers it is possible to draw extremely fine lines very close together, while the same lines on paper toweling would run into one big blur.

The scientific testing of a film's resolving power measures microscopically the number of reproducible lines per millimeter. Since light spreading is attributable to reflection, more of it usually occurs among the larger grains of high-speed films. Consequently the power to resolve fine detail is generally greater in the slower films which have small grains of a fairly uniform size.

No one factor is responsible to any appreciable extent for a film's resolving power because of the close relationship of all the emulsion properties. Higher contrast, such as black lines on white ground, will also raise the resolving power if exposure and development conditions remain constant. Variations in such factors as length of exposure, color of light, and method of development will affect the resolving power as well as the picture image as a whole.

PACKAGING. The availability of films in the size your camera accommodates is a final factor in determining what to use. Film comes in *rolls, packs,* and *sheets* in a variety of sizes and types. "Rolls" subdivides into most of the finished films bought by amateurs. Naturally the most popular sizes will offer a wider choice of emulsion speeds, and the other qualities just reviewed, than those sizes in lesser demand. This applies to color film as well as black and white. The broad classifications of *film sizes* follow.

35mm Films. For the different types of cameras using 35mm film, see the section on 35mm cameras in Chapter 2. The relative economy of 35mm film and the convenience of shooting 20 or 36 frames without reloading undoubtedly contributed to the popularity of this diverse and versatile camera size; this in turn makes 35mm the most popular film size. Although 35mm film does come in rolls, "roll film" has come to mean the wider strips, without sprocket holes along the edges, that are used in box and twin-lens cameras.

Since a distinguishing feature of miniature cameras is their wind-rewind mechanism, 35mm film is packaged in lightproof metal cases, called cassettes, designed to fit such cameras. Standard holes along the edges of the film strip, to engage the sprockets of the winding wheel, are characteristic of 35mm film and a reminder of its movie origin. Because it has no protective paper backing and to reduce the chance of its tearing at the sprocket holes, 35mm film is slightly thicker than roll films or film packs. After the last exposure, it must be rewound into its original cassette before it is removed from the camera.

The advance-rewind mechanism of 35mm cameras makes it possible to remove a partly exposed roll without wasting the rest of the film and to change the film if you decide to go to the races instead of to a museum. For instructions, see Chapter 2 (section on camera loading). This thrifty aspect and the low cost per exposure make 35mm one of the most economical kinds of film.

Roll Films. Unlike 35mm, roll films come in more than one width and are identified by a number—for example, the popular size 120. There are roll films for various box types of cameras, for $2\frac{1}{4}$ x $2\frac{1}{4}$ twin-lens reflex cameras, and a few less standard sizes. Most roll films have twelve exposures.

The .opaque paper backing that is characteristic of roll films has the vital statistics about exposure index, as well as the necessary frame numbers, printed on the paper leader. Roll films have no sprocket holes but wind onto a removable spool. The protected roll is removed from the camera after the last of the strip has been wound; it cannot be rewound.

A roll film for pictures $2\frac{1}{4}$ x $2\frac{1}{4}$ inches or larger costs more per frame than 35mm since it uses more emulsion, more protection, more developing materials. On the other hand, it offers a larger contact print and this, as a rule, cuts down on the enlarging costs.

8mm and 16mm films. These come in double cassettes for subminiature cameras, or in rolls and magazines for home-movie cameras.

Film Packs. Film packs are thin, like roll film, and are used professionally in press and view cameras when it is not possible or convenient to use a large number of film holders, which are bulky, heavy, and expensive. The very thin and unprotected material of film packs makes them a bit tricky to handle and more vulnerable to damage than other films. Probably the most useful size is the 4 x 5 but there are several others commercially available.

Sheet and Cut Film. This has a sturdy base, less flexible than other films, and comes in numerous emulsions, for general or specialized purposes. It is used only in professional types of cameras.

It is important to know your film as well as your camera. Look at the information sheet each time you open a package of film: it is a good reminder even when it contains no surprises. Practice with a few rolls to find out which film you like best for certain purposes. If you ask a fellow picture-taker what film he is using and he answers vaguely, "Oh, I think it's Kodak-this, or maybe it's Ansco-that," you can be sure that he is not very interested in how his pictures turn out—and they probably won't.

COLOR FILMS

The reason for separating color photography from black-and-white, in classrooms and in books, is that there are significant differences to note, digest, and keep in their proper places. Since there are also numerous likenesses in both categories, it is not possible to keep them completely separate. Color in photography, including the structure of color films, is covered in more detail in Chapter 9.

Basically, the structure of color film is three color-sensitive emulsions on three layers of film, with a yellow filter between the top layers, supported on a single base—somewhat like a layer cake on a

Fig. 47.—Structure of color film.

plate. The base is the kind used in black-and-white films and has an antihalation coating. The bottom layer of emulsion, applied directly to the base, is a specific panchromatic type which, with filtering, reacts to red only. The middle emulsion layer is orthochromatic, sensitive to green only. The top layer is colorblind, sensitive to blue only. Coatings of clear gelatin protect the emulsions from scratches before and during processing.

Contrast. In black-and-white photography the contrasts in the negative are governed mainly by the difference between highlights and shadows and the angle of the light source. In color photography the contrasts in the negative are produced by the different colors of the subject. Extremes of lights and darks are not desirable in color work as a rule.

Exposure Latitude. There is a much wider leeway in the exposure range within which you can get a perfectly good black-and-white print than there is in color films. The multilayer construction of color films results in lower ratings and this, in turn, sharply curtails the exposure latitude. The latitude is further limited by the fact that variations in color are less acceptable to the eye than variations in black-and-white tones.

Relative Speeds. A major difference between black-and-white films and color films is in their emulsion speed. Furthermore, while it is possible to rate a color film higher than the printed index, it is not recommended since the color ratings are not always held down by the ASA safety margin of black-and-white films. Moreover, faster and faster color films have been narrowing the difference between black-and-white and color films.

For many years the original Kodachrome, at ASA 10, was the only color film as far as some photographers were concerned, even while a few faster films became popular. These ratings remained constant for a long time, and it was possible to publish the short list of color-film speeds with some accuracy. Now, however, the ratings of various old and new brands range from ASA 25 to ASA 200, with changes too frequent to tabulate with any certainty. Even an old black-and-white favorite like Plux-X has had three different ASA indexes within the past few years. Moral: Don't forget to look at the instruction leaflets.

Chrome vs. Color. The brand names of domestic color films have an element of potential confusion in their suffixes. You should therefore remember that those ending in "chrome" produce *transparencies* for color slides. Those ending in "color" produce *negatives* for making color prints.

Although it is possible to obtain prints from color transparencies and slides from color negatives, this involves extra steps and extra expense. Thus, it is advisable to determine in advance whether you want to show most of your pictures by slide projection, or by prints to be passed around and mounted in an album, and to choose your film accordingly.

The two main types of color film generally available for hand cameras are described as *reversal* and *negative* types.

Reversal-type color films are developed first as negatives and then, by re-exposing and redeveloping, are reversed to produce positive images directly on the film that was in your camera. That very same film eventually emerges, in small mounted pieces, as *color transparencies*. Agfa*chrome*, Ansco*chrome*, Ekta*chrome*, and Koda*chrome* are examples of color reversal film.

Negative-type color films record the opposites of the colors being photographed, which are later transferred in their true values to appropriate sensitized paper as *color prints*. Koda*color* is a color negative film. This film comes in daylight type only for use outdoors or with clear (white) flashbulbs.

Color reversal films come in daylight or tungsten emulsions. While the tungsten type is for artificial light generally, fluorescent lighting usually requires daylight film for natural effects. Whether a film is for daylight or artificial light, and whether it is a reversal or negative type, is printed on the film package.

The "chrome" and "color" differentiation is not always true of the brand names of foreign films. When buying an unfamiliar color film in another country, look carefully to see whether the package is marked "For Slides" or "For Prints" and, if in doubt, ask the shop.

Color Variations. There are noticeable differences in the colors produced by various color films under similar or even identical conditions. One may give you blue skies that verge toward a purple tone while another may give skies of bright ultramarine. Grass and other foliage may be reproduced in quite dissimilar greens. Yellows may be slightly orange or more golden. Reds can be dazzling or subtle. You will find softer pastel shades in some films and a more saturated color brilliance in others. White can vary a great deal and can be one of the most difficult colors for the photographer. It is up to you personally to decide which color film pleases you best. Not everyone prefers redheads, and not every photographer votes for the same color film.

A further difference in color films is that some can be processed in home darkrooms but others cannot. (For more on this subject, along with others relating to color, see Chapter 9.)

7

Principles of Exposure

EXPOSURE refers to the amount of light that reaches the film. In the uncomplicated days of the early box camera, exposing a film correctly was a relatively simple matter, and good results were largely dependent on luck. For one thing, there were far fewer kinds of film to expose; and because the old-time camera was preset to do its own focusing and to take pictures at one fixed speed through a fixed aperture, there were not too many mistakes you could make. You picked a nice sunny day, placed your subject in a nice bright spot, and click!—it was a snap, and most of the time a fairly good one.

Into this easygoing picture technologic progress gradually pushed its way. The eager camera fan was first intrigued by an influx of improvements, then baffled and frustrated by them. No longer could he rely on a constant light beam of about $f/16$ at $1/25$ of a second; the camera seemed suddenly to have shifted its responsibility for exposure and printability to the bewildered photographer. As it became necessary to cope with the capacities of more and more powerful lenses, multiple-speed shutters, depth-of-field devices, and the varied ratings of a growing complex of new film types, timely aids kept pace with the problems. The technical skills and vast experience that produced the innovations also furnished the basis for reassuring and reliable advice, including helpful exposure recommendations, and it is now possible to enjoy a satisfying degree of control over picture results.

The printed instruction leaflets that accompany 35mm films, compact printed dials, and various light meters are modern guides to correct exposure and, consequently, to good, printable negatives. It is important to recognize that these are only guides; there is still discretionary ground in which the thoughtful amateur must exercise judgment and observation. The factors to be considered in determining the setting for accurate exposure, all of which have been discussed in the preceding chapters, are: light conditions, reflectance of your subject, kind of film being used, and speed of your lens.

STEPS TO CONTROL EXPOSURE

Basic Exposure. To learn to estimate exposure, begin with a basic or key setting for an average outdoor scene. *Average* in a photograph means a nearly equal distribution of lights and darks in normal sunlight, with the subject front lighted. The generally accepted starting point is an *f*/16 stop and the index number of the film as the shutter speed. To illustrate: if you are using black-and-white film with an index of 125, your basic exposure for an average sunlight picture will be 1/125 at *f*/16; if your film is rated at 60, your basic exposure will be 1/60 at *f*/16 (or 1/50 in case your camera has the alternative shutter markings explained on page 54).

The *index number,* or rating, of film is based on its emulsion speed and on other known factors affecting the amount of light the film records, such as the lens' transmittance and the camera's degree of reflectance. The index is an accepted measurement for which we can thank the American Standards Association. This association also developed another useful tool, the *ASA Computer,* at the request of the U.S. Navy during World War II. It was designed originally for setting cameras in combat conditions where it was not possible to read a meter successfully.

The ASA Computer and the Eastman Kodaguides each merge so much researched data into compact printed form that you can get off to a running start in your exposure calculations by using one of them. But it is still up to you to supplement this valuable information with your individual evaluation of light conditions and relevant factors. (Incidentally, if you are traveling in Europe and buy film with DIN ratings, just ask the shop for a card with a conversion table to ASA ratings.)

EV Numbers. In the Exposure Value System (EVS), mentioned in the chapter on lenses, each number from 2 to 18 represents the amount of light admitted to a lens by a given aperture and shutter speed. When these two controls are cross-coupled, changing one makes an automatic compensation in the other. EVS allows you to keep a shutter speed and *f*/stop combination in mind as a single number. If you accustom yourself to the system, it is very useful in reading light meters, which generally include EV numbers. The following table of equivalent values shows how EV numbers compare to conventional shutter speed and f/stop combinations.

TABLE 1

EV SYSTEM NUMBERS

(Conventional equivalents in shutter speeds shown below the corresponding f/stops)

EV	Aperture	f/2	f/2.8	f/4	f/5.6	f/8	f/11	f/16	f/22
2	Shutter Settings	1							
3	(seconds)	1/2	1						
4		1/4	1/2	1					
5		1/8	1/4	1/2	1				
6		1/15	1/8	1/4	1/2	1			
7		1/30	1/15	1/8	1/4	1/2	1		
8		1/60	1/30	1/15	1/8	1/4	1/2	1	
9		1/125	1/60	1/30	1/15	1/8	1/4	1/2	1
10		1/250	1/125	1/60	1/30	1/15	1/8	1/4	1/2
11		1/500	1/250	1/125	1/60	1/30	1/15	1/8	1/4
12			1/500	1/250	1/125	1/60	1/30	1/15	1/8
13				1/500	1/250	1/125	1/60	1/30	1/15
14					1/500	1/250	1/125	1/60	1/30
15						1/500	1/250	1/125	1/60
16							1/500	1/250	1/125
17								1/500	1/250
18									1/500

Only relatively recent cameras have EV markings, since this exposure system (originally called the "Light Value System") was introduced in 1954. Most cameras with coupled lenses can be uncoupled for greater flexibility. If you check your meter or exposure guide to determine the EV number for a particular shot and later decide to vary the basic exposure, you should be able to change the aperture setting without disturbing the indicated shutter speed.

CONDITIONS GOVERNING EXPOSURE

We have said that exposure refers to the amount of light that reaches the film; now let's look at what is meant by *correct exposure*. When you have chosen the right combination of f/stop and shutter speed to control the exposure correctly, you will be able to see distinct detail in both the light and the dark areas of the negative. Regardless of weather, the highlights and shadows of your picture will show up clearly, with a good range of middle gray tones, and your print will have contrast and brilliance. Basically, the aim of correct exposure is to record the different areas of a scene with as nearly equal densities as possible in the different areas of the negative.

Basic Light Conditions. The printed leaflet packaged with film includes a little chart, similar to that in Figure 48, which applies to

Fig. 48.—Basic exposure must be increased or decreased according to sky conditions.

all hand cameras. When you know your basic exposure, the next step is to look at the chart, look at the sky, and learn to interpret these light conditions.

Bright sunlight is, well, bright sunlight, with clear skies. So you set the camera at your basic exposure which is, say, 1/125 at *f*/16.

Hazy sunlight is less intense, with the sun visible through a thin curtain of clouds or fog. There are shadows, but not as definite a contrast in lights and darks. This condition calls for *two times* basic exposure, which you get either by decreasing your shutter speed to 1/60 of a second or by opening up to *f*/11.

Cloudy bright has very little trace of shadows; you know the sun is up there but you can't find it because of the unbroken layer of fairly thin clouds. Contrast is so low it seems flat, yet this lighting is fine for some subjects when you want maximum detail in all tones. *Four times* basic exposure should compensate for this lower intensity: either change your shutter speed to 1/30 or enlarge your lens aperture to *f*/8.

Cloudy dull is not very different from cloudy bright except for further weakening in the intensity of the illumination: quite thick clouds, with no sign of the sun. Now you may need as much as *eight times* basic exposure, which would bring your setting to either *f*/5.6 at your original speed of 1/125 or *f*/16 at 1/15. Please note that it is almost impossible to hand-hold a camera steady for a quarter of a second.

Cloudy dark is when you will probably decide that you didn't want to take. pictures anyway. This flat and dismal condition may be in very early or very late hours or when a storm is imminent. Such lack of intensity requires up to *sixteen times* basic exposure: open up to $f/4$ for $1/125$ of a second or change the shutter speed to $1/8$ of a second for your original $f/16$ aperture. The same negative density can be obtained with these equivalent combinations: $1/60$ at $f/5.6$, $1/30$ at $f/8$, and $1/15$ at $f/11$.

Any slight variation in exposure due to a different series of shutter markings—for instance, $1/25$ and $1/50$ instead of $1/30$ and $1/60$—is negligible. Whichever standard series of markings your camera carries, your exposure calculations can be made in the same way.

Color and Intensity of Light. When we refer to *normal sunlight* in arriving at a basic exposure, it is important to remember that the *color* of light, as well as its *intensity,* varies at different times of year and at different hours, especially toward the beginning and end of the day. The white light of the sun at midday blends about equal parts of all colors. During the hours near sunrise and sunset, however, the light not only decreases in the intensity of all wavelengths, but also loses proportionately more in the blue zone of the spectrum.

Since film is most sensitive to this blue light, the exposure should be increased by a half to a full stop for the hours farthest from the peak light of the day: in general, the two hours after sunrise and the two hours before sunset. With practice the photographer learns how the results can be expected to go at various hours.

Extreme variations in the intensity of the sunlight, such as midsummer in areas toward the tropics or winter in the far north, can also alter the basic exposure by one stop. Say basic exposure is $1/125$ at $f/16$; then, stopping down your lens to $f/22$ for more intense light, or opening up to $f/11$ for weaker light, may give you a more normal exposure even though, with the latitude of modern panchromatic films, $f/16$ would probably be satisfactory.

Direction of Light. In evaluating light conditions, you must also consider where the light comes from and the angle at which it falls upon the subject. As already mentioned, front lighting is the direction on which basic exposure is predicated.

In *front lighting,* the sun, or other source of illumination, is more or less directly behind you and striking the subject head-on. Because the sun direction is constantly changing, you get variations on the front-lighting theme, which apply also to illumination other than the sun: *45-degree front lighting* is usually the most desirable and is what you get on a sunny day during most of midmorning and midafternoon when the sun slants downward over your shoulder. *Top front lighting* is the kind that makes dark shadows under noses and chins and objects because the sun is almost directly overhead. These shadows can be softened by a fill-in flash (see Chapter 11) and can be quite flattering if the sun, though very high, is not quite directly overhead.

Side lighting means that the illumination is coming pretty much at a right angle to the imaginary line between the lens and the subject. This, especially in bright sunlight, makes an interesting contrast by throwing half of your subject in shadow and keeping the other half well lighted. In bright sunlight the basic exposure should usually be increased by a half to a full stop for side lighting; but if the light is weak or diffused, no increase is needed.

Cross lighting refers to illumination falling on a subject from two directions. It may be fairly soft lighting from a main light and a fill-in reflector, or it may be two lights placed to lighten strong shadows or to accentuate texture details.

Back lighting means that you, rather than your subject, are facing the source of light. On a bright day, back lighting can produce pleasing highlights on a person's hair and shoulders and a soft, even lighting of the face. Be sure that you do not allow the light to shine directly into your lens, or you will get a glare instead of a good picture. Basic exposure should be increased by a full stop for back lighting; if the illumination is very intense, you may need an increase of two stops, but on a dull cloudy day no increase is required.

The reason no increase is needed for side lighting or back lighting in dull or diffused light is easy to understand if you stop to realize that your exposure estimate will already have been increased to compensate for the lessened light, whatever its direction.

Back lighting can also be used for dramatic silhouette effects, for a tree or a building or a foreground figure, for instance. In this case you do not want detail in the dark areas; so instead of opening up your lens, you close down one f/stop below your basic exposure.

Subject Reflectance. The color and amount of light reflected into the lens from the subject being photographed is termed *subject reflectance*. This principle was covered in the chapter on light and is summarized here.

Light or bright-colored objects will reflect a considerable amount of the light striking them, sometimes more than 80 per cent; a brilliant white surface will reflect nearly all of the light. A surface that is sufficiently smooth to be nondiffusing will reflect a larger percentage of light than a rough-textured surface which scatters the rays.

Exposure should be decreased, usually by a full stop, *for lighter than average subjects:* for example, a sunlit snow scene, a beach with bright sky light striking the sand and water, a gleaming white steeple, or a brilliant blue sky with white clouds.

Darker surfaces, on the other hand, absorb much more of the light, often reflecting only a small percentage of it to the lens. When nearly equal wavelengths are absorbed, the object will appear to be a neutral gray, becoming a deeper gray tone as light absorption increases until it finally seems black. But if the surface absorbs one wavelength more than the others, it will take on the color tone of the least absorbed wavelengths; then it will no longer look neutral but will appear as a lighter or darker gray tone. *Exposure should be increased* by at least one stop *for darker than average subjects;* for example, a rainy landscape, a dark-skinned person, a dull bronze statue, a dark building, or people in dark clothes when the focus is on figures rather than on faces.

OTHER FACTORS AFFECTING EXPOSURE

Window Exposures. Taking a picture through glass is a common condition that nearly always calls for opening up one stop. Suppose you are shooting a street scene through a closed window, or a view from a train window, or a display in a shop window. Although a transparent medium such as glass will transmit almost all of the light reaching it (see Chapter 3) and although some glass will have more refraction than others, it is a fairly safe bet to increase the exposure by an additional f/stop. If a window has not been washed for some time, better not consider it a transparent medium.

If you are taking a picture through an airplane window, the brightness of the aerial view generally makes it unnecessary to increase the basic exposure. If you are shooting through a car window, however, you may need to increase the exposure by two or three stops because the relatively dark interior absorbs light, and the car roof can keep a good deal of the sky light from reaching the lens.

Nearly all filters call for some increase in exposure. These variations, and others as they apply to different conditions and types of subjects, are discussed in subsequent chapters.

Brightness Range. Obviously, if you select a scene with extremes of bright and dark areas, it is not possible to expose the film evenly. The span of light values within a scene, from brightest to darkest tones, is called the *brightness range* of the scene. For satisfactory reproduction, exposure must be within the latitude of the emulsion you are using, as explained in the preceding chapter.

The brightness range is represented as a ratio, which takes into account the capacity of the film to convert silver halides into the metallic silver of the image. When an emulsion is asked to respond to an unreasonable range, it can only do its best for the highlights, the shadows, or the middle tones—not all three. It is as if you were to measure a wall with a yardstick: the yardstick can take in only three feet at one time, but those three feet can be at either end of the wall or in the center or anywhere in between.

The ratio expressing the maximum brightness range (of arbitrary light units) with which a film can cope adequately is 128:1; in other words, the lightest part of a scene to be reproduced acceptably must not be more than 128 times as bright as the darkest part, even when you are using a black-and-white film with great latitude. Color films, having far less latitude than black-and-white films, cannot be expected to reproduce satisfactorily all the detail in a scene with more than an 8:1 brightness range.

On an extremely bright day a scene with high contrast may have a brightness range of as much as 1600:1; for such a scene no exposure could produce detail in both the highlights and the shadows. On the other hand, on a dark day a scene with very little contrast may have a range of only 30:1; it could be exposed to produce a thin negative with faint detail in the dark areas and moderate density in the lighter areas.

Sensitometry. The measurement of an emulsion's response to light is known as *sensitometry* and is primarily the concern of manufacturers of films, printing materials, and developers. It is scarcely necessary for a photographer to go into the technicalities of the subject or to acquaint himself with the "characteristic curve" of the film he buys. The first scientific study of the relationship between exposure and development was made in 1890 by a team named Hurter and Driffield; hence the term *H & D curve* which is still applied to the measurement of film sensitivity, as shown in Figure 49.

Tone Scale. What *is* necessary, however, is for the photographer to develop an awareness of a black-and-white tone scale in what he sees. Curiously enough, this is very easy for a colorblind person; for one with normal color vision, more studious observation is often required. Start by giving your imaginary scale a specific number of gray values, such as those in the film strip in the center of Figure 49, with a neutral gray having about equal parts of black and white in

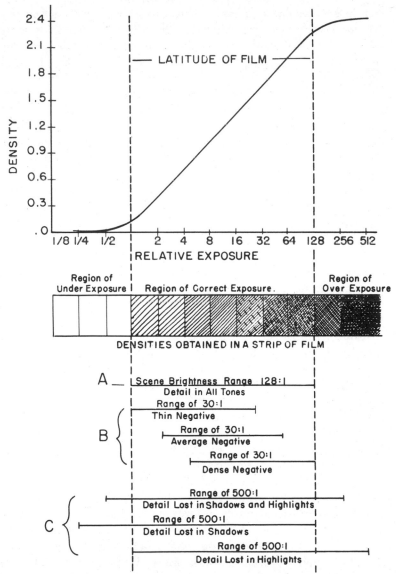

Fig. 49.—A typical film characteristic curve (H&D).

the middle of the scale. Then learn to evaluate colors and light in terms of these gray tones when making an exposure.

Overexposure and underexposure can be measured in this way for deliberate effects with predictable results. No photographer wants a neutral gray all the time, and frequently he must choose from an extreme brightness range which areas he wishes to emphasize or to sacrifice. You will notice in the illustration that, within the film latitude, there are three gray tones on either side of the middle gray. *Overexposing* one stop from this neutral gray will produce the slightly lighter gray of an average flesh tone or of flagstones; two stops will produce a very pale gray; an overexposure of three stops will produce an off-white. *Underexposing* by one stop will result in a slightly darkened gray comparable to open shade; two stops will result in a darker gray more like that of definite shadows; three stops will result in a very dark gray with little or no discernible detail.

How the brightness range of a scene affects the number of gray tones that a film can encompass is shown in the lower half of Figure 49. When the brightness range is 128:1 or less, an exposure for all values can be made within the film latitude; otherwise, you must decide whether to shoot for highlights, or shadow detail, or an average brightness. Sometimes an extreme brightness range can be compensated for in processing: for example, if the film is exposed for shadow detail, then developed less than normal time, the density of the underexposed areas will be reduced.

Kind of Film. Film was discussed at length in Chapter 6 and was mentioned earlier in this chapter in connection with the exposure index, which is the numerical scale of the sensitivity of various films to light. When you buy a film rated 50, for example, you know it is approximately half as fast as one rated 100; in other words, a film rated 50 will require twice the exposure of one rated 100, other factors being equal, to produce the same degree of density in the negative. Because the more orange color of tungsten light can reduce the speed of panchromatic films to about two-thirds that of daylight, black-and-white films should usually have an increase in exposure over the ASA index when used in artificial light.

If you switch from one brand or type of film to another having the same index number, there may be a slight variation in the density obtained by the same exposure setting. This small difference can safely be ignored in black-and-white films. With color films, however, because of their far more limited latitude, it is a good idea to make a few test shots and to note the most favorable basic exposure for using a particular film in your camera.

The very great latitude of black-and-white films for outdoor photography makes it possible to use them quite satisfactorily without a light meter. Under average light conditions and with some practice in estimating correct exposure, you can get a fair percentage of really good negatives. Color is another matter, however; there the latitude is much less and guesswork much riskier. Since color films are more expensive than black and white, and errors in exposing them more costly, it is worthwhile on all counts to use a reliable light meter for color materials. Light meters (described in the next chapter) are advisable also for poor or unusual light conditions.

Age and unsuitable storage can affect the speed of film, which is rated under controlled processing conditions. The manufacturer's instructions for care and handling should be observed, as well as the printed advice about developing the negative, in order to avoid a diminution in sensitivity. In fact, reading all labels and directions of photographic materials is a wise precaution and may prevent some picture failures; at the least, it helps you to keep track of a few of the continuous changes.

Speed of Lens. Your choice of exposure is defined, in the final analysis, by the maximum effective aperture of your camera's lens and by its range of shutter speeds. As an example, assume that, for the film you are using, a meter reading or other estimate of light conditions gives you a choice of these equivalent exposures:

$f/2$	$f/2.8$	$f/4$	$f/5.6$	$f/8$	$f/11$	$f/16$	$f/22$
1/500	1/250	1/125	1/60	1/30	1/15	1/8	1/4

If the speed of your lens happens to be $f/3.5$ (a half stop), obviously you cannot use the first two exposures; or if the lens closes down only to $f/16$, you cannot use the slowest shutter speed in the series above. Similarly, you cannot use the first two exposures if your lens has a maximum shutter speed of 1/200 of a second. *Which setting,* when you have a wide choice, depends on your subject and particularly on how much depth and action it involves.

Speed vs. Depth. As you will recall from the study of lenses, increasing the aperture to stop fast action in a picture decreases the depth of field. Conversely, decreasing the aperture increases the depth of field. You can't have it both ways, as a rule, so the exposure must sometimes be a compromise.

When movement is of major importance to your picture, naturally you choose a fast shutter speed and the corresponding f/stop. When depth of field is essential, choose one of your smallest aperture settings and a slower shutter speed. Remember, too, that it is difficult to hand-hold a camera steady for exposures longer than 1/50 of a second; anything slower than 1/25 should have a tripod or other brace.

Presetting the exposure of an adjustable camera to give it box-camera simplicity for casual outdoor shooting on sunny days is a frequent practice of some amateur fans. To do this with a standard lens, select a film with a rating recommended for box cameras. Set your shutter speed at 1/60, for example, for most color shooting and your aperture at *f*/11 or *f*/16—depending on the speed of the film. Set the distance at about fifteen feet (the "universal focus" previously mentioned) and everything in an average sunlit scene will be reasonably sharp from approximately nine feet to infinity.

If you are a newcomer to this great all-America game, you may feel at first that there is too much to remember just to set your camera for one picture. But it is like driving a car or a golf ball; once you get the hang of it and reinforce your knowing with some doing, taking pictures becomes a surprisingly easy and natural operation.

8

```
┌─────────────────────────────┐
│  Exposure by Light Meter    │
└─────────────────────────────┘
```

A RELIABLE light meter can be a photographer's best friend. But a meter should serve as a guide and should not be expected to carry the entire burden of decisions about the best exposure. That is the responsibility of the photographer.

An exposure meter is a must for color pictures generally and, by and large, will assure a more uniformly consistent density in all your negatives. With correctly exposed black-and-white negatives you can count on obtaining good prints with a full range of gray tones. Furthermore, a meter's ability to help you cut down on wasted film can justify its cost in a short time.

Selenium and CdS Meters. Photoelectric meters with a selenium cell have long been the standard method of measuring light intensity to determine correct exposure, the best-known brand names probably being Weston and General Electric. Relatively new on the market are meters with cadmium sulfide (CdS) cells, and it is possible that they may eventually supplant the photoelectric type (or be supplanted themselves by an even newer type). The fundamental difference is that selenium meters have an extremely delicate wire for transmitting the energy generated by light falling on the meter window, and the size of the photoelectric cell is comparatively large. CdS meters have a tiny hearing-aid type of battery in conjunction with a tiny photoresistive cell; they offer greater sensitivity, ruggedness, and compactness.

The wide and constantly changing choice of meters includes a variety of sizes and prices in both selenium and CdS types; at this writing new models of CdS meters cost about twice as much as new models of selenium meters. Figures 50 and 51 show some of the popular meters offered by Sekonic, a large company which also designs and produces meters for other firms, including built-in types for manufacturers of still and movie cameras.

A   B   C

Fig. 50.—Some selenium exposure meters: (A) An inexpensive small meter for general use; (B) Meter with built-in booster for low light, hinged mask for bright light; (C) A studio-type meter mainly for incident readings.

Basic Meter Construction. Exposure meters, like individuals, have certain similarities despite their infinite variations in design, as you can see in the examples illustrated. Curving behind the cell is a calibrated scale with numbers representing light values and a needle indicator ready to point to a number. The circular calculator on the meter case is a kind of compact computer into which you feed the index number (speed) of your film and the light-value number of the subject which the meter has sized up for you. When you have wheeled this number to the spot indicated by the fluctuating needle, the calculator displays an orderly choice of equivalent combinations for f/stop and shutter speed, any one of which will admit the same amount of light.

This meter reading may be the best exposure for normal conditions or it may be merely a guide to the correct exposure, which could be influenced by any number of specific conditions requiring the photographer's judgment. It is especially important to learn to assess subjects as average, lighter than average, and darker than average— as discussed in the preceding chapter.

Boosters and High-Low Devices. Another exposure problem relates to average, lower, and higher intensities of light, and to the fact that a given film may be slower in dim light than in bright light. In extremely weak light a selenium meter may be a trifle less accurate than when used in ordinary illumination because the amount of current in the photoelectric cell is proportional to the intensity of the light. There is a separate little accessory, called a *booster,* that can be jacked into some meters for reading unusually low light that the meter alone cannot measure. Figure 50B features a built-in booster for dim light and a mask for bright light. The newer and more sensitive CdS meters incorporate some device for reading high- and low-light levels, such as a switch for an "H" or "L" setting.

Special-Purpose Meters. Most modern exposure meters provide for reading reflected or incident light; a hinged or separate disk of

A   B

C

Fig. 51.—Some cadmium sulfide meters: (A) A popular CdS meter, compact and versatile; (B) Ultra-sensitive meter with attachment for night shooting; (C) Miniature precision meter attachable to camera accessory shoe.

opal glass to cover the regular meter window is a usual means of converting from reflected to incident readings. However, some meters (such as the studio type in the illustration) are designed primarily for incident readings. Most meters read still or movie settings; but for the few home-movie cameras without built-in meters there are inexpensive little movie meters.

Special-purpose meters are designed for a good many unusual conditions which even the most serious amateurs are not likely to encounter. As examples: there is a super-sensitive meter that measures moonlight and reads to 0.14 foot candles; there is a "spot meter" that takes readings at great distances from the camera; there is a "long lens" meter that, when inserted into the lens barrel, reads only the light seen by that lens. The outer space of photography, one might say.

Methods of Reading. There are two basic methods of measuring light quality by a meter reading: (1) *Reflected Light* is the amount and quality of the light that reflects *from* the subject when you point the *meter toward the subject* and away from the lens. (2) *Incident Light* is the intensity of the light that falls *on* the subject and is read by pointing the *meter away from the subject* and toward the lens.

Most meters are designed primarily for reading reflected light. For landscapes and distant scenes, as a rule, the meter should be slanted downward slightly because the sky is usually the brightest part of an average picture. This is not true of snow or some beach scenes; so, if you get a brighter reading by slanting the meter downward, then hold it level. To get a reflected-light reading for average brightness, you can point the meter toward the brightest area of your subject, then toward the darkest, and split the difference. If highlight detail is more important to your picture than shadow detail, take your meter reading toward the lighter areas. If your picture needs shadow detail, possibly at the expense of the lightest tones, then take your meter reading toward the darker areas. The quality of back lighting —that is, with camera facing the sun or other illumination—can be read by turning your back on the picture, reading the meter in the opposite direction, then increasing the indicated exposure by one or two stops.

Incident light is read through an opalescent glass adapter or with an incident-light exposure meter. And be sure to read the manufacturer's instructions. Hold the meter near the subject and direct it toward the lens: in other words, away from the subject. This method can be particularly useful in very weak illumination. Some photographers find that an incident-light reading for average subjects may frequently produce a more uniform density, but it is not recommended for subjects that have a wide brightness range. Furthermore, you must remember that the meter is measuring the light before it reaches the subject and, therefore, does not allow for the bright or dark quality of the subject itself.

Built-in Meters. As far as possible these should be handled in the same way as separate meters. Obviously, if the meter is part of the camera, it cannot be pointed toward the lens; but it can be pointed away from the subject. Think of the camera as a meter when taking a reading and hold it accordingly. On adjustable cameras you will probably find some dial to turn for setting the exposure at the meter reading, and the manufacturer's instructions should be followed.

Similar to built-in meters are a few detachable coupled meters. These are designed to engage the shutter dial and the diaphragm of a particular camera and cannot be used on cameras generally.

Palm Reading. Some meter manufacturers and some professionals advise taking a meter reading from the palm of the hand rather than from the subject. The reason for this is that you can always hold the palm of your hand two or three inches from your meter, but you cannot always hold the meter close to a subject. Since skin color is one of the criteria of tone values, this provides a constant measurement. Cup the palm slightly in order to obtain an *average* light reading and compare the subject matter. If the major subject interest is a little or a lot lighter than your hand, close down the lens aperture by a fraction to a full stop. Conversely, if the subject is darker in tone, open the lens proportionately more than the meter reading indicates.

Gray Card. Another technique is to direct the meter toward a neutral medium-gray card (at least a foot square). Place the card beside or in front of the person or object so that the card is getting the same light as the subject. A major purpose of the gray card is to bypass slight variations in the response of some meters to different colors, and thus produce a more consistent measurement of light intensity.

Color Sensitivity of Meters. The photoelectric and photoresistive cells used in exposure meters may vary somewhat, as films do, in sensitivity to different zones of the visible spectrum. To the midzones of yellow and green their response is not far from that of the human eye, but this is not true of their sensitivity to the blue and red ends of the spectrum. These minor variations are generally compensated for in the meter design, and in most instances they are negligible unless the blue or the red rays predominate in the subject being photographed.

Acceptance Angle. The angle of view included by an exposure meter is called that meter's *angle of acceptance*. Since this is quite often different from the angle of view taken in by the camera lens, inaccurate readings may result, especially when there are sizable lighter or darker areas outside the lens' view but within the meter's acceptance angle. Most of the early designs had very wide angles, but for some time there has been a tendency to narrow the angle of meters. Slight variations in the angle of acceptance are sometimes necessitated to avoid infringing on the patented designs of other meters.

Learn the acceptance angle of your meter by studying the instructions which come with it and by making a comparative study of your exposure results. If a meter has a relatively wide angle of acceptance, it should generally be read close to the subject rather than from the camera position. This helps to limit the light by which the meter is influenced to the subject itself.

Which Exposure? A light meter can furnish useful statistics; it cannot tell you which exposure you should select. As long as you understand your own meter and what you are doing with it, it doesn't matter whether you read reflected or incident light, whether you take single or multiple readings, whether your meter has a wide or narrow acceptance angle. How you interpret the data supplied by the meter and how you evaluate the tones of your subject are the fundamentals on which correct exposure depends.

Suppose that you have taken a reading of a scene and that your meter indicates an exposure of 1/125 at $f/5.6$ or 1/30 at $f/11$ and other equivalent combinations. This is where your judgment comes in and where you can begin to ask yourself some questions such as: Is the scene average—that is, composed about equally of lights and darks, front lighted? Is there any fast movement in the scene? Is there any source of extra brightness, such as snow or white sand? Is there any exceptionally dark object or area in which detail is wanted? Is the picture to be a close-up, or is depth of field important? And what are the color values in terms of a gray tone scale?

Procedure Summary. Following is a step-by-step summary of the general procedure for using a light meter. First of all, be sure that the flap of the snug leather case in which the meter is probably enclosed is not interfering with the light reaching the meter; best to fold it back under the case. Then:

(1) Set the ASA index or other numerical rating to correspond to the film being used. The calculator dial of the meter may be set between the numbers shown if the film speed is different from those numbers.

(2) Point the meter toward the subject to read the intensity of reflected light. Point the meter away from the subject for an incident-light reading. For distances, read from camera position. For correct close-ups, read six to twelve inches from subject.

(3) For an average brightness reading, check the necessary darks and lights in either distant or close subjects. If you are taking several pictures in the same location under the same light conditions, take your readings once for all the pictures before starting to photograph.

(4) Be sure to read only the areas within the frame of your picture, not those outside your viewfinder.

(5) Set the meter dial to correspond to the light-value reading. More combinations of aperture and shutter speed will appear on the dial than will be found in any one make of camera, since meters are designed for use with all cameras.

(6) *Think*. Evaluate tones and compensations needed, then choose one combination of shutter speed and f/stop. They are all equal in exposure value. As a starter, this is suggested: For average pictures, try 1/125 of a second and the corresponding f/stop. For action shots, select a shutter speed of 1/250 or faster and the paired f/stop. If you need depth of field, pick a small f/stop, such as f/16 or f/11, and its corresponding shutter speed.

Maintenance. Proper upkeep of a meter is normally a matter of reasonably careful treatment. It requires no periodic inspection or lubrication and generally is not subject to deterioration. However, an exposure meter is a delicate little instrument, and it should be protected from damage and abuse. Dropping definitely disagrees with it; and dangling it at the end of a long cord or chain can easily disturb its proper functioning. Excessive heat and moisture are confirmed enemies of the key components of a meter, so do not leave it in the glove compartment of your car or on a handy windowsill. In a damp climate a meter can be used with impunity, but it is not wise to use it in pouring rain. The meter's glass window should, of course, be kept relatively free of dust and dirt.

Zero Check. On all meters it is the fluctuating needle or arrow that indicates the quality of the light. Therefore, you should check occasionally to be sure that the needle points to zero when no light is entering the cell. You can do this simply by covering the meter window with something dark, like a notebook, or with the palm of your hand, while holding the meter level—that is, with its needle in horizontal position. Practically all meters have a small adjustment screw for resetting the needle at zero, if necessary.

Rules and suggestions for meter use can only generalize, can only give you an approximation or take-off point. After a good many pictures you may want to make a slight modification of your meter's zero setting, depending on whether your negatives show more or less density than you consider desirable. In that case, base any adjustment on color work as it will give you a more precise calibration than black and white. With every meter it is the photographer's personal satisfaction with the results that determines its ultimate accuracy.

9

Color in Photography

PRESENT-DAY color photography can achieve a wide variety of results which are affected by choice of film, choice of subject, light conditions, and processing controls. Exact realistic duplication of a scene is generally not possible, nor should it be the goal of an original photograph. Just as a painting of a garden in bloom, or of a glorious sunset, may inspire unlimited admiration—along with such comments as "But tulips aren't *quite* those colors" or "That doesn't look like a *real* sunset to me"—so a transparency alive with unbelievably beautiful color may sometimes seem to have surpassed reality. Make it a practice to study your own color photographs and the various factors that may have influenced their success or failure.

BASIC CONSIDERATIONS

Color Perception. Color photography derives from the fundamental premise that all color perceptions result from single or combined responses to three basic color sensations. Some sensations to which the brain-nerve-muscle mechanism reacts are distinctly unpleasant, like the energy waves radiating from an overheated stove and threatening to burn the hand that tries to control them. The waves of energy that we classify as color, however, are apt to be quite pleasant sensations, on the whole—and certainly not destructive ones, even when the color is "hot."

Different Primary Designations. A great deal of confusion (and a few arguments) results from the ill-considered use of the term "primary colors" without specifying which primaries are meant. As noted in Chapter 3, primary colors for mixing paints are not the same as primary colors for mixing light rays. Likewise, the subtractive primary colors which control photographic color processing are different. Finally, if you pause to think about the everyday colors you look at and live with and wear, you will realize that every one of them is some variant of red, yellow, green, or blue; these, with black and white, are referred to as the psychological primaries.

White Light. Fundamentally and photographically, the subdivisions of white light are *the primary colors:* BLUE, GREEN, RED. All other colors are combinations of these in different proportions. The respec-

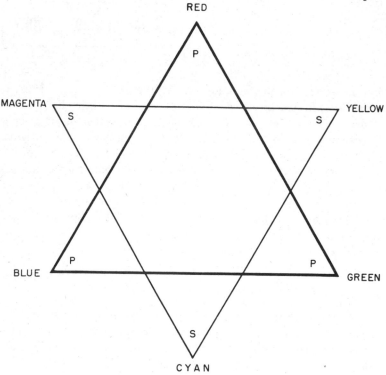

Fig. 52.—Primary and secondary colors.

tive *complementary colors* of the primaries are YELLOW, MAGENTA, CYAN, each being a combination of the other two primaries. (See Figure 52.) When a primary color and its complementary (secondary) color are combined to bring all basic color together again, the result is *white light.*

All this adding and subtracting is what makes color photography possible and is why there are two different processes by which to obtain results: namely, the *additive* process and the *subtractive* process.

ADDITIVE PROCESS

The principle of color addition was demonstrated in a rudimentary way more than a century and a half ago. Any method that produces color by blending three primaries, in whatever amounts, from three discrete sources, is termed *additive*. Figure 53 shows diagrammatically the result of color addition, which can be demonstrated by the following steps:

(1) When separate filters of BLUE, GREEN, and RED are placed in front of three light sources, such as projectors, and the three beams of light are superimposed in a kind of off-register projection, a core of WHITE color results.

(2) If only the blue and green beams are mixed, the result is a blue-green for which the technical term is *cyan*.

(3) When just the blue and red beams are mixed, a blue-red results; and if you aim to sound like a photographer, better call it *magenta*.

(4) Mixing the red and green beams produces yellow which, surprisingly, is called *yellow*.

How Photographic Color Is Added. Using the additive color process, you can produce a color photograph by taking three separate

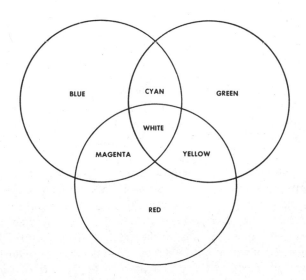

Fig. 53.—Additive color process.

but identical black-and-white exposures of a subject and employing three different color filters. If you expose one of the black-and-white negatives through a blue filter, the next one through a green filter, and the third through a red filter, the three negatives will have recorded all the blues, greens, and reds in the subject. When superimposed, after development, the three will appear to be one negative.

From each of these negatives a positive black-and-white transparency can then be made, in which the color-dense areas of each negative appear as clear areas in the transparency. The three positive transparencies should, if the film has been correctly exposed, transmit the proper amounts of light from the original subject. In this additive process a color transparency is obtained by projection. The three black-and-white positives are then placed in individual projectors, and a filter of the color through which the negative was first exposed is placed in front of each projection lens. Next, the three filtered images are superimposed on a screen to duplicate the original subject in colors that should be a fairly accurate reproduction—though slightly less brilliant because of the blackened metallic deposits in the black-and-white transparencies which hold back more than half the light rays of the projector.

Summary. Thus, *adding* red, green, and blue light *from separate sources,* in amounts calculated to duplicate a given color, is the basic premise of the additive process.

SUBTRACTIVE PROCESS

Subtraction is the opposite of addition; black is the opposite of white. In the subtractive process of color photography, the three primaries and three complementaries of the additive process swap places: YELLOW, MAGENTA, and CYAN now become the *subtractive primaries*. When projected in overlapping beams of light, they absorb their complementaries of blue, green, and red, and a BLACK core results. (See Figure 54.)

How Photographic Color Is Subtracted. It is easy to demonstrate this absorption by the subtractive primaries of their complementaries. If you project a beam of white light through filters of yellow and magenta, the yellow filter will absorb the blue from the light beam, and the magenta filter will absorb the green, leaving only the transmitted color *red* apparent on the screen. Then overlap the yellow filter with a cyan filter: again the yellow absorbs the blue rays from the

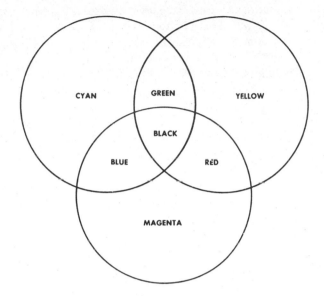

Fig. 54.—Subtractive color process.

light; the cyan subtracts the red and you see only the green. Now, this time overlap cyan and magenta filters; both filters absorb the red and green, respectively, and you see the transmitted blue.

Summary. A color print or a transparency is produced by dyestuffs which transfer, by transmittance or reflectance, the colors absorbed in the dye, with certain opposite colors cut out. Thus, *subtracting* red, green, and blue *from white,* by using cyan, magenta, and yellow in controlled proportions, can duplicate any desired color in the subtractive process.

STRUCTURE OF COLOR FILM

As noted in the chapter on films, there are two main types of packaged color films, *reversal* and *negative,* both of which are subdivisions within the *subtractive process* category of film manufacture. Reversal film, for color transparencies, is the more popular type. Both are similar in construction to the diagram shown in Figure 47.

Three color-sensitive layers of emulsion are supported on a single base of the same type used for black-and-white film. Each layer after processing contains the image of one of the three subtractive primaries: yellow, magenta, cyan. Each layer absorbs the complementary color to which it is sensitive. The top layer is a blue-sensitive (color-blind) emulsion which contains the *yellow* dye image. Under this layer is a yellow filter which absorbs blue but transmits red and green. The middle emulsion layer reacts to green and contains the *magenta* (blue-red) image. The bottom layer is sensitive to red and records the *cyan* (blue-green) image.

Reversal-type Color Films. There are two methods by which modern films achieve the color you see: (1) selective color development, the outstanding example being Eastman Kodachrome, in which the dye-forming substance is incorporated in the positive developers, requiring separate exposure and development for each of the three positive images, and (2) color-forming chemical development, used by the other popular color films such as Anscochrome and Ektachrome, in which the dye-forming intermediates are contained in the emulsions, permitting reversal development of all three layers in one developer.

Selective Color Development. This technique, used in processing Kodachrome, requires precise laboratory control of temperatures, solutions, and timing. It is definitely not a do-it-yourself game—unless you have a backlog of professional knowhow and about $100,000 worth of equipment. In this method the color images corresponding to the blue, green, and red of the picture you took are developed in the film's three emulsion layers by means of different couplers and filters.

The film is first developed to a black-and-white negative, forming the usual minute silver particles in all emulsion areas not occupied by the positive color image latent in each layer. Then a different coupler (a substance that couples to a chemical brought out by the color developer) is introduced for each of the three subtractive primaries, or controlling colors as they are sometimes called: yellow, magenta, and cyan.

When the film is exposed to blue light and developed in a yellow coupler, a positive yellow image forms in the blue-sensitive top layer. In the next key step the film is exposed to green light and developed in a coupler that forms the middle layer's magenta image. Afterward, it is exposed to red light and developed in a cyan coupler to produce the cyan image in the bottom layer.

Finally, after these major steps and numerous minor steps—including stop baths, hardening baths, washes, rinses—the negative silver particles remaining in any areas devoid of color images are removed by a special chemical bleach. The wondrous result of this scientific progression is a three-in-one *color transparency* with its rich variety of subtle shades.

Color-forming Chemical Development. Used in processing other films including Anscochrome and Ektachrome, color-forming chemical development is much less complex and, with a relatively inexpensive kit, can be processed in the kitchen sink. This is because the chemical couplers, which bring forth the color images in each layer of these triple-decker films, are combined with the sensitized emulsions during manufacture. After a negative black-and-white developer is used and the film re-exposed to white light, *a single color developer* brings out the yellow, magenta, and cyan images simultaneously.

Next the film, which now contains a negative silver image, a positive silver image, and three dye images, is bleached to remove the silver particles—and *voilà!* your color transparency. Fundamentally all films that use this type of processing are the same, with minor variations in the makeup of the coupling substances and in the color-developing agent.

Negative-type Color Films. The principal advantage of this type of color film is its relative flexibility. Basically the reason for this is that the film in your camera and the finished pictures are *not* the same bit of material—as they are in reversal types. Although negative types have the standard three-layer structure of all color films, they are somewhat akin to black and white in their tolerance of exposure variations and their allowance of some correction between developed negative and positive print.

Eastman's *Kodacolor* is a popular example of a negative-positive color film. When this type of film has been exposed, then developed, fixed, washed, and dried, it is printed on a specially treated paper. Another similarity to black and white is that on the negative the darks show as light areas, and vice versa. Negative colors also appear as opposites of what the finished print will show: magenta lawns, yellow skies, little cyan schoolhouses—all very weird. The orange which shows during the development of Kodacolor is due to two color-corrective masks of red and yellow in the film itself.

Exposure Latitude. Because of the second-chance opportunity to compensate in the printing for slightly inexact exposure, films like Kodacolor have an exposure latitude not countenanced by reversal color films. Although one particular aperture and shutter speed may be *the* best exposure, you can still expect a good printable negative if it is exposed anywhere within the manufacturer's recommended range of three *f*/stops.

The sensitized paper on which the color prints are made contains an emulsion similar to the film's except that the coupling substances are colorless so that they will not affect the values of your color picture. Color transparencies, or black-and-white prints, can also be made from negatives of this type of film.

10

Filters

A FILTER in photography is a transparent piece of glass or gelatin used to alter or control the color of light reaching a film during exposure. Filters are for black and white *or* for color, not for both. The exception to this are the "neutral density" filters which have essentially no color characteristics; they are used to reduce light transmission and to prevent overexposure of fast films.

Filters are designed to transmit certain colors you want brightened in the final picture or to absorb colors you want toned down; thus they can compensate for differences between what the eyes see and what the film records. Although primarily intended for a more accurate translation of the color values of the subject, whether in color or in gray tones, filters can also be employed in unconventional ways for deliberate dramatic effects.

PRELIMINARY CONSIDERATIONS

Materials. Filters are made of glass or gelatin. Of the hundreds available from various manufacturers, the most permanent and highest in quality are made of molten *optical glass* to which coloring substances have been added. They are in the minority, however, since their absorption abilities leave something to be desired when they are used with many panchromatic films; further, and more importantly, only a limited number of dyes can be added to glass.

Gelatin filters, the most commonly used, are available in practically any color you might want. To make them, appropriate dyestuffs are added to a solution of high-quality gelatin, which is then solidified into very thin sheets. To avoid fingermarks or other defects, these sheets must be handled with extreme care.

Mountings. Individual gelatin filters for hand cameras are cut from sheets, cemented between two layers of optical glass, then mounted in metal holders—like colored monocles. They should be handled carefully and should be kept from undue moisture or heat which could overtax the cement. Some are sized and threaded to fit a specific camera; others can be used in an *adapter ring,* which has the effect of converting the filter size to fit your camera; the threaded collar of the ring permits it to be attached in front of the lens. Identification of the filter type is engraved on the metal mounting.

Filter Factors. The number indicating the additional exposure required to compensate for the reduced light transmission when a filter is used is called the *filter factor;* it can vary from zero to six or eight times basic exposure, depending on the type of filter. For example, the almost colorless "skylight" filter for color films has no factor, but a red filter for black and white has a factor of 8.

These numerical factors are usually applied only to filters for black and white, and those for the most popular filters are printed on the leaflets packaged with black-and-white films. For color films a different exposure index is generally indicated, or flash *guide numbers,* instead of a factor by which the basic exposure must be multiplied.

Filter factors or guide numbers, like meter readings and basic exposures, should be regarded as *average* suggestions, to be supplemented by the photographer's evaluation of specific conditions. Differences in camera lenses, direction of light, and the particular effect wanted are some of the considerations that may dictate a slight departure from the recommended key.

Suggested Review. Since the subject of filters concerns the modification of the color of light reaching the film, it might be well to review the characteristics of light transmission and absorption and the characteristics of different film emulsions. These are detailed in Chapters 3 and 6, respectively. The basic principle of filters for hand cameras is the same as that of color addition and subtraction explained in the preceding chapter; that is, a primary color transmits its own color and absorbs its complementaries.

FILTERS FOR BLACK AND WHITE

How the myriad hues all about you will appear in several shades of gray is a basic question for every photographer. You will recall that, while normal human eyes are most sensitive to the yellow-green portions of the spectrum, the greatest sensitivity of all films is to the blue and violet zones—and to the ultraviolet, which we do not see at all. For this reason a film sometimes records light and dark densities contrary to those you expect; an apparently brilliant yellow dress may turn out a very dark gray, or the bright blue sky you admired in a scene may be a washout in your black-and white print. The basic fact to remember is that a filter *lightens its own color and darkens its complementaries.*

Filters for black-and-white films are divided, according to their transmission abilities, into two general types: correction, or compensating; and contrast, or over-correction. *Correction* and *contrast* should not be thought of as sharply separate divisions since the correction of related colors rendered as black and white may seem to require more contrast or exaggeration for a true appearance to one photographer than to another.

When filters transmit all the colors of the visible spectrum in varying degrees for different wavelengths, they are broadly classified as *correction* filters. By equalizing the rays of light, they compensate for discrepancies between what the eyes see and what the finished print reveals in terms of black and white. When this type of filter has the transmission characteristics appropriate to the film and the light source, it is possible to obtain the correct values of the gray tonal range, "correct" being that which most nearly corresponds to what normal eyes see.

The second general group of filters for black and white are usually called contrast filters. These are more selective, absorbing certain colors almost completely and shifting the percentages of the rays transmitted from the other colors. An over-correction, or greater than normal separation of colors, is thus produced, showing in the print as increased contrast between the light tones (transmitted by the filter) and the dark tones (absorbed by the filter).

Fig. 55.—Haze penetration.

Fig. 56.—No filter results in washed-out sky.

Fig. 57.—Light yellow filter shapes clouds, gives pleasing contrasts.

Fig. 58.—Red filter exaggerates contrast for dramatic effect.

Haze Penetration Filters. Probably the most useful filter for general photography is one of the yellow group, which illustrates the principle of color addition and subtraction. When you use a yellow filter to clear up a distant landscape that appears to be wearing a misty blue veil, you are simply subtracting some of the blue so that the red and green can get through to the film; otherwise you would get indistinct gray on gray in your print, as in Figure 56. Haze consists of air, moisture, and particles of dust which scatter more blue-violet light than reds or greens; therefore, a yellow filter will help cut the haze by absorbing the light rays at the blue end of the spectrum, as illustrated in Figure 55.

The choice of a filter for haze penetration depends on the amount of haze, the principal subject, and the effect desired. Orange or red filters are used for greater contrast, for example, since they cut out most of the green. On the other hand, a light green filter will produce a result similar to that of a yellow filter, but will render skin tones and foliage colors generally lighter and softer.

Wratten Filters. If you wonder about the origin of the term *Wratten,* that was the name of the first English manufacturer of present-day filters. Although they have been made by Eastman Kodak for some time now, they are still called Wratten light filters; and the letters and numbers assigned to them are arbitrary labels which have become more or less standard during the past thirty years. Good filters by other manufacturers will have different numerical designations.

Only a few of the hundreds of commercial filters are used by amateur photographers to any extent. As a rule, filters are practical only for panchromatic emulsions since pan films record all colors. A handful of favorite filters, with their factors for popular films of medium speed (such as Kodak Plus-X), follows:

Filter & Color	Factor (for Plus-X)	
	Daylight	Tungsten
K-1 LIGHT YELLOW	1.5	1.5
K-2 MEDIUM YELLOW	2	1.5
G ORANGE	2.5	1.5
A RED	8	5
F DEEP RED	16	8
X-1 LIGHT GREEN	4	4
B GREEN	8	8
C-5 BLUE	5	10

Filters for Beginners. Most amateurs use only two or three of the filters listed; some are content with one or none. An initial choice is often one of the yellow group (including orange, which can be considered a deep yellow). The five described below are the most common choices.

K-2 *medium yellow* is usually regarded as the best general-purpose filter for outdoor pictures in black and white. It cuts haze, increases contrast, gives patterns and puffiness to clouds (Figure 57), makes lighthouses and steeples stand out, softens skin tones slightly, and helps produce (to borrow a Kodak phrase) "correct monochromatic rendering of colored objects." The factor of 2 means one additional stop for daylight exposure.

K-1 *light yellow* gives less correction than the medium yellow and is less popular. The factor of 1.5 is approximately 3/4 of a full stop.

G *orange* filters give greater contrast than yellow ones and are preferred by some photographers, especially for thick clouds, marine scenes, and a somewhat more emphatic separation of tones. The factor for daylight is 2.5, which is slightly more than one additional stop. (A factor of 3 would be one-and-one-half stops.)

X-1 *light green,* by absorbing blue and red and transmitting colors that contain green, gives a more natural tone to foliage and to the complexions of people photographed with the sky as a background. In artificial light, this green filter can be used "for correct monochromatic rendering of colored objects." It is a great favorite, but it does require more exposure compensation than the yellow filters: a factor of 4 for daylight or tungsten, meaning two additional full stops.

A *red* filters are used for exaggerated contrast (see Figure 58) when you are striving for a dramatic rather than a realistic effect and when you have enough bright light to compensate for the daylight factor of 8. Clouds, sailboats, and such will come out almost starkly white, while the landscape and other darks will seem almost black. Definitely not for a gray day! In artificial light (factor of 5) a red filter is especially useful for copying work—reproducing blueprints, for example. For daylight, if your normal exposure calls for 1/125 at *f*/16, for instance, the exposure with a factor of 8 would work like this:

Open 1 extra stop—twice the exposure—to 1/125 at *f*/11
Open 2nd extra stop—four times the exposure—to 1/125 at *f*/8
Slow shutter speed once—eight times the exposure—to 1/60 at *f*/8
(Alternatives would be 1/125 at *f*/5.6 or 1/30 at *f*/11)

Caution. Again we mention *average* in determining your exposure. A darkish day is not average; neither is back lighting. In such conditions remember that you may need an additional stop besides the extra exposure required by the filter. Conversely, if the subject is glaringly bright, you may need less. Refer to the filter factors recommended on the film information leaflet; then consider whether or not your subject is average.

Box cameras, since they do not permit an increase in exposure, can use filters only to a very limited extent. For example, if the doubled exposure needed by a K-2 filter corresponds to a preset aperture and shutter speed for a given scene, then of course the filter can be used. On the whole, however, filters are impractical for preset cameras.

Effect on Sharpness. Most single filters do not contribute to any loss of sharpness, even in standard enlargements. As a matter of fact, the increased contrast usually makes the print seem sharper, unless other conditions are affecting the definition. If you fail to obtain the effects expected, you may be overexposing; and you cannot get cloud-sky contrast on a gray day when there are no clouds and no blue sky!

Summary. Before looking at the quite different species of filters used only in color photography, it might be a good idea to list briefly some very general helpful hints for the use of filters in black-and-white photography:

(1) Check the recommendations of the manufacturer as to the sensitivity of the *type of film* being used; also check the *factor* of the filter you are using.

(2) To reproduce a color as *dark gray,* use a filter which *absorbs* that color. The color to which a film is least sensitive will print dark.

(3) To reproduce a color as *light gray,* use a filter which *transmits* that color. The color to which a film is most sensitive will print light.

(4) To emphasize a color, determine first whether it should be *lightened or darkened*. Details in a relatively large color area will show more clearly as a light gray. A small area of color will be more prominent as a dark gray against a lighter ground.

(5) Filters are often unnecessary. If you are doubtful about the right filter and film combination, your best bet may be an *all-purpose panchromatic film with no filter*.

(6) Not that you would, but don't use a filter that is going to absorb *all* of the light reflected by your subject!

FILTERS FOR COLOR PHOTOGRAPHY

Filters are used far less in color photography than in black and white. Very few of them are used by amateurs—usually only the so-called skylight filter and a conversion type which permits the use of indoor film outdoors.

Haze Penetration Filters. For a slight haze correction, a faintly pink-tinted filter, such as the Kodak Skylight filter (Wratten 1A), is widely used. It requires *no increase in exposure*, nor does Ansco's UV-15 (ultraviolet) filter; they simply hold back some of the sky's blue color to which all film is most sensitive. Some photographers like to leave this no-factor filter attached to the camera for all outdoor color shots; others argue that some pictures are better without the filter. Try it both ways and see which theory suits you and your camera.

Conversion Filters. The other type of filter which is popularly used is one that converts indoor film to outdoor use by cutting out much of the excessive blue contained in daylight. Most popular of these is a salmon-pink 85 filter which converts certain color films balanced for artificial light to be used satisfactorily in daylight. Since manufacturers are continually changing the available films, it is a good idea to obtain current information regarding filters for a specific film and to consult the film leaflet for any recommended change in the exposure index.

While it is quite practical, and frequently very convenient, to convert indoor film to outdoor type, the reverse is not true as this would slow down the film too much. However, some home-movie cameras feature a built-in filter to permit indoor and outdoor shooting on the same reel.

Polarizing Filters. The principle of polarization was discussed as one of the characteristics of light on page 31. Different makes of polarizing filters can be used to eradicate glaring reflections and to control the brightness of the sky without causing any change in the colors of the picture. To be effective, a polarizer must be used with the sun coming at right angles to your subjects. First you look at the sky through the filter, which is rotated by moving a little handle or knob. You will see the sky darken gradually as you shift the filter's angle. When you have the effect desired, leave the filter at that angle and place it on the lens mount. Some polarizing filters are mounted so that their angle can be adjusted while on the camera.

The additional exposure required depends on the angle used, the greatest degree of polarization calling for the largest exposure increase.

Color Compensating (CC) Filters. Designed primarily for professional work, these filters come in graduated densities of primary and secondary colors. Some are used only in the color head of an enlarger to correct the balance of color between illumination and a particular film in color printing. Some may be fitted into a special holder and used experimentally in front of a camera lens; the adventurous can also use the colored filters for black-and-white film in this way. Probably the greatest use of CC filters among amateurs is in slide remounting when one or more colored "gels" from a packaged assortment can be sandwiched into the finished slide.

11

Artificial Light for Photography

PHOTOGRAPHIC ILLUMINATION from any source other than the sun is generally regarded as *artificial light* and referred to as *tungsten* or as *flash*. "Daylight" is used almost synonymously with "natural" light and refers to any normal sunlight, from very bright to very dim. Here, however, is another instance of inexact terminology, since moonlight and starlight are natural illumination and call for daylight films; admittedly there is not much photography in this area, but a few amateurs do attempt pictures by natural night light.

PRELIMINARY CONSIDERATIONS

Sources of Artificial Light. For photographic purposes artificial light includes all tungsten-filament incandescent lamps: photofloods, photoflashes, and ordinary service bulbs; also fluorescents, gas lamps, carbon arcs, candles, and oil lamps. Photofloods require electrical connections and are standard equipment for pictures that need relatively prolonged lighting and have little movement—such as portraits, still lifes, interiors. Flash is used for action subjects, such as an active child or pet, for sports events, for night shots away from electrical outlets, for fill-in lighting, and for any subject requiring momentary illumination. Increasingly popular are the repeating speedlights known as electronic flash.

Fluorescent lighting varies because its color depends on the particular substance with which the inner walls of the tubes have been coated. The mercury vapor or similar gas within the tube does not produce color but merely activates the coating when an electric current passes through. Since most fluorescent lighting is closer to bluish daylight than to reddish tungsten, daylight-type color films are generally recommended. However, fluorescent lighting is often combined with tungsten, notably in places like museums, making it difficult to judge which is the prevailing light. Furthermore, there are slight differences in the color balance of different brands of color films. Here as elsewhere, the variables affecting satisfactory results are governed to a great extent by the judgment, experience, and preference of the photographer.

Bounce Light. This term describes the diffused illumination produced by directing either a photoflood or a flashbulb at the ceiling or wall instead of directly at the subject. The quantity and quality of the light that is bounced will be affected by the color and distance of the surface at which it is directed.

In an average-size room with a height of about eight feet, the floodlamp or flashholder can be placed about halfway between ceiling and floor for even distribution of the illumination; a lower white ceiling will require less than basic exposure, a high or dark ceiling will require more. When using color film, you will usually find it better to bounce the light from a portable reflector, such as white cardboard or sheeting, since even the palest off-white ceilings and walls can change color results.

Lighting Variations. The different types of artificial light can be used in combination with each other and with daylight. As noted earlier, *available light,* which is also called *existing light,* generally refers to dim or otherwise unsatisfactory light conditions under which you may wish to take a photograph, indoors or outdoors, without supplementary illumination.

Artificial lighting was once equated with taking pictures indoors, but improvements in film speeds and lens efficiency have made it practical and convenient to take many pictures under what were formerly "adverse" light conditions needing supplementary flash or flood. Pictures indoors are often taken by natural window light or by the available light of room lamps without photographic lighting equipment. Moreover, flash is not confined to indoors; and it is well to note that there is a good deal of *un*natural light outdoors: in city streets, at carnivals, and around campfires, for example.

The Kelvin Scale. Developed by the British physicist William Thomson, Lord Kelvin, this system in its application to color is based on the fact that white is the sum of all color and black is the absence of all color. (See color addition and color subtraction in Chapter 9.) Carbon, which absorbs light and was used by Lord Kelvin as a basis for comparison, was found to reflect no light at all at $-273°C$. This point of blackness became zero in the Kelvin scale; therefore, a temperature stated in degrees Kelvin is always 273 degrees higher than when stated in degrees centigrade. For example, when the carbon body was heated to a redness of about 2000° C., this emission of light was found to have a color temperature of 2273° K. Thus it was determined that as the temperature of an object goes up, it produces progressively whiter light with a correspondingly higher color temperature, which is indicated in degrees Kelvin.

It is interesting to note that the popular impression of warm and cool colors is contrary to scientific theory—a difference reminiscent of the widespread misconceptions about primary colors (see page 25). In the everyday world about us, in scenery and paintings, in fashions and furnishings, blues and greens are usually described as "cool" colors, reds and oranges as "warm" colors. To the man in the laboratory, however, the opposite is true. The first visible light to appear when Lord Kelvin heated the carbon body was red; when maximum heat was applied, the carbon reached a blue-white color.

Measurement of Color Temperature. The color quality of a light source in color terms of red to blue is generally referred to as that light's *color temperature,* variations in these color temperatures being

APPROXIMATE COLOR TEMPERATURES

CLEAR BLUE SKY ——— 10,000

9,000

OVERCAST SKY
HIGH SPEED ELECTRONIC FLASH TUBES

8,000

7,000

DAYLIGHT FLASHLAMPS (BLUE)
AVERAGE 10 A.M. TO 3 P.M. SUNLIGHT

6,000

WHITE FLAME CARBON ARC
DAYLIGHT FLOODLAMPS (BLUE)

5,000

CLEAR FLASHLAMPS
WHITE FLUORESCENT LAMPS

4,000

PHOTOFLOOD LAMPS (3400 K)
FLOODLAMPS (3200K)

3,000

INCANDESCENT HOUSE LAMPS

2,000

CANDLE LIGHT

1,000

Fig. 59.—Approximate color temperatures of common light sources.

expressed in degrees Kelvin. Like the Fahrenheit (F.) and centigrade (C.) scales, the Kelvin scale is simply an approximate measurement used at present to describe the degree of whiteness of a particular photographic light. Although sunlight has a color temperature, the Kelvin scale has been customarily applied only to the various artificial light sources.

Color temperature is not dependent on light intensity. For example, a fluorescent tube burns at a very low Fahrenheit temperature, yet has a high color temperature. In black-and-white photography the important considerations are the intensity of the light in relation to the subject and the speed of the film being used. The same factors apply to color photography; but advanced amateurs who take their color work seriously will want to consider also the color temperature of the light. The chart in Figure 59 indicates the approximate temperatures of common light sources.

ARTIFICIAL LIGHTING EQUIPMENT AND ITS USE

Ordinary tungsten or fluorescent room lights, floodlamps, or single and multiple flashbulbs may be used in combination with each other and with daylight to illumine a photographic subject. Flash is the briefest illumination and the most mobile; other lamps supply sustained illumination and must be plugged into electrical outlets. Since floods have a useful life of at least three hours, as compared to a flashbulb's split second, they are relatively economical despite their large consumption of current. With the versatile flash, one must visualize how the briefly lighted subject will appear; with floods one can preview the lighting effects.

Photofloods. A *photoflood* is essentially an electric lamp using an excess voltage for sustained illumination. This type of light bulb was introduced at the start of the 1930's, about the same time that panchromatic film became available, and the two innovations combined to make photography by artificial light practical for amateurs.

Photofloods, which should generally be inserted in a metal reflector, resemble standard frosted bulbs, fit standard sockets, and operate on ordinary house current of approximately 110 volts. However, the tungsten filaments of floods are designed to produce more intense light per watt for a relatively shorter lifespan per bulb. A No. 1 photoflood looks like a regular 100-watt bulb but burns as if it were a 750-watt bulb and has a life expectancy of three hours. No. 2 photofloods are slightly larger (like 150-watt regular bulbs) and give twice as much light (1500-watt intensity) for twice as long (about six hours).

The letter *B* with a photoflood number indicates that the bulb has a blue filter and should be used with daylight-type color films. If you use regular photofloods with Type F (for flash) color films instead of with the usual artificial-light type of color films designed for tungsten, you can sometimes obtain improved results with a light blue filter (Wratten 82A) because the photoflood color is a trifle yellower than most clear flash.

There is a much more powerful lamp, the No. 4 photoflood, which draws four times as much current and gives about four times as much light as a No. 1 flood; but this type does not fit ordinary sockets and is intended for professional studio use.

REFLECTOR LAMPS. A letter *R* with the photoflood number, such as the popular R-2 reflector photoflood, indicates that the lamp has a reflector lining which eliminates the need for a separate metal reflector. The filaments of the R-2 are about the same as those of a standard No. 2 flood, but the bulb itself is shaped like a funnel; its neck tapers toward the screw base, which fits a standard socket, and its broad flattened top is frosted inside. The reflective aluminum deposit in the funnel concentrates the R-2's light over an angle of approximately 60 degrees. Almost identical in appearance and performance is the RSP-2, a reflector photospot; but the light beam of this lamp has been concentrated into about 20 degrees on a fresnel lens (a small positive lens circled by prismatic rings), giving the condensed spot of light more than seven times the intensity of the R-2.

CIRCUIT OVERLOADS. Most electrical circuits for household wiring are fused for maximum loads of 15 amperes to prevent overloading, and it is not considered safe to use more than 1500 watts on one circuit. If you are using the maximum number of photofloods, all other loads—such as customary room lights, television sets, radios, and clocks—should be turned off. An additional precaution against blowing fuses is to disconnect major appliances, like refrigerators, while the floods are in use.

BASIC USE OF PHOTOFLOODS. Artificial lighting employed in such a manner as to simulate daylight can achieve a natural effect. Whether the subject is a person, a piece of machinery, or a small object, it should be carefully lighted to bring out detail and avoid harsh shadows. Outdoors, the sun is the one main source of light, with the sky serving as an immense reflector. Indoors, therefore, one photoflood should be your main source of illumination, and it should be kept above an imaginary line from the camera to the top of the subject. If a second flood is used, it should generally be placed near the camera, but not turned directly on the subject. A third lamp should be used only for background illumination or special effects.

For stepped-up but natural lighting, a No. 1 photoflood can be used instead of an ordinary bulb in a table or floor lamp, with the other lights balanced so that the shadows will not be too dark. This device is best employed when the lampshade is large enough to keep its distance from the scorching heat of the flood.

Exposure for incandescent or fluorescent lighting is determined by reading a meter in the same way you would for natural light. If a combination of artificial and natural light is being used, always expose for the *main* light source.

"PAINTING" WITH LIGHT. This technique is sometimes used for soft, even lighting when you wish to photograph a larger interior area than your quota of floods can cover. It involves handling a single photoflood as if it were a spray gun during a time exposure. If near objects appear too bright and background objects too dark for a good black-and-white print, "painting" may be your best lighting method. Set up the camera, focus for the area to be included, and select an exposure of *ten seconds or more;* time depends on the size of the interior since the shutter, of course, must remain open while you are light-painting. *Keep the floodlamp moving constantly* across the subject area, up and down and sideways, making sure that you do not allow the beam or any reflective glare to strike directly into the lens. If the depth of the subject necessitates your walking into the picture to paint the far corners, wear something dark, keep moving, and hold the light away from you and away from the lens. Don't paint any one part too long, but try to cover the entire area evenly.

BASIC LIGHTING SETUPS. The placement of photofloods, while applying to photography generally, is particularly important to formal photographs of people and is therefore examined in detail in Chapter 16.

Flash. The forerunner of modern flashbulbs was a form of powder flash, touched off amid noise, smoke, and some justifiable apprehension. By contrast, today's safe and silent flash is a small sealed bulb coated inside and out with cellulose acetate to make it shatter-resistant. There are a dozen or more sizes and types from which to choose, all standardized by the manufacturers and designed to fill the needs of different cameras, shutters, reflectors, and photographic purposes.

Flash photography falls into two general categories: *synchronized flash* which employs a mechanism for controlling shutter action so that it coincides with the peak intensity of the flash; and *open flash* which is without mechanical synchronization and can be used with any camera having a time or bulb shutter setting.

WHY FLASH? Although it is possible with fast films and modern lenses to take nearly any picture by available light, there are a number of reasons why some photographers frequently choose flash. For one thing, a specific type of flashlamp always discharges the same amount of light and, if properly used with a camera and reflector with which you are familiar, makes exposure more certain. Furthermore, flash can be placed where you want it when the existing light does not give the desired effect. A third reason is that the additional light permits you to use smaller apertures, even at action-stopping shutter speeds, thereby increasing depth of field. Still another consideration might be whether you intend to have enlargements made, since in that case the high-speed films you might otherwise choose for existing light could be undesirable because of coarser grain.

BASIC LAMP CONSTRUCTION. A standard flashlamp is filled with hair-fine flammable material and sufficient oxygen to assure fast and instantaneous combustion. A smaller and speedier midget type is filled with oxygen but, instead of foil or wire, has a chemical paste heavily applied at the business end of two little lead-in wires which are readily fused to produce an intense light of very brief duration.

The most popular flashlamps have a "bayonet" base, and some larger lamps have a screw base (both types are illustrated in Figure 60). There are also a "miniature" base and a "baseless" (AG) lamp. A flashholder accepts only one kind of base.

Because of the brevity of the light discharged by flash, its duration is measured in terms of a *millisecond* (abbreviated *ms*) which is 1/1000 of a second; that is, 1000 milliseconds equal one second. *Lumen,* or lumen second, is the term used to measure light intensity; it refers to a somewhat smaller unit than the more familiar candle-power. It is unnecessary for you to use these measurement units since you will find the essential data calculated for you in the exposure tables published for all flashlamps.

USABLE LIGHT OUTPUT. When a flash reaches approximately half-peak intensity, it is giving off enough illumination for normal ex-

Fig. 60.—Flash synchronization.

posure conditions. The useful light output of a lamp is generally calculated from that half-peak point to the same level on the downside curve. (See Figure 60.) Since an average between-the-lens shutter takes less than 5 milliseconds to reach wide-open position and a standard flashlamp takes 20 milliseconds to reach peak intensity, it is obvious that most shutter action must be delayed to give the lamp a headstart if the exposure is to receive maximum light from the flash.

Duration of flash refers to the usable and fairly constant output of illumination at or above half-peak intensity.

TYPES OF LAMPS. Flashlamps are classified mainly according to light output and delay, which is the length of time required to reach peak intensity after current has been applied. *Type F (fast)* lamps, which have a 5-millisecond delay (about 1/200 of a second), are not in general amateur use. The most popular standard lamps have a 15- or 20-millisecond delay (about 1/50 second) and are classed as *type M (medium)*. Class or *type S (slow)* lamps, which are principally for professional studio use, reach a sharp peak intensity about 30 milliseconds after current has been applied.

There is also a *type FP* flash for *focal plane* shutters; these lamps are similar to type M and reach useful half-peak intensity in about the same time. Their chief difference is in their greatly extended burning time after half peak. Some combustible materials burn faster or longer than others; variations in light output and burning intensity are governed by modifications of the bulb and its filling. For example, by increasing the diameter of the combustible wire filling, an FP lamp can be designed to supply a usable light output during the time it takes a focal-plane shutter to traverse the film.

Clear flashbulbs are designed to emit light that balances correctly with color films for artificial light. *Blue-coated* lamps are used with daylight-type color films and also for fill-in flash in outdoor shooting. If you are not sure which flashlamp type or size you should have for your camera and for the photographs you intend taking, ask your photo dealer for specific advice about basic types and new items.

GUIDE NUMBERS. The principle back of flash guide numbers is the inverse square law (page 41), which explains how the intensity of light is related to distance from the source of illumination: the nearer a subject is to the light source, the greater will be the quantity of light falling on the subject. Guide numbers, like basic exposures, are merely key suggestions for *average* conditions and should be altered to meet given conditions as you appraise them. Variations in synchronization and reflectors also influence individual use of guide numbers, which are based on the light output of a particular lamp in relation to the speed of the film and shutter speed being used with that lamp.

A *flash guide number* represents the approximate lamp-to-subject distance in feet multiplied by the *f*/stop to be used. Conversely, if you divide the guide number by the lamp-to-subject distance, you will get the recommended *f*/stop for that lamp at that distance. The chart for a particular flashlamp will list guide numbers according to the different shutter speeds you may use and according to whether the lamp is being used in a 3-, 4-, or 5-inch reflector and whether the reflector has a matte or polished surface. Lower guide numbers in a series indicate higher (faster) shutter speeds.

INSTANT FIGURING FOR FLASH. An accepted procedure for quick calculation on flash is to figure on ten feet as average and to drop the last zero of the guide number—for instance, 170 to 17. At closer than ten feet, the flash is brighter, so set the exposure down one stop. If the flash travels more than ten feet to the subject, open up one stop.

Charts of guide numbers accompany packaged flashlamps and may also be found on the instruction leaflets packaged with films; many individual flashholders have all essential data right on the holder. Inexpensive little dialguides for flash are also available in photographic stores. Guide numbers, flashlamp numbers, film exposure indexes, and flash equipment are all subject to change.

OPEN FLASH. This nonsynchronized method of firing flashlamps is not in wide use today since most modern cameras are designed with built-in synchronization. However, open flash, which can be used with any camera having a T (time) or B (bulb) setting, is sometimes desirable, and the method is simplicity itself. Exposure is determined from the guide number recommended for "Open" or "Time" and, after setting up the camera on a tripod or other firm support, you open the shutter manually, flash the lamp, then close the shutter. Because a standard type M flashlamp produces effective illumination for about 1/50 second, your choice of subject should be limited to relatively still matter for which a 1/50 shutter speed would be appropriate in natural light. Also, the existing light should be at a fairly low level, otherwise the room lights or window light may register too brightly.

Although open flash can be used on the camera, it is not recommended as this position tends to overexpose near objects in relation to more distant areas of the room. Detaching the flashgun from the camera permits you to place the light in a more advantageous spot. It is further possible to use a variation of the "painting" technique explained for photofloods to light a sizable area with flash; the principal differences are that with flash you should keep yourself out of the lens' field of view and should cap the lens between flashes. For using open flash outdoors after dark, see Chapter 18.

SYNCHRONIZED FLASH. The objective of synchronization is to time the shutter action so that it reaches maximum aperture at the same time the flash reaches peak intensity. For open flash there is a single guide number for a specific lamp; for synchronized flash there are several guide numbers, one for each principal shutter speed. Accurate adjustment of the synchronizer is especially important at the faster speeds because of the reduction in effective light output; at 1/250, for example, considerably less than half the illumination fired by a standard flashlamp is utilized.

Synchronizers can be either electrical (usually a solenoid core in a battery case) or mechanical (a device using gears, springs, and so forth). If you intend to photograph at higher shutter speeds, it is desirable to have a synchronizer with an adjustable delay which can be regulated for different speeds. When a battery system is used, be sure that the batteries are fully charged; or better still, have an outfit which stores the battery charge in a condenser.

BUILT-IN "SYNC." On the newer cameras having shutters with built-in synchronization, an "X" or "F" near the markings for shutter speeds indicates a setting for electronic or fast flash; an "M" indicates a setting for medium flash. These letters are also found on current charts of guide numbers for flash exposure.

Class F flashlamps can be used with between-the-lens shutters which have type F "sync," but only up to speeds of 1/100 or 1/250, depending on the particular shutter. It is extremely important to *read the camera instruction manual* about this to avoid damaging the shutter or the synchronization.

SINGLE FLASH. The majority of all flash photographs are made with a single flashlamp in a unit attached to the camera. This is by far the easiest way to use flash and very convenient for snapshots of people, pets, and various activities. The main objection to this popular procedure is that it often results in a strong flat lighting on the foreground subject and a background of black shadows. Nevertheless, on-camera flash is entirely adequate for many pictures, particularly when the flashlamp reflector is positioned to one side and somewhat higher than the camera lens—again imitating the direction of natural light. Be sure that the flash is not aimed at a surface which would reflect light back into the lens.

Single flash can also be used *off the camera,* not with simple box types but with most adjustable models. Detaching the flashgun, and using it on a flash extension cord, allows you to hold the unit at arm's

Fig. 61.—On-camera flash should not be too close to lens or subject.

Fig. 62.—Off-camera flash permits adjustment of lighting balance.

length to one side and above the level of the subject; the resultant highlights on one side and shadows on the other will create an effect of modeling and depth. Unless you are adept at operating your camera with one hand, you will also need someone to hold the flashgun, or you can get a flashgun clamp for attaching the unit to some support such as a shelf or chair. (See Figures 61 and 62.)

OFF-CAMERA FLASH TECHNIQUES. Direction and distance of flash off the camera can be controlled in various ways, except for action pictures when there is no time to manipulate the equipment. By aiming the flash toward a central area of your subject, you can balance the lighting to some extent and avoid an overexposed foreground. This is especially desirable if your subject is a group of people: by directing the flash toward the farther members of the group, you obtain a more even lighting of the group as a whole. Another technique for groups is to place the flashgun appreciably higher than the group, then tilt the reflector slightly upward so that the flash will be directed toward the group but not full in their faces. This method is sometimes called *feathering* and, being indirect, requires about two stops more than the basic exposure, which would be calculated from the lamp to the nearest person. Figure 63 illustrates the kind of indirect lighting that can be obtained by bounce light, feathering, or multiple flash.

Diffusion of the sometimes harsh light of flash is accomplished simply by draping a white handkerchief or its equivalent in front of the lamp, whether it is on or off the camera. Or you can *bounce* the flash from a white ceiling for a softer effect. Any lessening of the light intensity will require a compensating increase in exposure.

MULTIPLE FLASH. For large rooms and groups of people in relatively stationary arrangements, multiple flashlamps are sometimes used to provide cross lighting and background illumination for the elimination of black shadows and exaggerated contrasts. Since it is difficult for all but very experienced photographers to visualize how flash exposures will turn out, it is not advisable to attempt two- or

Fig. 63.—Girl scouts and their shell collections both benefit from indirect flash lighting.

three-flash setups until you have had some practice with single flash and have considered whether the photographs you plan to take are worth the expense and inconvenience of the additional equipment.

For multiple-flash photography, the flashholder which is coupled to the shutter should have a battery-condenser unit to forestall power failure. You will also need one or more extra flashholders and metal lampstands, clamps, or live aides to direct the additional light where it is wanted. Self-contained flash units which can be used away from the camera are called *slave units;* they are usually of the battery-condenser type and, although not connected by wires to the camera, are set off by a primary flash that is connected.

The basic setups for multiple-flash units are essentially the same as for photofloods (see Chapter 16). In black and white you will probably get more depth and modeling if one flashlamp is about one third farther from the subject than the key lamp; in color, however, placing two flashlamps at approximately equal distances from the subject seems to work out better. If all the lamps are the same size, exposure should be based on the key lamp, the one supplying the most direct illumination on the subject. Secondary lamps are generally for fill-in and background lighting.

FILL-IN FLASH OUTDOORS. The same principle of supplementary light to fill in shadows and cut down contrasts is applicable to outdoor pictures (see Figure 64). Formally this is called *synchro-sunlight* photography, but "fill-in flash" is its more familiar name. For most sunlit subjects the brightness range (page 85) is too great for satisfactory rendition of detail. The highlights, especially in color, should be no more than three or four times as intense as the shadows, and a fill-in flash can help solve the contrast problem. This technique is most frequently used to photograph people in back or side lighting; such lighting avoids the discomfort or squinting occasioned by full front lighting on a bright day but causes unflattering shadows which fill-in flash can lighten. (See the two photographs in Figure 65.)

With daylight color films, blue flashlamps (any bulb with a "B") should be used to match the natural light. Exposure is based on the main light which outdoors, of course, is the sun. While expert use of this technique requires considerable practice and depends to a great extent on personal preference, fill-in flash is a valuable addition to a photographer's skills.

Calculation of Fill-in Light. Since synchro-sunlight photography is

Fig. 64.—Filling in shadows with flash: placement of flash and fill-in result.

Placement of flash for fill in

Result of fill in

subject

60° Maximum

flash

sun

predicated on using the sun as the key light, the fill-in flash should always be less intense than the existing sunlight. This ratio is governed by the *lamp-to-subject distance*, which is calculated as follows: first, take a meter reading of the brightest sunlit area in which detail is wanted and determine your exposure for that part of the subject —say it is 1/60 at $f/8$. Next, determine the flash guide number for

Fig. 65.—Flash can solve some snapshot problems in bright sunlight. Left: Full front lighting. Right: Side lighting with fill-in flash.

the shutter speed, film, and type of flashlamp you are using—for example, 80. Finally, divide the guide number by the *f*/stop of your exposure setting—about ten feet is your lamp-to-subject distance.

If the camera-to-subject distance at which you wish to take the picture is not the same as the correct distance between flash and subject, you must position your flash unit by means of an extension cord and move your camera to the desired distance. Or you can move the camera-with-flash closer to the subject and lower the estimated brilliance by diffusion; one thickness of a white handkerchief reduces the flash intensity by about half.

EFFECT OF SHUTTER SPEEDS. At faster shutter speeds the relative intensity of the fill-in flash is high, so the correct lamp-to-subject distance is relatively greater; at slower shutter speeds you can bring the flashlamp nearer the subject. The explanation for this is that at 1/100 or 1/125 of a second the shutter cuts down the amount of sunlight reaching the film but cuts practically none of the flash output. At a typical slow shutter setting of 1/30, however, the film is exposed to sunlight for 1/30 of a second while the flash output reaches the film during only part of the longer exposure.

FILL-IN FOR CASUAL SNAPSHOTS. If you wish to make reasonably good synchro-sunlight photos without a lot of figuring, follow these simple suggestions: Set your camera for the basic exposure in normal sunlight (see page 82). Then place your subject so that the sun is at the person's back or side, but do *not* increase exposure as you normally would for back or side lighting. If you are *more than 8 feet* away, use the flash without diffusion; if you are *8 feet or less* from the subject, drape a white handkerchief over the reflector to avoid overexposing the front view. You can also use a simplified dial computer, similar to that in the Kodak Photoguide, to help you calculate distance and amount of fill-in.

ELECTRONIC FLASH. An invention of Dr. Harold Edgerton provided photographers with a new type of flash, the *electronic discharge lamp*. In lightweight portable models this flash unit usually has a slim strobotron tube filled with xenon gas and connected to one or more battery condensers by a kind of triggering circuit. When condenser-stored power is discharged through the tube, a practically instantaneous flash of extremely brief duration is released. This action-freezing speed and a capacity of thousands of flashes without changing tubes give electronic flash its principal advantages.

Since the flash from an electronic unit is between 1/500 and 1/2000 second, virtually all of the brilliant illumination is utilized.

There is no problem of peak intensity; hence the *guide number* recommended for a particular film is the same regardless of shutter speed. The color temperature, intensity, and duration of electronic flash equipment in proper working order are generally more consistent than they are with other types of flash. Daylight-type color films should be used, indoors or out, with electronic flash which is similar to the spectral quality of natural sunlight. Electronic flash is especially well suited to sports and other events where it is desirable to stop fast action. It is also good for informal portraits where you wish to stop momentary facial expressions and body motions.

X-SYNCHRONIZATION. A majority of modern adjustable cameras are provided with synchronization identified as "X," which means that the shutter can operate on contact (a delay of zero—or less) as well as on "M" (a delay of 20 milliseconds). To avoid damaging the shutter, you should not only follow instructions as to voltage and operation of the specific equipment but also use an electronic unit recommended by the manufacturer of your lens or camera.

Focal-plane shutters usually cannot be synchronized with electronic flash at high shutter speeds because the brief burst of light would strike only one strip of the exposed film; however, the amount of coverage varies in different cameras. At 1/60 second or slower, most focal-plane shutters expose the complete film area, thus allowing an accurately synchronized electronic flash to reach the overall picture.

COMPARATIVE COST. Electronic flash units vary greatly in size, design, and price. They are expensive and impractical for occasional casual snapshots, but for a serious amateur, who plans to take perhaps two hundred flash shots a year, an electronic device can be an economy compared with the same number of expendable flash-lamps. When auxiliary lighting is required, electronic flash can be combined with other less expensive illumination through application of the basic principles already set forth.

FLASH SAFETY. The common sense applicable to electricity generally should be exercised in the handling of flashlamps—which are considered quite safe unless treated carelessly.

Flashlamps are packaged to protect them—and you. Keep them in their packages until you are ready to use them; never carry them loose as friction may damage the protective coating of the glass or the glass itself might become cracked, causing the lamp to explode when fired. Some lamps have, inside the bulb tip, a blue spot of cobalt chloride which turns a light pinkish color if even an invisible crack has admitted any air.

When the low voltage supplied by the flash batteries is inadequate, house current (110 volts) can be used if the flashlamps are designed for safe flashing on house current; be certain the package states that such lamps are designed for 3 to 125 volts. If the carton states "for battery flashing only" the lamps are unsafe for house current. Disconnect the power before inserting the first bulb and aim the flashgun away from yourself or other persons when plugging in the cord. *If you are unfamiliar with your equipment, ask someone experienced to demonstrate it for you.*

The intense heat generated by flashlamps makes them too hot to touch immediately after firing. Your flashgun will probably have an ejector; if not, wait for the spent bulb to cool before removing it manually. Eject hot bulbs over an appropriate container, such as a metal can or wastebasket which contains nothing flammable.

Do not use flash in an explosive atmosphere, such as around gasoline vapor. Be cautious about picking up a flashlamp if you have built up an unusual amount of static electricity at the time.

Never drop a lamp you have just fired into a camera gadget bag or any other place where it might contact new lamps which could be ignited by the residual heat.

If you are photographing anyone within six or eight feet, the flashlamp should be screened by a transparent or translucent shield over the reflector.

Fluorescent Lighting. Fluorescent lamps, while varying greatly in types and sizes, have some common characteristics. They draw relatively few watts, and they supply a soft light of considerable photographic intensity that gives off very little heat. This comparative coolness is an advantage in studio portrait work where a sitter can be spared the twin discomforts of excessive heat and blinding floodlamps. The chief disadvantage is the softness of the illumination which, although sometimes quite flattering, is too diffuse to be concentrated into a small area and thus produces a flat kind of lighting. If you are arranging your own subject and lighting (not simply taking a picture where the lighting happens to be fluorescent), you can counteract this flatness by using photofloods and spots for background and highlights.

Fluorescent lighting is not often used in color photography. Although a white fluorescent lamp has a normal color temperature of about 3500° K., the temperature fluctuates with the age of the lamp, making it undependable as a light source. Fluorescents, unlike tungsten lamps, give better and more economical service if they are not switched off frequently but left on during the time you are arranging and taking your pictures.

12

A Look at Composition

COMPOSITION, being a subjective term, cannot be arbitrarily defined, nor can any set of rules ensure a successful composition in all situations. When the elements of a picture have a pleasing, unified arrangement, that picture can be said to have good composition. If it looks right to you, it *is* right. If you sense, however vaguely, some confusion or conflict, the composition is *not* right. In short, a composition should satisfy a viewer's innate sense of harmony and proportion.

Certain general principles can help you to develop a feeling for effective photographic composition. By being sufficiently aware of these guides to apply them where they fit and to forget them where they do not, you can often gain the emphasis and the organization of shapes and tonal values without which even the most interesting subject matter can fail as a composition.

MAIN INTEREST

Have you ever looked at a photograph and felt impelled to ask, "What is it a picture *of?*" If nothing draws your attention to any one area, the eyes wander all over the scene, consciously or unconsciously looking for some meaning. When the components of a scene are well integrated, they direct attention to a dominant element in the composition. This *center of interest,* or *point of interest,* should be the focus of everything in the picture and, as mentioned in the first chapter, should seldom be the geometric center of the photograph but, ideally, the *dynamic center.* Since "point" might imply restriction to a single object and "center" might suggest the central area, these customary usages can be misleading if accepted literally.

One idea only should be presented in a single photograph. This does not mean that a picture should be limited to one object, or even to a few objects; what is important is that all the elements included in your composition support and emphasize the one basic statement you wish to make. Any irrelevant material detracts from the subject and should be eliminated as far as practicable.

It is quite possible to have a pleasing photograph in which some design or overall *pattern* comprises the picture. Such compositions do not depend on a specific area of emphasis: the main interest is the whole pattern. This kind of picture can be dramatized by a break in the pattern; for example, suppose you intend to make a pattern shot of the circular shapes and textures offered by the sawed ends of a pile of logs: You can break the pattern by introducing an axe, or a cooperative cat, into the composition.

"Rule of Thirds." One of the most helpful techniques for positioning the main interest of a photograph is to divide the picture area roughly into thirds, horizontally and vertically. This is usually done with imaginary lines, although some photographers with larger cameras actually draw four lines on the groundglass viewfinder. By

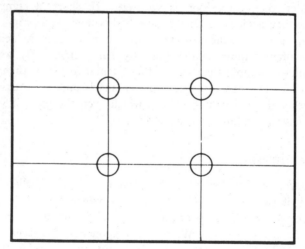

Fig. 66.—"Rule of thirds" pinpoints logical areas for main interest.

placing the principal object of a composition somewhere near one of the four intersections indicated in Figure 66 and keeping the supporting lines and shapes in a balanced arrangement, you can often strengthen an otherwise flat composition.

It is a mistake to follow this or any other "rule" blindly. Look to see what happens to a scene when you place your point of interest

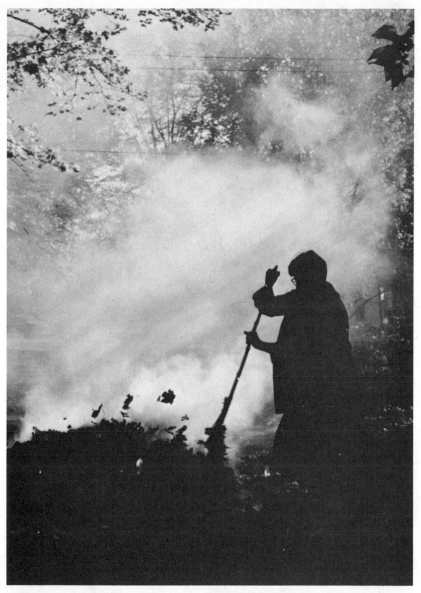

Fig. 67.—Active and atmospheric shot gains impact by "thirds" placement. (Courtesy of the Newspaper National Snapshot Awards)

Fig. 68.—Left: Good placement of camera. Below: Poor choice of camera angle.

A

B

near one of the intersections and when you place the same element at an imaginary central intersection of one horizontal and one vertical line; note how this applies to the award-winning snapshot in Figure 67. Fundamentally, the thirds guide is an extremely simplified, applicable version of the specialized art principle known as "dynamic symmetry," and its purpose is to help place photographic emphasis where the eye instinctively prefers to find it. A less obscure reason is that a central placement of the main interest tends to divide a composition into halves; this can create confusion for the viewer and give him the uneasy feeling that he is looking at two pictures instead of one.

Camera Viewpoint. The satisfactory arrangement of elements in a composition depends to a great extent on where you decide to place you and your camera. As a simple test, try the rule of thirds on the two views of an arbitrary "scene" shown in Figure 68. In view A you will note that the figure on the bridge is near the upper right intersection of the thirds, while the point at which the arc of the seemingly larger tunnel meets the water is at another intersection. Since the dark figure, although relatively small, is looking directly at the camera, it can be considered the point of interest, supported at the secondary intersections by the tunnel, the water, and the trees. Now notice how the various other darks all flow into an integrated pattern which gives unity and balance to the composition.

A poor choice of camera angle is apparent in view B. The figure not only falls near the geometric center but also is too far away to be significant, the upper line of the bridge span seems to cut the picture in two, the dark tree stands apart from the other elements, the tunnels have no depth, and there are no unifying darks pulling the elements together.

Leading Lines. Any object, or series of objects, which serves to draw attention to the center of interest is called a *leading line*. Among the more familiar natural leading lines are roads, pathways, fences, hedges, tree trunks, shorelines, shadows, and the horizon. These directional lines can be strong and obvious, like a dark hedge directing the eye to the entrance of a white chapel; or they can be subtle, like the long shadows, the footprints, and the tree trunk which lead unmistakably to the figures in the snow scene in Figure 69. Notice also that, due to the arrangement of lights and darks, the two figures constitute one main interest.

Although the word "line" might suggest a lack of weight, as compared to other shapes and masses, this is not true of leading lines.

Fig. 69.—Leading lines.

Generally they are substantial elements of the composition and contribute importantly to the overall balance. A figure which is not the main interest can be a leading line, either in tonal values or because it looks in the direction of the principal object rather than at the camera.

Horizontal lines suggest tranquillity and repose more often than other lines; typically they are found in a low landscape or a reclining figure. Compositions that rely entirely on horizontal lines are apt to appear somewhat static, but they can acquire strength and interest when combined with vertical lines. *Motion* in a horizontal direction, such as that of a speeding car or of a charging bull, immediately creates an action photograph. When there is action in a photograph, have your subject move *into* the picture by allowing more space in the direction in which the action is going and less space in the direction from which it is coming.

Vertical lines, usually in combination with other lines, can denote dignity and strength, as in Figure 70. The classic example is a towering cathedral whose blend of many lines, dominated by soaring verticals, adds up to an impression of power and peace.

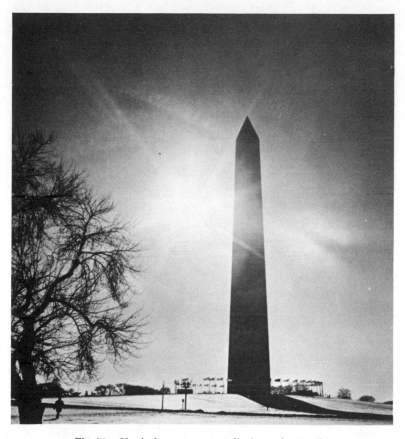

Fig. 70.—Verticals can represent dignity and strength.

Diagonal lines, with their off-balance look, lend themselves to more dynamic arrangements. As they lead the eye to or away from other lines or objects, they suggest activity and movement in varying degrees and often increase the dramatic impact of a composition, as in Figure 71. *Angular lines* formed by two or more lines from different directions can be very sharp, like a "Z," or open like an "L"; they may converge in a pyramid-like "A" or meet in a "T" formation.

Curving lines usually lend grace and a smooth flow of movement that can enhance and coordinate other lines. These, too, tend to assume alphabet tags, the most popular being known as the *S curve,* which is most pleasing in landscapes, as in Figure 72. Curving a diagonal into a "C" introduces a softened line which can lead the eye to the point of interest as surely as a straight line, but less urgently.

Fig. 71.—Diagonal and angular lines add to impression of coordinated activity. (Courtesy of Scholastic High School Photo Awards)

Fig. 72.—A nicely handled example of the classic S curve. (Courtesy of the Newspaper National Snapshot Awards)

Fig. 73.—Effective use of parallel lines. (Courtesy of the Newspaper National Snapshot Awards)

Parallel lines can be effective in directing attention to a subject if they run in a contrasting direction to the subject's dominant line, as in Figure 73. If the parallel lines run in the same direction as the subject's, they usually weaken the composition.

Looking for letters or other familiar formations of compositional lines can be an interesting and sometimes instructive game. Generally speaking, however, it is inadvisable to embark on any picture taking with a fixed idea about photographing some scenery in an "S" curve or a figure in a symmetrical "Y." These terms serve merely to describe what we have seen in some photographs, not to dictate how the elements of a composition should be arranged.

BALANCE

Consciously or unconsciously we seek in photographs the state of balance that exists in ourselves and in nature. Quite automatically we keep upright on two feet, place chairs so they will not tip over, and estimate the weight of objects we pick up. Although we may not be aware of doing it, we also assign weights to the elements that make up a photographic composition. *Weight* in a composition signifies a value in relation to all the elements, not necessarily heft or size.

A *balanced* composition refers to one in which all parts in opposing areas within an arbitrary frame appear to be of equal weight and to belong to an integrated whole. This must include a balance between primary and secondary objects, between unlike shapes and masses, between various color values, and between highlights and shadows. Tones, lines, perspective all affect the balance of a composition.

Like Objects. Placing two similar objects of equal weight equidistantly from the center of a photograph (as if they were on a pair of scales) will produce a balance but usually not an interesting composition. Three like objects can be balanced in an equilateral triangle. Such an obvious balance may be appropriate for comparative purposes, for certain merchandise and machinery or for a close-up of identical twins, but it will lack a dynamic point of interest and rarely succeed as an interesting photograph.

Triangle and *pyramid* arrangements of seemingly dissimilar masses can achieve balance with fairly dull subject matter, as shown in the two matter-of-fact industrial photographs just below. The same

Fig. 74 (left) and Fig. 75 (right).—Triangle and pyramid balance of masses.

principle may be applied to more appealing material, as in Figure 76; you have probably seen it in captivating shots of two youngsters with heads together over one book or one upright tot manipulating a pulltoy. By observing your subject and noticing these patterns, you can learn to judge when they might serve a specific composition.

Unlike Shapes and Masses. Dissimilar objects of different weights can also be balanced by placing them at *unequal* distances from the center of a composition. The object of lighter weight in this instance should be farther from the center to create an illusion of balancing the heavier one. At a much greater distance from the center, a fairly small mass can balance a considerably larger mass near the center.

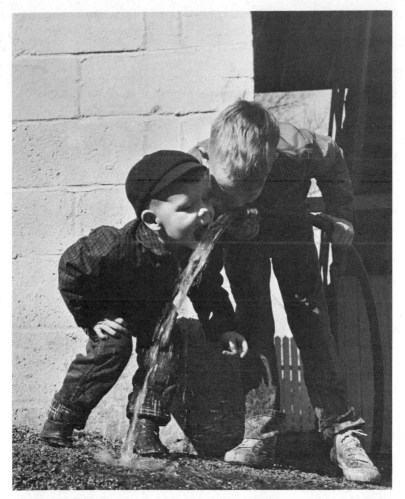

Fig. 76.—See what the boys in the backyard will have with a balanced triangular composition.

Dark tones have more weight than light tones, as can be seen in various photographs. For this reason shadows, clouds, and other intangible "objects" are important elements in balancing a composition, as are the leading lines already discussed in connection with main interest.

The impression conveyed by light and dark masses in a composition can be partially controlled by lighting. *High-key lighting,* which has predominantly light tones from medium gray to white, can lend airiness or softness to scenes and portraits. *Low-key lighting,* which has mainly darker gray to black tones, can impart a mood of mystery or seriousness. More often than not, you will want a balanced lighting between the two extremes.

Depth. Depth, or perspective, is simply the illusion of distance, the creation of space where none exists. It is possible to achieve this three-dimensional effect on a two-dimensional plane by the selection

Fig. 77.—Depth.

of camera viewpoint and lighting and by the placement of foreground and background objects.

The relative sizes of near and far objects determine the apparent distance between them, and our recognition of familiar shapes becomes a kind of mental measuring device. For example, in Figure 77, the apparent sizes of the foreground and background trees on a wide road which converges to the point described as infinity all add up to an impression of distance. This is the way such a road actually appears to normal eyes, so this is how we see a picture of it on a flat piece of paper. If you were to look at a photograph showing a vast expanse of desert sand with no footprints, no indication of plant, animal, or human life, nothing except sand, you would get no impression of depth even though the lens might have taken in a greater distance than in the snowy road scene.

One of the simplest ways to relate size and distance is the use of a foreground figure. A person admiring the craggy grandeur of a canyon wall or a mountain vista, for example, immediately establishes a dramatic contrast between the immensity of the scenery and the smallness of a recognizable object. Placing the figure at one side and looking into the picture can help to frame the composition as well as increase the apparent distance. The fact that framing is usually accomplished with identifiable objects related to the main interest— such as people, shadows, tree trunks, branches, doorways—tends to strengthen the illusion of depth.

Depth can often be gained by focusing sharply on the principal object and using a medium or large aperture to allow the background to go slightly out of focus. Back lighting, or a strong side lighting, can add depth by giving better separation and making the subject stand out more sharply from the background.

SIMPLICITY

Perhaps the one quality that more than any other distinguishes a strong composition from a weak one is simplicity. What simplicity is *not* is lack of interest; rather, the main interest is emphasized by the elimination of unessential or distracting elements, as illustrated in Figure 76. When all the elements of a composition are successfully concentrated on stressing a single idea, the result is simplicity.

Contrast is one of the primary factors in clarity and simplicity. Except for deliberate effects, mergers of nearly equal tonal values should be avoided; dark hair against dark foliage or a white kitten against a white fence, for example, will almost certainly lack impact. For better separation and contrast try to get dark objects against lighter backgrounds and light objects against darker backgrounds. In color pictures, of course, you must consider not only the tonal values but also the ability of different colors to complement or blend pleasingly.

Backgrounds. A busy background can be even more confusing than one that lacks contrast. If your subject is up against a distracting clutter as in Figure 78, try another camera angle—or another background. You can look at a scene and subordinate everything in it to your main idea, but the camera lens does not automatically distinguish a center of interest from its surroundings.

One of the best ways to cut out unwanted background is to get close to your subject, as in Figure 76. Most amateurs stand too far away because they see a scene selectively, mentally isolating the main interest without realizing that the lens sees unselectively everything within the range for which it is exposed. Studying your view-finder carefully and learning to move in closer will solve some of the background problems.

One of the best ways to change a background is to change your camera angle. Compare the two snapshots in Figures 78 and 79: the

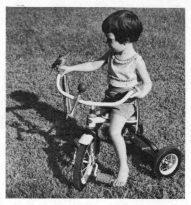

Fig. 78.—Left: Busy background overwhelms subject.

Fig. 79.—Above: Camera angle catches subject against grass background.

pretty subject of the first picture is all but lost among windows, rooflines, lamppost, fence, dark driveway, white snow, carriage handle and wheels; in Figure 79 a well-chosen camera angle has concentrated on the child's complete interest in the visiting bird. Frequently it is possible to eliminate houses and telephone poles just by aiming up instead of level and getting your subject against a fine blue sky, or aiming down toward a green lawn, as in Figure 79. Sky, grass, water, and sand are among the most desirable natural backgrounds. Indoors, a plain wall or plain drapery makes a much better background than a patterned fabric or distracting furniture; even the most attractive furnishings can take away from a main interest.

Selective Focusing. You can retain an interesting and appropriate background without loss of emphasis on the main subject by a sharp focus on the subject. You might be aware that there is space between a man and the tree beyond him, for example; but the lens sees them on one plane so that, if both are sharply focused, the tree may appear to be growing out of the man's head. Suppose you plan to photograph a fisherman and wish to include the rocks and surf of the locale:

By choosing your exposure for a relatively shallow depth of field and focusing narrowly on the man, you can subordinate the background and give eye-catching prominence to your main interest.

Foregrounds. Much of what has been said about backgrounds applies also to foregrounds. Simplicity should be the keynote, with unessentials eliminated. Extreme close-ups of people, flowers, insects, and small objects obviously have no foregrounds to consider.

As a rule, foregrounds should be in focus; the eyes accept a fuzzy background more readily than an out-of-focus foreground. Leading lines usually appear in a foreground and, while these elements should be less emphatic than the area to which they lead, it is generally objectionable to have them blurred.

Large objects, such as buildings and trees, should have sufficient foreground to support the object. An example of this is shown in the

A   B

Fig. 80.—Left: Lack of foreground support. Right: Foreground of proper depth.

facing illustrations that comprise Figure 80. In photograph A the building seems to be standing on practically nothing and to be overwhelmed by a topheavy sky. In photograph B the same building has been given appropriate foreground depth with a proportionate amount of sky.

Cropping. Often a composition can be improved by a kind of reframing. Masking the negative or print along any of its borders to cut out those areas is called *cropping*. The handiest way to study a print with a view to cropping is to use two L-shaped pieces of white cardboard, moving them to cover parts of the print until they border an area that satisfies you as a complete picture. (See Figure 81.) Color slides can best be studied in projection by tilting the projector to block off a strip along any border. Since the projector cannot be tilted in all directions at once, it is sometimes necessary to study a slide on a lightbox to be certain of the effect of cropping opposite borders; or you can put tentative strips of masking tape on the shiny (base) side and have another look by projection before actually remounting the transparency. Larger negatives can always be cropped more easily than 35mm or smaller.

Fig. 81.—Use L-shaped cardboards to mask print for cropping.

Composition and technique must also be balanced for successful photographs. Do not become so absorbed with framing a subject that you forget to focus correctly, nor so concerned with technical calculations that you neglect to notice a bad background. Consistently keeping a record of what you do with your camera, and constantly checking on the results, can develop an instinctive feeling for what makes a good picture.

13

Landscapes and Other Scenery

OUTDOOR SCENES photographed by natural light in the daytime or at night will be discussed in this chapter; the subjects covered have in common their predilection for daylight-type color films as well as for black and white. Other subjects usually associated with night photography, such as electric signs, Christmas trees, fireworks, and campfires, are considered in Chapter 18.

Scenery in black and white can be greatly enhanced by the use of filters, especially for sky-cloud contrasts, if light conditions permit proper exposure. (See Chapter 10.) In average light, it is best to use slow to medium films for their finer grain and a relatively slow setting (small f/stop) for depth of field. Beware of overexposure on bright days; it is better to err on the side of underexposure.

When taking scenery in color, remember that the continuous change in the color of the daylight itself—from the warm golden glow of the rising sun to the cool blue shades of early evening—can affect the tones and mood of a landscape. In most outdoor color photography, the "skylight" filter which has no factor helps hold back some of the excessively bright blues. A polarizing filter for darkening blue skies and diminishing reflections requires variable exposure increases. Before using a polarizing filter you should carefully study the instructions supplied by its manufacturer.

A *lens shade* is advisable for both black-and-white and color to keep the film from being lightstruck.

LANDSCAPES

The pictorial wealth of great and small wonders in nature almost invariably entices the tyro in photography. Quite rightly, too, for a beautiful picture of a beautiful landscape is one of the easiest successes. And being an easy success it permits a learner to become

151

better acquainted with his camera. Beyond that, however, there is the difficulty of finding original versions of grand views or more intimate scenes which may have been dulled by duplication on thousands of postcards, calendars, and magazine pages.

One way to avoid trite photographs of old favorites is to take pictures under unusual conditions of weather and lighting, of clock and calendar. Black storm clouds can be more arresting than fleecy white shapes; rain furnishes reflections on rocks and pavements as a change from sun and shade. Back lighting can make water sparkle or trees loom darkly. Seasonal changes provide new pictures of the same place continually, as do the hours of each day. Distinction is often achieved by breaking rules: by refraining from obvious framing, planted foreground objects, and S-curved pathways. Confidence and authority about rule-breaking, however, generally grow out of a knowledge of the rules you elect to break.

Spectacular Views. For spectacular scenery a selective viewpoint can make the difference between a travel ad and a personal expression. If time permits, study your viewfinder from many angles for a

Fig. 82.—Mountain masses need small aperture, infinity focus, and foreground object.

composition that really pleases you, and don't attempt to get everything into one picture. Increase dimension by having a person or strong foreground object at one side, but focus at infinity, using a small aperture and fairly slow shutter speed for maximum depth. (See Figure 82.) Predominant horizontals and a low horizon line will add to the impression of vast space.

To give mountains greater apparent height, keep the horizon line close to the top of the picture and let the steep verticals of cliffs and peaks dominate. At high altitudes on a clear day pictures are apt to be too contrasty because there is little moisture and dust to reflect light into the shadows; it is easier to get shadow detail on a slightly cloudy day. Unfiltered haze frequently adds realism to photographs of mountains.

When you wish to avoid excessive dark areas, especially with color film, try to keep your back more or less toward the sun so that the view you are taking will be well lighted, with enough cross lighting to bring out contours.

Masses vs. Shapes. The fundamental difference between spectacular and less pretentious scenery is that at a distance of miles you are dealing with masses, while at distances within a few hundred yards you are dealing with definite shapes. A towering mountain can be masses of snowy slopes, dark forests, and stark cliffs; but church steeples or haystacks or oak trees are known shapes with characteristic detail.

Small-scale Scenery. More intimate landscapes should have the focus on the main interest, which may be at infinity or nearer. (See

Fig. 83.—Rural scenes need small aperture for depth, some foreground interest.

Figure 83.) A peaceful meadow with mostly horizontal lines usually captures more attention if it includes grazing animals, a figure or two, a brook, or a rural mailbox, for instance, as leading lines in the foreground. Whether you find picture opportunities along country roads or in urban settings, the basic principles of composition and exposure apply.

Buildings in Landscapes. When a barn or house or other building is part of a composition, it should seem to be straight—unless you are after a deliberate angle shot or an abstract of one part of the building, as in Figure 84. Standard practice is to align one of its dominant verticals—for example, the left side of the barn in Figure 83—parallel with the edge of the viewfinder, making sure that you maintain a level horizon line. With a small camera it is usually necessary to stand well back from a building to get its lines acceptably straight, and the foreground should be filled in with shadows, shrubbery, or other elements appropriate to the composition as a whole.

Normally the eyes accept the illusion of lines converging horizontally in a landscape, but there is less occasion to observe that tall buildings have the same kind of "perspective" vertically. Shooting up at a building or colonnade, one cannot expect *all* its verticals to

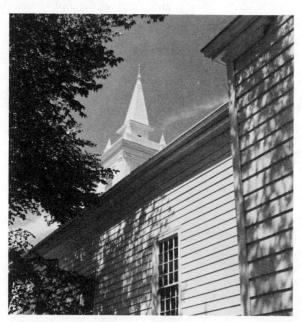

Fig. 84.—Angle shot of steeple is dramatized by diagonal lines and shadow patterns. (Courtesy of Scholastic High School Photo Awards)

appear parallel, any more than one can keep those hypothetical railroad tracks from appearing to converge in the distance.

Architectural photography should not be confused with amateur pictures of incidental buildings or with record snapshots of a new home, a favorite inn, or a famous museum. Architectural photography is highly specialized, requiring a view camera with swings, lenses of different focal lengths, and devices for counteracting distortion. Like outdoor portraits, architectural photographs benefit from a skillful selection of angles and backgrounds, accurate judgment and timing of light conditions, and a large negative size to facilitate cropping.

Good professional photographs of cathedrals, monuments, and historic landmarks can usually be purchased on location to fill gaps in your album or slide collection. Often they blend very well indeed with amateur photographs; they are especially welcome on sightseeing trips when time or weather may curtail your own picture taking.

SEASCAPES, BEACHES, INLAND WATERS

Filters for Haze. Except for deliberately hazy effects, you will want to use a filter for most marine scenes. Yellow and red filters for black-and-white photographs will penetrate haze, decrease glare, and deepen contrasts. When lakes, rivers, and waterfalls are surrounded by foliage or shadows, a light green filter may soften contrasts and give good sky tones. A skylight (no factor) filter, or a polarizing filter, is frequently used for marine scenes in color.

Exposure Suggestions. Because sunlit pictures of sand and water are generally brighter than average, basic exposure should usually be decreased by a full stop. Foam and sparkle on rolling waves can be caught with a fairly fast setting, 1/250 for example. A mass of surging water, like Niagara Falls, gains realism from the immense moving blur you get with a very small aperture (for greatest depth) and the correspondingly slow shutter speed. To catch detail in surf, try exposing for the highlights in the water, at a medium fast setting. If your composition is to include a natural dark frame of rocks or cave, as in Figure 85, it should be exposed for the bright area beyond the frame.

Back lighting can be used to give a shimmering radiance, a feeling of animation to water scenes. By sending elongated shadows toward the camera, backlight imparts an illusion of greater depth, as well as a more pronounced separation of lights and darks; a low camera

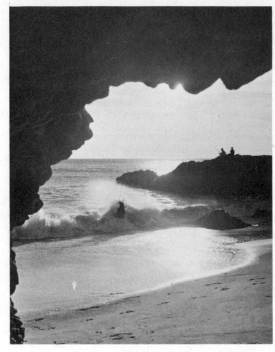

Fig. 85.—Exposing for lighted water catches sea and sand textures, silhouettes fishermen and rock framing.

Fig. 86.—Fog, sun, and solitary silhouetted subject were exposed at $\frac{1}{125}$ second, $f/11$, for this winner. (Courtesy of the Newspaper National Snapshot Awards)

angle further increases the depth illusion. Texture of wet sand can also be reproduced by back lighting. When facing the light source, remember to shield your lens from direct rays.

Focusing on Objects. Moving objects, such as people, birds, and boats, usually become the main interest when introduced into the picture; therefore the lens is focused on them rather than on the water itself, as in Figure 86. However, when objects at a distance appear as little more than dots on the horizon, they cannot be the focal point of interest unless you are using extreme telephoto equipment.

Marine scenes offer many pattern possibilities, especially in reflections which are often the main interest. In Figure 37 the focus is on the the massed boats with the rippling reflections contributing secondary interest. Figure 87 shows a telephoto close-up in which the reflections themselves, enhanced by technical skills, form the main interest.

Fig. 87.—Reflections caught by a 300mm telephoto lens make interesting marine pattern. (Courtesy of the Newspaper National Snapshot Awards)

Lens Protection. A filter, which is nearly always desirable for water scenes, helps protect the lens. Keep your camera from splashes and especially from salt spray and sand—particularly when there is action near you: people diving, hauling in fish, beaching a boat, building sand castles. When you are not actually using your camera, keep its case closed; if it does not have a case, keep it in a plastic bag or a closed gadget bag. In case of accident, wipe the camera with a cloth wrung out in fresh water and take it to a repairman as promptly as possible.

SKYSCAPES

Sunsets. The infinite splendor of a sky at sunset is an irresistible challenge to photographers, perhaps because the colors are always different, the light never quite predictable. If you are going after sunsets, don't take *a* picture but as many as you can, for one picture can record but a single instant of the elusive beauty we admire in a sunset's constantly shifting colors. Take the pictures when a cloud, or some foreground silhouette, obscures the direct rays of the sun coming toward your lens. Try to select a camera angle that will give you a good composition, with the sky filling at least two-thirds of it.

Black-and-white tones can hardly do full justice to such a colorful subject, yet effective shots are sometimes obtained. Some photographers prefer orthochromatic film when the sunset colors are mainly reds and yellows; when mauves and blues are more in evidence, especially after the sun has gone below the horizon, a panchromatic

Fig. 88.—Expose for sky colors in sunset scenes.

film such as Plus-X or Verichrome is needed. As a start, try the pan film with a red filter at fairly slow shutter speeds.

When photographing a sunset in *color* choose daylight-type films for their warmer tones. But remember that no color film will have sufficient latitude to encompass the entire brightness range of a flaming sky and a darkening land.

In deciding on exposure, take a meter reading toward the sky. The dark silhouetting of everything below the horizon will emphasize the sunset drama above. A slight *overexposure* will tend to intensify the colors; a slight *underexposure* produces softer colors, which sometimes resemble the delicacy of moonlight. If you are doubtful about your exposure setting, or do not want to lose too much time, try basing it on 1/60 at f/6.3 for regular Kodachrome or Kodacolor while the sun is still above the horizon. If the sun has already sunk below the horizon, open up to f/3.5 at 1/30. Then, if time permits, bracket your shots by taking a full stop on either side of the suggested exposure. Shorter exposures have the effect of making the sunset seem more advanced, while longer exposures tend to make it look earlier.

Fig. 89.—Heavy pre-sunrise mists bend reeds for a winning picture taken from canoe. (Courtesy of the Newspaper National Snapshot Awards)

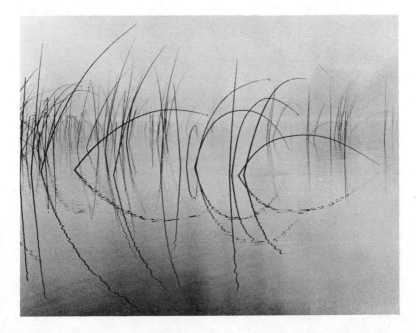

Sunrises. Most people are asleep at dawn and awake at dusk, so sunrises get less photographic attention than sunsets; but the basic suggestions apply to both. Sunrise colors are softer, on average, and early mists create a peculiar subtle radiance, particularly in the milder months when early rising can prove pleasant and rewarding. Figure 89 shows how one wide-awake photographer caught not only the mood of heavy morning mists but also the pattern of fish shapes made by reeds bending toward their reflections. The color of the sunrise light progresses in the opposite direction from that of sunsets, starting with pale grays and growing brighter and warmer as the sun climbs into the sky.

Rainbows. For greater saturation of color, a very slight underexposure of less than half a stop is recommended; otherwise the exposure should be what you would use for sunlight alone.

LANDSCAPES BY MOONLIGHT

Although a moonlit scene is not a daylight picture, it is related to landscapes and needs daylight-type color film. Since even the brightest moon gives only a tiny fraction of the illumination supplied by the sun, time exposures are required. This entails a consideration of reciprocity failure, which is why color films of different speeds are grouped together in the following suggestions. (For more on time exposures, see Chapter 18.)

Because all such photography is experimental and results are thoroughly unpredictable, any suggestions must be regarded as mere starting points. Amateur consensus seems to be that the best bet for a scene lighted by a bright full moon is a time exposure of 15 minutes at $f/11$ for regular Anscochrome or Kodachrome II. This should produce silhouettes in the landscape but not detail. The moon itself should be kept out of the picture, and the scene should have less exposure if there is water or snow reflecting some light.

Growing interest in astronomy and outer space has produced a corresponding increase in *astrophotography* and special books on the subject. Shooting *at* the moon with an average small camera will not produce much of a picture; but if you would like to try it anyway, pick a clear night and a fast daylight film, such as Super Anscochrome or High-Speed Ektachrome (or Plus-X for black and white). Try 1/50 or 1/60 second at $f/6.3$ for a crescent moon, at $f/8$ for a quarter moon, at $f/11$ for a three-quarter moon, and at $f/16$ for a full moon.

AERIAL VIEWS

Any standard camera, including a simple box type, can be used to photograph from planes or other great heights. Waist-level types of viewfinders, such as those on twin-lens reflexes, are the least convenient in planes.

On commercial airliners, the best seats for picture taking are back of the wing or well forward of the wing, on the side away from the sun. Occasionally a wing comes in handy for framing, but generally it is preferable not to have any part of the plane obstructing your view. Your shots will be *oblique* views, as in Figure 90; *vertical* views are mostly for mapping and are taken from special small craft. Since

Fig. 90.—Aerial views of landmarks or home town can help fill in record shots of a trip.

there is a good deal of vibration on even the smoothest flights, avoid resting your elbows on the seat arms or leaning against any part of the plane structure. Try bracing the camera against your cheek and keeping your arms in tightly; then hold the camera as close to the window as you can without actually touching the pane, which should be reasonably clean.

Various Altitudes. Below 1000 feet, exposures are about the same as on the ground. For takeoffs and landings, which cause additional vibration, very fast shutter speeds are recommended. Moreover, scenery seems to whiz by too fast for satisfactory shots when the plane is within 2,000 feet of the ground. As an airliner gains altitude, exposure should be gradually decreased, closing down by a full stop at about 4,000 feet. Unless the atmosphere is exceptionally clear, it is impractical to try for any pictures above 10,000 feet.

With mountain scenery, the matter of haze should be considered in deciding on an exposure and whether or not to use a filter. Aerial landscapes are best on a clear day because clouds often cast dark shapeless spots on the ground. Shooting through clouds, however, for a partly obscured but distinctive landmark can prove interesting. Midday light when the sun is directly overhead is the poorest time for aerials—and for most pictures. Side lighting improves detail, while back lighting increases the haze effect.

Exposure Suggestions. Black-and-white pictures benefit from the use of a yellow filter to reduce blue haze. With medium-speed panchromatic film and a light yellow filter on a bright day, you should find $f/11$ at 1/250 (or 1/200) about right for up in the air. A red filter, by holding back green as well as blue and ultraviolet, will give greater haze penetration and extremely sharp contrasts. Sometimes infrared film is used for similar striking results, but its major application is in reconnaissance; it is not very practical for general photography.

Exposure for aerials in color is, in general, less critical than for landscapes because the shorter range of contrasts presents no problems of highlights *vs.* shadow detail. There may be some slight color in a plane's window glass, but the effect is usually negligible. Since haze increases with altitude, a Kodak skylight filter or an Ansco UV filter is advisable. An average aerial exposure on a bright day for a color film rated ASA 25 would be about $f/4.5$ or $f/5.6$ at the 1/250 shutter speed. For sunset pictures in early evening, use the same aperture as if you were on the ground but a faster shutter speed, an average being $f/4.5$ at 1/125.

SNOW SCENES

Photography outdoors is less popular in winter than in summer for basically the same reason that sunrises are less popular than sunsets. Nevertheless, there are many hardy individuals who appreciate, through lens instead of window, the gleaming white brilliance of a snow scene. For those who do, the favorite time is soon

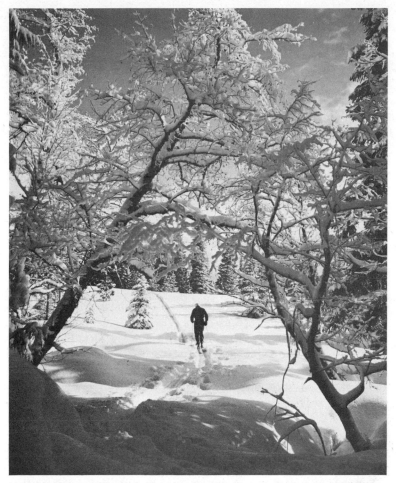

Fig. 91.—For snow scenes choose fine-grain films to bring out subtleties of pattern and texture.

after a snowfall so as to capture the unspoiled whiteness and sculpture surprises which may soon deteriorate into drabness and slush, especially in cities. In country or park areas, the tracery of fresh snow on tree trunks and branches, as in Figure 91, creates myriad compositions for alert photographers.

Snow Textures. One of the most fascinating aspects of fresh snow is that it is never just plain white but several different shades of white which can be played against each other as well as against interesting shadows. Because the comparatively large grains of medium- and high-speed films tend to obliterate snow texture, it is necessary to use slow films with very fine grain to reproduce the white-on-white subtleties.

Snow scenes are natural black-and-white subjects and should be printed on glossy or semi-glossy paper to enhance the brightness and texture; matte prints cancel much of the brilliance. A yellow filter is desirable for normal contrasts when the shadows are due to a sunny blue sky. If there are dark evergreens which might come out black, a green filter may give a better balance of tones.

Color film is more effective when the snow is a background for people rather than the primary interest. Colorful play clothes and winter activities will then determine your choice of film; for just the subtle colors of snow and the landscape, a very fine-grain film will give best results. The standard Skylight filter is recommended for contrast and to tone down the dominating blues in sky, snow, and shadows.

Shadows on Snow. These are always present, even at noon, because in this part of the world the winter sun is never directly overhead. Especially against the lightness of snow, winter shadows assume definite importance as design elements, and the snow itself acts as a natural reflector to bring out shadow detail. For snow artistry, backlight is probably the favorite technique; it throws long shapes into the foreground and gives good separation to lights and darks. Also, shooting into the sun will light up any stray flakes which may still be drifting down. Sidelight, or any crosslight which strikes the snow surface, is best for emphasizing snow textures, as in Figure 82. A low camera angle helps take full advantage of winter shadows and increases the impression of quantity and height in the snow.

Exposure Suggestions. A sunny snow scene, being a lighter than average subject, takes the usual decrease from basic exposure. However, the customary half- to full-stop increase for side lighting or back lighting is *not* necessary because of the low contrast range of most snow scenes. On a gray day the range is even lower; therefore your exposure should have a half-stop more than the meter reading indicates when the sky is completely overcast.

Falling snow (or rain) can be photographed most effectively with a slow shutter setting: 1/25 or even longer if you are using a tripod and if light conditions permit. Unless you are under a shelter which positions you at a distance from the falling snow, the flakes just in front of the lens will be out of focus and consequently somewhat blurred.

While gaining practice in photographing snow at really accurate exposures, remember that underexposure will result in muddy grays and darkened colors. Since you are trying to capture light tones, it is better to err slightly on the side of overexposure. If it is a picture you really want, the best insurance is bracketing.

Cold Weather Cautions. Camera lenses, like eyeglasses, will fog when transferred from a warm shelter into bitter cold, particularly if unprotected by a filter. Carrying a camera under your coat or outer jacket should keep it sufficiently warm to forestall fogging and keep the shutter operating smoothly. If fog or moisture freezes on the lens, do *not* attempt to wipe it off while frozen. Comparatively warm film should never be loaded into a very cold camera, or vice versa. Film becomes increasingly brittle as the thermometer drops and should be advanced very slowly, not only to avoid breaking but also to prevent the scratchy marks caused by static electricity.

In extremely cold weather a cable release is almost a necessity, as it is difficult to operate a camera with covered hands. Mittens are much better than gloves for keeping fingers warm and workable; beware of bare hands when using a camera: fingers can stick to icy metal parts, causing painful skin damage.

Winterizing is done only by expert camera technicians, usually for professional photographers working in subfreezing temperatures. Cameras can freeze, however, and if you expect to use yours in prolonged cold, it might be well to confer with a good mechanic and spend the few dollars charged for this kind of protection.

Fig. 92.—Low camera angle and $\frac{1}{500}$ shutter speed freeze leaping lad against plain sky background. (Courtesy of the Newspaper National Snapshot Awards)

14

Action in Still Pictures

THE ILLUSION of motion is sustained quite easily in a speeding "movie" sequence by the very rapidity with which the individual pictures are projected. What appears to be action in a "still" photograph, however, results from catching a sharp image of the moving subject at a single telling instant, as in Figure 92.

Stopping Action. When film is exposed to record a moving subject, the image is in contact with the film for a fraction of a second. A shutter speed of 1/300 second permits one-tenth as much movement on the film as a 1/30 shutter setting; in other words, the 1/30 second allows ten times as much chance for blur on the film as 1/300. A shutter speed that records action without blurring is said to stop, or *freeze,* the action. Your choice of subject, the effect you visualize, and the end use of the negative will determine whether a certain amount of blur, as in Figure 71, can be appropriately tolerated or whether a completely stopped action is desirable. Figure 93 shows an effective combination of completely stopped action at the originating end of a whopping splash and a convincing amount of blur at its receiving end.

Factors affecting sharpness are (1) the speed of the action, (2) the direction of movement in relation to the camera, (3) the distance between the moving subject and the camera, and (4) the lighting conditions. In addition, the flexibility and limitations of your camera must be considered. A box camera, for instance, will have a much slower shutter speed than an adjustable camera. Some adjustable cameras will have lenses of greater focal length than others, thus forming larger images which create more blur than smaller images.

Box-camera Techniques. While a preset lens is certainly not ideal for action pictures, it is quite possible to get creditable snapshots that have a feeling of motion. If you have a shutter speed of 1/40 sec-

Fig. 93.—Shutter setting of $\frac{1}{250}$ second recorded this summer-camp fun. (Courtesy of the Newspaper National Snapshot Awards)

ond, it is highly impractical to attempt to capture fast sports action; a shot of the particular sports atmosphere at a relatively inactive moment will probably yield a more satisfactory picture. Suppose you wish to photograph some diving events at a pool, for example: If you shoot when the diver is poised at the end of the springboard, you can retain an impression of activity, whereas clicking the shutter during the actual dive would result in blurring the film.

When using a box camera for any actual motion, such as children on roller skates or a dog ambling up a path, try a position that will bring the moving subject directly *toward* the camera (or directly away from the camera) as this will create a minimum of blur, as compared to movement *across* the focal plane which will emphasize the motion on the film. Even if you have a preset camera, you should note the recommendations for adjustable cameras, as well as the general instructions included in this chapter, in order to learn how to use your own aperture and shutter speed most effectively.

Panning. This technique can be practiced with a box camera for action shots of subjects moving at a fairly even pace in one direction. It contradicts all admonitions about holding your camera steady, for *panning* means swinging the camera horizontally with the moving subject, to record a *panorama;* it requires steadiness of a sort, however, as the follow-through camera motion must be very smooth and level. It works this way: assume your target is a boy on a bike. Center the subject in your viewfinder and, turning your body smoothly from the waist, follow the approaching subject in your finder until boy and bike are where you want them, then click your picture and continue to follow the subject for a moment—the way a golfer swings through after his driver has made contact with the ball. In this way it is possible to maintain a smooth motion throughout the entire operation. Practice pressing the shutter release gently; you cannot shorten the 1/40 second by a hurried, jarring jab at the trigger.

When the panning is done correctly, the subject will be in reasonably sharp focus, and the blurred background will have moved across the film in a direction opposite to the apparent motion of the subject, thus creating a definite illusion of movement. If you swing the camera slowly, there will be less blur; if you swing it faster, there will be more blur which will heighten the impression of speed, as in Figures 94 and 104.

Fig. 94.—Short distance, camera angle, and appropriate blur increase impression of speed. (Courtesy of Scholastic High School Photo Awards)

Effect of Distance and Direction. It is interesting to observe what happens to a passing scene from a speeding car or an express train. The trees and telephone poles a few yards from a train whiz by too fast to be counted. Shift your focus to trees at a middle distance and they will seem to move past very slowly. Then if you look at trees way off toward the horizon, they will appear to be standing quite still, and you can watch the same trees for a relatively long time.

This basic principle is true for photographic subjects actually in motion. If you watch a car or train several hundred feet away, it is not readily apparent that it is moving at all. As it comes nearer, however, it appears to become much larger rapidly and to race past with accelerated speed. As you turn your head (or camera), the same effect can be seen in reverse as the speeding vehicle appears to dwindle in the distance—all this despite the fact that it has been traveling at the same miles-per-hour during the time you have watched it. This is why faster shutter speeds are required to stop action at short distances from the camera than to stop action at longer distances.

Viewed from even slower rates of motion, external objects appear to move in a direction opposite to the viewer's movement. For example, if you walk alongside a picket fence at a brisk pace (say, a military cadence of 128 steps per minute) and look at the pickets, the effect will be downright dizzying. But if you look beyond the pickets at the landscape, the houses and trees will be reassuringly stationary.

In observing a speeding object, you will notice that the angle, or direction, of the movement affects the way you see and interpret the speed. If you stand in the middle of a road on which a car is approaching, the car's speed seems much less than if you were watching it at the same distance from alongside the road; and its greatest speed will appear to be when the car passes at a right angle to your line of vision.

Choosing a Shutter Speed. Developing an awareness of how distance and direction affect the way you see a moving object will help you judge which shutter speed is most likely to succeed in stopping the action you want to catch. The table of Recommended Shutter Speeds for Action Photographs on page 171 should be studied carefully for the fundamental principles on which it is based. Theoretically the correct exposure can be worked out by a mathematical formula; in actual practice, even assuming that you could be

TABLE 2

RECOMMENDED SHUTTER SPEEDS FOR ACTION PHOTOGRAPHS

Typical subjects	Approximate speed (in miles per hour) of moving subject	Distance between subject and camera	When motion relative to camera is . . .		
			directly head-on	at about 45° angle	at right angle
Slow Motion Pedestrians Street scenes & construction Slow-moving water & boats Parades, etc.	5 to 15 mph	10-15 feet 25 feet 50 feet 100 feet	1/200-1/250 1/100-1/125 1/50-1/60 1/25-1/30	1/300-1/500 1/200-1/250 1/100-1/125 1/50-1/60	1/400-1/500 1/300-1/400 1/200-1/250 1/100-1/125
Medium Fast Action Active sports Horse racing Scenes from trains, etc.	15 to 30 mph	10-15 feet 25 feet 50 feet 100 feet	1/500 1/200-1/300 1/100-1/200 1/50-1/100	1/500 1/250-1/500 1/200-1/300 1/100-1/200	1/1000 1/500-1/1000 1/400 1/200-1/300
Swift Action Speeding cars & trains Motorcycles Aircraft, etc.	over 50 mph	12 feet 25 feet 50 feet 100 feet	1/1000 1/400-1/500 1/200-1/250 1/100-1/125	1/1000 1/1000 1/400-1/500 1/200-1/250	1/1000 1/1000 1/1000 1/400

sure of the exact distance, the exact angle, and the exact rate of speed at which your subject was moving, the subject would have come and gone during your calculations.

Actual practice, in fact, is the answer to this problem. When in doubt, it is better to select a shutter setting that may be too fast than to risk using one too slow for a specific subject.

Timing. After you have decided at what shutter setting you wish to photograph a moving object, the next question is when to trip the shutter release. Usually it is a matter of anticipating where the action is going to be and clicking just before you actually see it take place. This gives the camera a fair chance to record the image on film at the same time it is recorded on your retina. In the panning technique just described for box cameras, the action follows a prescribed course; this is also true of the action of some sports, such as those in Figures 95 and 96. But if you are attempting to stop motion which is being controlled by the subject, you will probably find yourself in a fast guessing game. For stopping most sports action, the best times generally are at the start, finish, and middle.

The comparative inaction before and after some exciting movement, such as the throwing of a ball, can be recorded with a fairly slow shutter setting and often provides better pictorial possibilities than the action at its liveliest, such as while the ball is in flight. For example, in the brief instant when a basketball player is poised to toss the ball at the basket, or when a baseball has just landed in the little leaguer's mitt, there is a vivid suggestion of brisk activity.

Different people react at different rates of speed, so one cannot be arbitrary about how action shots should be timed. Your own timing of the actual click will doubtless become instinctive and practically automatic with continued practice.

Peak Action. Somewhere in the middle of most sports action, between the rise and fall of a complete motion, there is a split second of suspense termed the *peak action*. This refers to a pole-vaulter drifting over the bar (see Figure 97), a skater at the top of a spinning leap, a halfback whose raised foot has just come into contact with the football, a rower ready to dip oars again, a youngster clearing a large puddle or a jumprope, a rubber ball at the top of a bounce—any action during which the moving object seems, at the height of activity, to hang almost motionless in the air before resuming the movement.

Catching peak action depends more on alertness, familiarity with

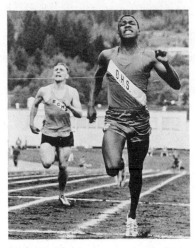

Fig. 95.—Finish (or start) of most sports events offers best chance for action-stopping photo. (Courtesy of Scholastic High School Awards)

Fig. 96.—Fast start-or-finish sports shot needs less shutter speed if action is toward the camera. (Courtesy of Scholastic High School Awards)

Fig. 97.—Relatively slow shutter speed can catch mid-moment of peak action if timing is perfect.

the action pattern, and luck than on a super-fast shutter. For the "pros" who get such exciting shots into the daily sports pages, there is—in addition to skill, speedy shutters, and extra focal lengths— a small accessory called a press pass. At certain public events it is just not possible for a grandstand amateur with a lens of standard miniature focal length to record details of fast action when there is a considerable distance (and several dozen heads) between camera and action.

Films. The high exposure indexes of many films today are often more than enough to compensate for a relatively slow shutter speed; they also allow medium apertures for better depth of field than you would get at the fastest f/setting. In black and white a medium-speed film will produce less grainy prints than the extremely fast films. Some distinct advantages of black-and-white films for sport shots, if you are aiming at the action itself, include greater speed, far greater latitude, adaptability to lighting conditions, and an economy which invites taking many pictures for a better chance of getting some good prints.

For color slides, choose one of the fast films, such as High-Speed Ektachrome or Super Anscochrome. Spectators at sports events are sometimes more colorful subjects than the main action, but the lighting is apt to be a bit tricky. Outdoors in full sunshine the brightness range is usually too great for color film, and a gray day may provide too little light for the shutter setting you want to use. Indoors, if it is at all possible or convenient, you should observe the lighting before loading your camera and then choose the most appropriate film. Remember, too, that color films do not permit the darkroom corrections which add greatly to the flexibility of black and white.

Atmosphere Close-ups. Groups of spectators or general atmosphere can often be photographed quite well with a simple box camera. If you have an adjustable camera, plus the opportunity to move in closer and to focus more accurately, you can get individual shots of spectators or participants. A close-up such as the one in Figure 98 can be obtained with a telephoto lens or by cropping a suitable negative. The close-up in Figure 99 is obtained by focusing on the foreground figure with a large aperture so that the other figures become an out-of-focus background. Close-ups can be used in slides or prints, just as in home movies, to give a change of pace or a dramatic accent to your photographic record of an event.

Some Sports Suggestions. If you plan to take occasional pictures of sports action, your camera should have a minimum shutter speed

Fig. 98 (left) and Fig. 99 (right).—Close-ups amplify photographic record of sports events. (Courtesy of Scholastic High School Awards)

of 1/200 second, preferably faster. If sports pictures are a major photographic interest, you will need speedier equipment with a shutter time of at least 1/500 second; shutters of the focal-plane type are generally preferred for fast action. It is also helpful to have a camera with a *sportsfinder,* an open frame auxiliary viewer which makes it easier to follow a subject in motion without excluding the area around the subject from your view. Consistent, analytical study of professional sports shots can be very instructive, even when they are beyond the scope of your own equipment. A few starting pointers follow.

Sailing pictures can be made at fairly slow shutter settings, even with a box camera, if the boat is moving directly toward you; if it is sailing across your line of vision, it needs 1/200. *Wrestling* and *boxing* are relatively slow action, with brilliant overhead lighting; if you have a ringside seat (close enough to touch the ropes), keep the ropes as foreground interest. *Figure skating* can be photographed at 1/100 to 1/200 second on fast film.

Golf pictures depend more on where you stand than on shutter speed: at a right angle to a swinging club, you will get a blur at any setting, as in Figure 100. It is best to try for a spot off to one side just ahead of or behind the golfer and to catch the beginning or end of the stroke. In golf, more than in any other popular sport, it is particularly important not to disturb the player with your camera.

Baseball and *football* plays on a big-league basis are usually too far away for satisfactory shots, but sandlot and Little League games

Fig. 100.—Camera at right angle to swinging golf club intensifies blur.

offer good opportunities to snap peak-action moments at 1/200 to 1/400 second with a medium aperture. (See Figures 101 and 102.) Any thrown object—be it ball, pillow, box, or stone—requires a shutter speed of not less than 1/200 second.

A high viewpoint is generally good for *swimming* and *tennis* pictures. Sometimes lake or pool water is clear enough for photographing swimmers through the water, but watch out for glare; a light yellow filter for black and white, or a polarizing filter for color, may be needed. Low-angle shots of up-in-the-air action (see Figure 92) are more dramatic than high or level viewpoints; therefore, try to catch a *high dive* or a *ski jump* in midair, against a pictorial sky, at 1/200 or faster. A low angle is also good for leaping tennis smashes, *pole vaulting*, or a *steeplechase*.

Prefocusing. When sports action is too fast to permit focusing as it happens, you will be better off to focus on the zone in which you expect the action to happen and hope for a reasonably correct guess, as in Figures 102 and 103. If you are where you can move about, such as on an open ballpark or at an outdoor horse show, you can step back when you find the action coming nearer than you anticipated. Prefocusing works very well for informal sports such as you will find at group outings, family picnics, and backyard games.

Fig. 101 (above) and Fig. 102 (below).—Catching sports action requires practice not only in timing and prefocusing but also in holding the camera steady and level. (Courtesy of Scholastic High School Awards)

Fig. 103.—Above: Choose best lighted area to prefocus for indoor sports events. (Courtesy of Scholastic High School Awards)

Fig. 104.—Below: Action should move into, not out of, a photographic composition.

Lighting Conditions. Just as in non-action photographs, the illumination on the action you wish to record will affect your choice of exposure. The existing light, whether normal daylight outdoors or artificial lighting indoors, may vary over the area you are trying to cover; a subject in motion may move rapidly from sunlight to shade or from overhead floodlights to a relatively dim corner. You may find that your camera will give you an adequate exposure at only the brightest section of the action scene; in this case you can preset your lens for the best lighting and anticipate action in that area. (See Figure 103.) Even when the lighting gives you a choice of exposures, it is generally more satisfactory to prefocus for the best zone of a fast-action scene.

Action Composition. In photographing fast action you must more often than not catch the subject as best you can and attend to the matter of composition later by cropping. This is one of the main reasons that sports and press photographers like equipment that accommodates a large format. Moreover, the fact that the longer focal lengths of larger cameras and supplementary lenses can produce larger images makes cropping less of a problem than it is with miniature negatives.

When the action is comparatively calm and predictable, try to have it lead into the picture. For example, a walking figure or a horseback rider or a racer should appear to be entering the scene rather than moving out of it as if the action had already been completed. When the subject is moving directly toward you, as in Figure 96, there is no problem. But if the movement is across the focal plane, as in Figure 104, it is usually desirable to have the space ahead of the subject greater than the space behind the subject. Practice in handling your own camera and studying the results should give you more effective instruction than any rules.

15

Snapshots of People, Pets, and Places

INFORMAL pictures of family, relatives, and friends—including the dog and cat—account for the largest percentage by far of all classes of amateur photographs. Within this extensive category, pictures of babies come first, both quantitatively and chronologically, and much of what has just been covered concerning action applies to the popular sport of photographing youngsters of all ages and their pets. Babies in general are contentedly captive subjects, and teen-agers have been known to remain relatively still at a number of occupations; but in between there is action galore in the busy world of childhood.

This chapter deals with casual photographs of the snapshot variety, an area where there is only partial control of circumstances and subjects—especially on vacations and other favorite picture-taking occasions. The subdivisions are for convenience, not because the principles of catching expressive snapshots of children and adults are basically different; the various approaches, composition cues, and illustrations are pertinent to snapshot situations generally.

GENERAL SUGGESTIONS

Many of the basic recommendations for more formal portraiture in the following chapter can be used to advantage for snapshots. Therefore, it would be well to read the next chapter in conjunction with this one, paying particular attention to the section on lighting to familiarize yourself with the general "rules" and how they concern outdoor portraits. To avoid repetition they are not included here, although they will be referred to. Note that fast films make it easy to photograph people in existing light almost anywhere and that hazy sunlight or partial shade is preferable to bright sunshine. Note also that midday sun overhead or any strong light striking the subject's face directly should be avoided.

People vs. Backgrounds. Including people in a scenery photograph is not the same as photographing the people. If you are taking a picture of someone, don't try to photograph a landscape or a house at the same time: move in as close as practicable and focus selectively on the person so that there is a minimum of background. (Compare Figures 78 and 79.) Unless you have had quite a lot of practice, you will probably do better to postpone a detailed study of formal techniques and to concentrate for a while on your subjects, backgrounds, and the smooth operation of your camera.

BABIES

New Arrivals. Starting a photographic story from the very beginning usually calls for the cooperation of a hospital nurse, either to hold up the infant for a few moments or to move the bassinet to a suitable spot. If the glass of a nursery separates you from your subject, keep the camera at an angle, rather than head-on, to minimize reflections. Use fast black-and-white film—save that color for later on—and open one extra stop for available light through glass.

If you use flash close up, at hospital or home, be sure to cover the flashholder with two thicknesses of handkerchief or similar white material so your picture will not be overexposed. If you use a preset camera which does not focus as near as you would like, try one of the simple closeup attachments described on page 223.

At Home. Pictures of baby during the first few weeks are likely to reflect a repetitious regime of sleeping and eating. A new father might like to try some high-angle shots of mother and infant: standing on a chair, radiator, or other available perch is one way to keep background clutter out of your composition. Use a wide aperture, if possible, to focus sharply on the faces. If you are mother and homemaker as well as photographer, your first pictures will probably be taken at nap time, and a high angle will help simplify the background, as in Figure 105.

Window light and the reflective quality of white pillows and light-colored blankets will usually provide plenty of soft illumination for crib or bed pictures when you use fast or medium black-and-white films. Sometimes a bassinet or crib can be rolled nearer a window or onto a porch to permit natural-light pictures without disturbing the sleeping child. If you keep your camera loaded with black-and-white film, the exposure will be uncritical, and two or three shots every few days will not involve much time or expense.

Fig. 105.—High angle helps simplify backgrounds.

Nonsleeping snapshots usually require an assistant or another photographer, whether it be father, grandparent, or neighbor. Even if such early activities as eating and burping, bathing and dressing, are photographed only on weekends, you can still obtain a consistent and rewarding record.

Sitting Up and Taking Notice. When a baby reaches the age of two or three months, you are no longer obliged to photograph it lying down but can experiment with propped-up poses. Try a big soft bedpillow in a sofa corner or a well-cushioned chair, or try propping the baby in a carriage or crib where he can watch a mobile —which makes a fine frame to shoot through—or other suspended toy. A single toy not of the mobile variety should always be smaller than the baby's face. Still more important, a baby, whether held by pillows or by knowing hands, should always look comfortable and *be* comfortable for picture taking; so don't prop him against a hard surface or in an unnatural position. (See Figures 106 and 107.)

Part of the baby's comfort depends on your forethought: try to pick an hour when he is usually wide-awake and not apt to be fussing. Then have your exposure and distance determined and your camera

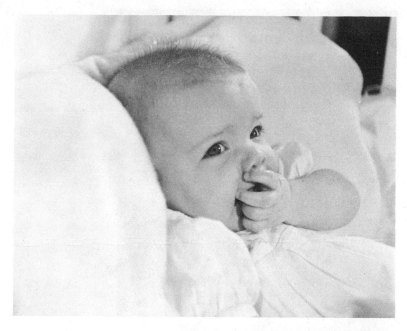

Fig. 106 (above) and Fig. 107 (below).—A comfortable position helps elicit smiling expressions; pale pillows and blankets help reflect light.

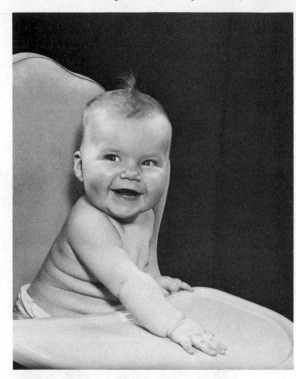

Fig. 108.—Choice of plain background, soft lighting, and close focus helps highchair pictures.

ready before posing begins. If the session seems unsuccessful, don't force the issue: patience puts a big plus in baby pictures.

Solo Sitting. When a baby is able to sit without propping in a stroller or high chair, you may have more control over the background. In any case, focus as close as your equipment permits and, if possible, get someone to stand off at one side and interest the subject in a toy or peekaboo game. This can produce delightfully expressive snapshots rather than a mere record of features. Plan ahead, perhaps with color film as well as an assistant, when you know that baby is to have a go at self-feeding, taking that first step, or some other eventful project.

Backgrounds are unwelcome distractions in pictures of people, and you cannot always get babies or other children in front of something plain. The solution is to get close enough to curtail the background intrusion and to focus on the face while letting background or foreground objects go out of focus. When you have a choice of equivalent exposures, select a large aperture so that there will be less depth of field; for example, 1/125 at $f/5.6$ will give a shallower zone of sharpness than will 1/30 at $f/11$.

Lighting should be comfortable and fairly soft. When the child is still young enough to stay where placed, as in Figure 108, a good scheme is to have the sunlight or other source of illumination behind him and something like a white cardboard or sheet beside you to reflect some of the light to his face. (See the suggestions about reflectors in Chapter 16.) A popular camera preference here is the $2\frac{1}{4}$ x $2\frac{1}{4}$ twin-lens reflex because you can look down at the ground-glass image without hiding your face from the child; and the negative is a good size for cropping.

Getting About on All Fours. Crawling opens up a world of new adventures and new snapshot opportunities. (See Figure 109.) As the baby grows more agile, the photographer must be more alert than ever and prepared to meet the subject on his own level. Don't think you can get a good picture of an exploratory crawl from your aloof

Fig. 109.—Crawling opens a world of new adventures. Framing tot in natural light of tall doorway tells a vivid story.

height: get down on the carpet or grass or beach blanket yourself if you expect the lens to see what is really going on.

Crawling pictures call for more flexibility than crib or high-chair pictures. You may not be able to focus quite as close up, nor to decide what the background will be. But you can decide on a likely distance for prefocusing your camera, load it with whatever fast film it accommodates, estimate the average light level of the area, and determine the best exposure guess. You may have time to change the exposure setting, and you may not.

Be ready too when baby meets another baby or new pet. (See Figure 110.) For either of these live shows, an offstage crew of two is imperative: one to cope with the cast, the other with taking the picture. A good "director" can help keep the subjects' attention on each other rather than on the camera. And take as many shots as practical: you may be lucky, but patience and the law of averages are more apt to produce winners.

Meeting Oneself in a Mirror. If you place a fairly large mirror where it can be discovered by the exploring tot, you can be quite sure of some very interested expressions. Focus on the image in the

Fig. 110.—Most child pictures should be taken at child level regardless of background.

mirror, and be sure that you and your camera are not in the picture; an angle of about 45 degrees to the mirror usually takes care of this. (See more about mirror snapshots later in this chapter.)

A Date with the Future. Don't trust your memory if you intend to keep a snapshot record of your children. It may seem at the time that you couldn't possibly *not* remember that Susie met her cuddliest doll on the second Monday in May, or that Billy met his first barber the last Saturday in. . . . Well, it just doesn't work that way. You should *date* your pictures right after you get them back from the photofinisher. When you get to album arranging or slide sorting, whether weeks or years later, you will be glad you made those timely notations.

CHILDREN

Keeping your camera handy around children does not mean that you must spend hours on end following their every move. But you should be set to seize sudden snapshot opportunities—sometimes called *grab shots*—which you can learn to recognize more quickly and surely with practice. (See Figure 111.) Habitual picture taking also accustoms children to having a camera in everyday use—like a clock or a lawnmower—and this in turn helps overcome excessive shyness or defensive mugging.

Down with Dignity! If you are as interested in your photographing as children are in their games, you and your camera will be some place down around their level (as in Figures 76, 110, 112, and 113), even if it involves a temporary forfeiture of dignity. Faces need not always be in the picture but, except for planned angle shots, looking down on children does not pay off in good pictures.

Catching children at their own games, as in Figure 112, generally results in better snapshots than asking them to pose. Sometimes one can unobtrusively observe a favorite pastime or daily habit for several days before deciding on camera positions and exposure, as in Figure 113. For more impromptu games you may be able to operate in the fringe areas of the activity without causing interruptions or self-consciousness. Plenty of absorbing games are played solo: if you come upon your small one curled up in a clothes basket, or sitting suddenly in a mud puddle, move in and grab a shot—naturally. But to request a child to assume such a pose would be unnatural, unsatisfactory, and unsporting.

Fig. 111.—Alert grab shot depicts happy relationship of a youngster and his dog. (Courtesy of the Newspaper National Snapshot Awards)

Fig. 112.—Children at their own games provide spontaneous and appealing pictures. (Courtesy of the Newspaper National Snapshot Awards)

Fig. 113.—Position of doll in background and unexpected peek in foreground result in a delightful winning snapshot. (Courtesy of the Newspaper National Snapshot Awards)

Small Fry in Motion. The principles explained in the preceding chapter on action can be applied advantageously here. Consider the direction of action as well as the approximate speed and remember that movement *across* the lens axis requires a faster setting than movement *toward* the lens. For average motion, such as skipping rope or scurrying about in hide-and-seek, a shutter speed of 1/200 or 1/250 is suggested. The capabilities of your camera will determine the advisability of certain snapshooting. For motion such as a tricycle coming down a predictable route or a youngster riding a pony, you might try panning, which is also described in the preceding chapter.

Props for Naturalness. Children as a rule have no objection to posing; in fact, some insist on doing so, as in Figure 114. Your problem is to maneuver the youngster into a natural pose, which is often accomplished by a helping hand and a well-handled prop. Advance planning is essential, especially with younger children. See that the camera is all set before revealing your *pièce de résistance,* which may be a toy, lollipop, flower, book, watch chain, kitchen timer, box of pebbles, or any other article that may enchant. The duration of the enchantment will be uncertain, so the prop should be kept out of sight until you are ready to click, then handed to the child by you or your helper. Total absorption may follow, or a bit of prompting—such as "Smell the posey" or "Hear the tick-tick"—

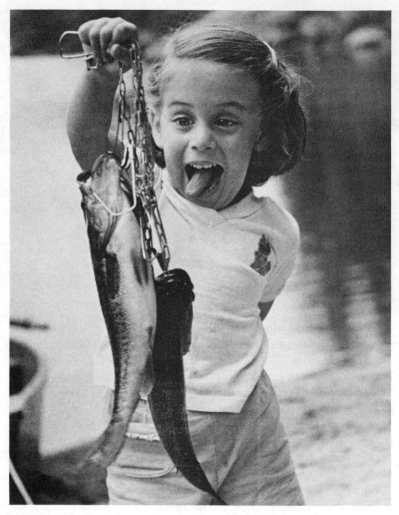

Fig. 114.—Very simple props, or spectacular ones like this, can produce animated expressions in children or adults. (Courtesy of the Newspaper National Snapshot Awards)

may seem in order. An empty-handed "prop man" may be able to elicit animated or serious expressions by engaging the subject in conversation or by clowning a bit out of camera range.

Picture-picking. Since black-and-white snapshots of children are usually the most numerous, calling for the most weeding out, this may be an appropriate place to mention a helpful little textile gadget named a *pick glass* and sometimes referred to as a "thread counter." This is a small but powerful magnifier, mounted on a tiny folding metal stand, which is used for counting the "ends and picks" in a fabric swatch to ascertain the number of warp and filling yarns per square inch. It is more convenient and efficient than many hand magnifying glasses and can save on enlarging costs. Contact sheets or strips from 35mm negatives are too small for average eyes to read unaided, but examining the details under a pick glass greatly facilitates picking the pictures which are worthy of larger prints.

ANIMALS

Household Pets. If there is one area where props are more valuable than in photographing small children, it is in photographing pets. Four-legged creatures seem to move approximately four times as fast as two-legged subjects and can be sixteen times as exasperating. There is no easy formula, but it is an interesting game, and patience plus watchfulness can win eventually.

Pets and children seem to possess an infallible affinity for each other and first encounters offer choice snapshot material. A puppy or kitten is normally gentle with youngsters and appears to accept mauling as a sign of the child's affection. Picture possibilities are limitless. If your camera is an adjustable type, you should not need flash, which is apt to scare pets and cause them to react by running off whenever a camera-with-flashholder makes an appearance. Available light with fast film generally produces more and better pictures.

Basically, the other suggestions for photographing youngsters apply to taking snapshots of pets. Like people, animals offer endless variations in personality and behavior; but they are generally less manageable than children, less dependent on adults, and less susceptible to obvious coaxing. Another point: because pets move faster than people, the snapshooter should approach his subject *slowly,* not stealthily but naturally, and refrain from sudden movements which might startle the animal. If your camera is on a tripod or otherwise vulnerable, watch out for sudden movements by the pet. And beware the dog whose friendly tongue may lick your lens as well as your hand.

Asleep at the Click. Sleeping cats and dogs often make appealing subjects, especially if they are considerate enough to nap in an uncluttered spot with a reasonable amount of light. If the animal

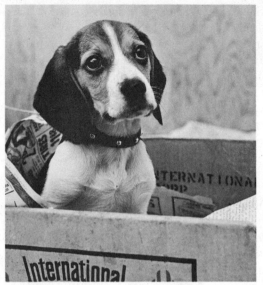

Fig. 115 (left) and Fig. 116 (below).—Subdued pup and fenced-in pet with nobody-loves-me expression make captive snapshot subjects.

(Left: Courtesy of Scholastic High School Photo Awards)
(Below: Courtesy of the Newspaper National Snapshot Awards)

Fig. 117.—Black cats need a light background for closeup or medium shots. (Courtesy of Scholastic High School Photo Awards)

Fig. 118.—Framed "cats" and large leaves make a fortuitous background for a favorite nap spot. (Courtesy of Scholastic High School Photo Awards)

Fig. 119.—Quietly occupied cats offer many possibilities to patient snapshooters. (Courtesy of Scholastic High School Photo Awards)

chooses the same spot frequently, you can study your viewfinder and calculate the exposure one day, then have your camera ready at the correct distance another day. You may even be able to improve the background between naps. Almost too easy, but good practice.

One improvement might be to place a light spread on a couch or chair for which a black pet shows a preference. Black cats and dogs are especially challenging since they need a light background and some light on the face; conversely, white or light pets need a dark background. Figure 117 shows a successful close-up; in Figure 118 a favorite nap spot has been used to advantage.

Cat Watching. Most cats go in for frequent periods of quiet alertness during which they may be contemplating a drapery cord, following a fluttering leaf, or bird-watching. Window sills, indoors and out, are favorite perches and provide interesting silhouette possibilities, even without the cat's face. (See Figure 119.) When snapping toward natural window light, set your exposure for back lighting (see page 84) and, if feasible, have a reflector or lamp on hand for fill-in light.

Props and Closeup Tips. Food is an almost surefire coaxer, though you may not want a dog biscuit or a saucer of milk in all your snapshots. A ball, a length of string, a fake bone, a catnip mouse, or other plaything can be useful. Try prefocusing on a spot to which you would like to entice the animal, then use a bit of masking tape, or an extra pair of hands, to anchor a suitable prop briefly on that spot.

With some assistance you can also attempt a neat little method for snapping a small kitten or puppy close up, either at the minimum focusing distance of your adjustable camera or with a closeup lens attachment (see page 223) for a preset type, remembering to tilt for parallax correction (page 58). *On your mark:* While the helper holds the pet, place a piece of paper or other marker exactly where you want the subject to land. *Get set:* After determining the distance and correct exposure, hold yourself ready to click. *Go:* At a signal from you, the helper should pick up the marker, place the pet in position, and move out of the picture—all in one swift step.

Tropical Fish. These little subjects should be photographed at an angle similar to that recommended for taking a new baby's picture through the glass of a hospital nursery. Unless your tank is exceptionally shallow, or contains very few fish, you might try placing a glass plate inside the back wall of the tank and moving it gently forward to keep the fish near the front wall. Plenty of patience will still be needed to snap the moving fish where you want them, so have your camera set before crowding them into close quarters. Flash is preferred to tungsten for less heat and because illumination from room lamps might cause problem reflections on the glass of the tank.

Public Pets. Flash is usually best at large aquariums where fish of various sizes are in display tanks, and also for relatively small inside cages like those for monkeys or tropical birds. But before shooting, be sure flash is permitted.

For zoo subjects in outside cages, including seals in an outdoor pool, use available light and a fairly fast film. Select a shutter speed of 1/100 to 1/250, if possible; if you have a box camera, simply try to catch the subject poised or resting but not actually moving. If you have a telephoto lens, you will probably want to take closeups like those in Figures 38 and 120.

Animals behind bars can be as perverse as a free-wheeling cat. You may be all set to snap a zebra in good light near the front of a cage only to have your prey suddenly decide to loiter in the farthest dark corner. There is not much you can do about this

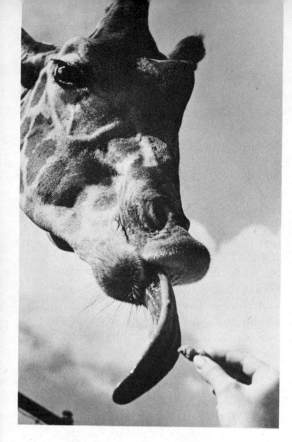

Fig. 120.—For closeup snapshots of most zoo animals a telephoto lens is needed. (Courtesy of the Newspaper National Snapshot Awards)

other than to accept the animals and backgrounds as you find them. Very often a camera can be held between bars to keep the bars out of the picture. If the animal is touching the bars, possibly reaching a paw or trunk through them, step back about four or five feet and take a picture with bars. If the light seems satisfactory but the animal's position is such that you cannot focus, hold the camera through the bars (or above a high railing), aim as best you can, and shoot blindly. You may get your picture, but it is not advisable to bet heavily on its being a good one.

ADULTS

The big difference between getting good shots of adults and good ones of children is that it is usually more difficult to capture naturalness in adults. But whatever the subject's age, a natural expression is seldom achieved by asking the subject to pose; stiffness and self-consciousness are average human reactions to facing a camera.

General Suggestions. Subjects preoccupied with a hobby or momentary interest generally show the most animated or characteristic expressions. This preoccupation is the equivalent of a prop, the same idea as diverting a child's attention with a toy. Photographs of people doing things are not necessarily action shots. A college student with an armful of books may be simply leaning against a campus doorway or pausing on the library steps; the books and background tell a story. An older person may be completely engrossed in a knitting project or a piece of hand carving or a grandchild.

Expressive snapshots of people need not always show their faces. You may recall, as a striking example, the prize-winning press photograph (Pulitzer Award, May 1962) of Presidents Kennedy and Eisenhower, taken from the rear as they strolled thoughtfully along a walk at Camp David in Maryland. Amateur snapshots can convey an impression of character and activity even with the subject's back to the camera. You might try it sometime with something like a fisherman reeling in a line or a farmer at a pump, a backyard chef or a stretching sunbather. Watch for opportunities without forcing the poses.

The Surreptitious Approach. If your intention is to photograph someone in a relaxed or characteristic attitude, a certain amount of stealth not only can be condoned but should be encouraged. On the other hand, subjects can be justifiably annoyed with unkind attempts to portray them in embarrassing or unattractive positions; such snapshooting among acquaintances may result in a collection of *former* friends.

Although furtiveness does frequently succeed in catching pleasantly natural poses, the major drawback is that it may not permit you to photograph as close as you might like to. The nearer you and your camera get to the unwary subject, the more likelihood there is of your being discovered before the picture has been taken.

Shooting from the Lap. There is a crafty little technique occasionally practiced by experts for snapping unsuspecting subjects on public premises, such as in a subway or on park benches. It is a little like aiming blindly at zoo subjects, and you might like to experiment among friends on private property.

The ruse is this: after pre-measuring the distance between two usually occupied seats, say a pair of lawn chairs, set your lens for that distance and the existing light; hold your camera down in your lap, or simply away from the intended subject. Then, while you are ostensibly examining a lens cap or light meter in your left hand, casually position the camera in your lap, training it on target as best you can *without looking at the subject* directly. Continue your feigned interest in the left hand, or in a fleecy white cloud, until well after your right hand has gently pressed the shutter release. Later, by faking a shot of some scenery in the opposite direction from your subject, you can reset your camera and try again. Nothing lost really if you are found out; the point is that you have gained some practice so you will know whether you would like to try the technique elsewhere.

The Conversational Approach. Probably the most effective means of inducing a natural expression, when you are neither being secretive about the picture nor utilizing a prop, is to engage the subject in light conversation. An easygoing query or comment which will get the person to talk is often better than talking *to* the person. Generally it is preferable to choose a rather innocuous topic, not one tending toward controversy or overenthusiasm which might promote gesturing and too much motion. If you have an accomplice to arrange a triangular chat, this makes it easier to catch the subject at an angle.

Practically any angle is an improvement over a wooden-Indian stance squarely facing the camera. Something to sit on, lean against, or rest a hand on usually contributes further to a relaxed appearance.

People in Pairs. When taking a photograph of two people, see that they present a unified appearance (as do the youngsters in Figures 76 and 112), so your photograph will not look as if two pictures happened to get on one snapshot. Seated or standing, the subjects may be very close together, or they may have a space between them that relates to the composition as a whole. Asking two posing adults to smile at each other, or to pretend to be talking to each other, is conducive to the same sort of stilted expressions that result from requesting any subject to smile, please, or to look at the birdie. Unless the subjects can be genuinely interested in some prop within the picture, try to interest them in something outside, perhaps in the conversation of another person standing a few feet to one side of your camera.

Groups of People. The basic principles of composition discussed in Chapter 12 are applicable to snapshots of two or several persons, and it might be worthwhile to reread that chapter with snapshots of people in mind, particularly specific groups which you may be planning to photograph. Masses and weights, whether scenery or

Fig. 121.—Above: Don't ask your subjects to stand in a row and look into your lens.

Fig. 122.—Below: Do try to catch subjects in some natural grouping, and not looking right at the camera.

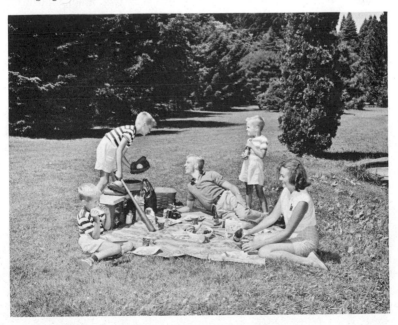

people, can be arranged in pleasing balance, and small or medium-size groups can often be arranged about an authentic center of interest: for example, family members grouped about the baby or pet, or school chums arranged in relation to a guitar player, or friends admiring some newly picked flowers.

Very large groups which must be arranged in compact rows in order to include everyone are bound to have a more formal and static appearance. The purpose is to show all the faces, as appropriately smiling or serious as possible; it is not to create a composition, and there is not much leeway to do so. A better feeling of balance can be achieved if you do not crowd the edges of your picture; it is preferable to crowd the subjects or arrange an extra row. Semicircles often fit the picture frame more satisfactorily than straight rows. Photographs of sizable groups really need a wide-angle lens.

If your viewfinder indicates that the group fits comfortably into two rows, you can seat the taller ones in front. A third row is often asked to sit on the ground or floor or a bottom step; be sure that their feet and legs are not thrust toward the camera. Try to keep an unequal number in the rows, so that rear subjects can stand between the heads of the row in front. A slightly higher camera angle than eye level can help to eliminate background areas. For a very formal group with a guest of honor, or some executives among business personnel, a standard arrangement is to place the senior subject in the center of the first row, seating other persons alternately in order of seniority to the right and left of center in that row.

TIPS FOR SPECIAL EVENTS

Birthdays, weddings, graduations, costume parties, vacation trips, Christmas Day and New Year's Eve are some of the special photographic opportunities for snapshots of people. Parties and pictures both benefit from preparedness, including a survey of lighting conditions and anticipated activities; and you will want to decide also whether to give prints to everybody or to show slides.

Children's Parties. Outdoor parties are easier on the parents and give the photographer a break as well. A camera seems less conspicuous outdoors, especially if a picture indoors requires flash; and usually the photographer can move about more freely outside, catching the subjects in more natural poses. Indoor parties, when given on a sunporch or other multi-windowed room, can usually be captured on fast film in natural daylight. Decide in advance what film should be in your camera when the party starts, and where any activities you particularly wish to photograph should take place—for example, the opening of gifts or the awarding of prizes.

Lighted Candles. The high point of festivities at birthday parties for children or grownups is normally a lighted cake. To photograph this feature, plan ahead where the cake should be placed, where you wish the candle blower to sit, and whether there will be a group of guests in the same picture. Lighted candles can make quite a glare in the foreground of a snapshot; this is halation caused by shooting across the candles when focusing on the person or persons back of them. You can focus on the candle lights, and the people behind them will be interesting although somewhat darker than the candles. Or you can arrange the people in the foreground, preferably a bit off to one side, and focus on the candles. A possible arrangement to catch someone blowing out the candles is to get the subject in profile so you can focus on puffed cheek and candle lights, leaving any watching guests slightly out of focus behind the main subject.

Mirror Snapshots. Sometimes at parties or other events you may have occasion to photograph a subject reflected in a mirror. As a specific example, consider a bride trying on her wedding veil in the foreground and her face reflected in the glass. This requires a slightly different exposure estimate than for catching a tot close to or touching a mirror, with no problem of depth.

For mirrored subjects in general it is necessary to allow for the distance from camera to mirror plus the distance from mirror to subject. If you have groundglass or rangefinder focusing, you can just focus on the image reflected in the mirror without measuring the distance. Choose a fairly small aperture to assure adequate depth of field; if you wish to be certain of having the bride's reflected image and the back of the veil both in focus, it is best to consult a depth-of-field scale.

Weddings. Even large affairs for which a professional photographer may be engaged usually leave ample snapshot opportunities for the amateur, especially during preparations for the ceremony. These may start with pictures of an engagement party; may include showers, fittings for the bridesmaids, the bride trying on her veil, the table of gifts, the floral decorations; and may conclude with an exit from a chapel, the reception and cake cutting, some just-married car tags, and goodbye waves at the couple's departure.

The first rule for taking pictures of any wedding events is to obtain permission of the principal participants; if there is any objection or hesitancy in granting it, refrain from photographing. For the actual marriage ceremony, be sure that you have express permission from the bride and bridegroom and from the person officiating. It should be understood, without even asking, that the picture-taking privilege does not extend to flash. Ordinary good manners prescribe further caution in not abusing the permission when given: be quiet, keep out of the way as much as possible, and do not obstruct a working professional. Even professional photographers, away from their studio lights, frequently encounter a problem in adjusting exposure for such shots as the traditional cutting of a large white cake, with the bride in a white gown and the bridegroom in a black suit; when something must be sacrificed, it is usually the dark suit.

Vacations. Whether taken on a honeymoon, a cross-country jaunt, or a tour abroad, many vacation and travel snapshots are pictures of people. However, pictures of landmarks or scenery or fiestas should not attempt to be snapshots of your travel companions at the same time, or they will be neither. People may be included as secondary interest if they are involved in the actual scene or are looking at it and not at the camera. When a group or a person, whether close friend or quaint foreigner, is intended as the main interest, get as near to your subject as possible and minimize the background.

There seems to be a rather universal urge among amateur photographers to interfuse pictures of places with pictures of people, as if to tell friends "That's us at the Grand Canyon" or "That's Mother in front of the Taj Mahal." Try to believe that this is not necessary. If a foreground figure looking into the picture happens to be John or Mary, well and good. But anonymous figures will often do equally well or better; and separate snapshots of yourself and friends, combined with pictures of places and things in your slide show or album, can be quite convincing evidence that you were there—and will probably provide you with a more satisfactory photographic record.

Travel Planning. A brand-new suitcase may be an excellent travel item, but an untried camera is not. Even though you have carefully reviewed the operation of a new model and studied the instruction manual, it is not enough for your head to know the camera: it is even more important for your hands to know it. When the camera is your first one, you should allow at least several weeks for practicing with different types of film in order to familiarize yourself with the camera and to decide which kinds of film your prefer to take with you. If you are replacing an old camera, plan to do this well in advance of a trip so that you can shoot a number of practice rolls and still have plenty of time for the camera to be checked if necessary. A minor slipup in some step of the camera operation can mean the difference between good pictures and the possibility of no pictures at all.

If you intend to take a familiar camera but have not been using it very recently, shoot a roll of black-and-white film and have it processed a couple of weeks before departure to be sure that everything is in good order; check other equipment, such as light meter and flash unit, at the same time.

TRANSPORTING EQUIPMENT. When you are traveling entirely by car, space is usually not a problem, but cameras and film should be safeguarded against excessive heat, vibration, and theft. The most desirable spot is on the rear floor, where bulkier items can be covered; the worst places are glove compartments and window ledges. A car trunk is all right unless sun and high temperatures make it too hot for film storage.

How much equipment to take when traveling on buses and trains, ships and planes, depends on your itinerary, probable climate conditions, and packing problems. Suggested minimum items, when you must consider weight restrictions of luggage on planes, would be camera, light meter, lens shade, filters, optional accessory lenses, and a good supply of film. Good films can be purchased in many places all over the world, but some of the brands may be unfamiliar. American films to which you may be accustomed cost more in other countries and are sometimes scarce.

PHOTOGRAPHING PERMITS, FEES, AND PROHIBITIONS. In quite a number of historic buildings, museums, and other places, both at home and abroad, cameras are prohibited for one reason or another. Museums, for example, customarily forbid cameras if all or part of the exhibition is on loan rather than in the permanent collection.

Sometimes a professional photographer owns the picture-taking concession at an interesting spot, and good photographs can be purchased on the premises. Other places may require a special permit or a nominal fee. If there is any doubt, ask permission. Asking permission is a courtesy which should extend also to people when you wish to photograph strangers while traveling.

No permission is needed to photograph many ready-made titles: road signs and billboards, city-limits markers, street and shop signs, plaques on monuments and landmarks, names over entrances, all sorts of public local identification items. Watch for snapshot opportunities which will help round out your album or slide collection.

U. S. CUSTOMS. When taking "imported" equipment on a vacation abroad, you should either register the items before leaving this country or carry proof of ownership in order to avoid re-entry problems. To register your camera, ask the Customs Department for the current form and explicit instructions. Proof of ownership is best established by a bill of sale; but a document such as an insurance policy listing the item or items by serial number should do. Equipment identifiable as of American manufacture need not be registered.

Because regulations vary from country to country and from year to year, even within the United States, it is advisable to rely only on up-to-date information. Customs offices, travel agencies, brochures of various countries and carriers, and local bureaus provide data without charge. In addition, there are numerous and frequently revised booklets, and monthly travel and photography magazines.

RETURNING FILMS TO THE U. S. If you are moving about a good deal while abroad, you may prefer to send your American films home for processing rather than try to find foreign photofinishers at the right times and places. Present regulations permit films of U. S. manufacture, clearly marked *For Processing,* to be mailed duty-free to yourself, your photo dealer, a processor, or the film manufacturer. Unused films may also be returned by mail if the parcel is marked: *Handle with care. Undeveloped photographic film of U. S. manufacture, for personal use only.* This declaration also cautions customs examiners and other officials against storage or handling that might cause film damage.

Note that some foreign color films are sold *with processing,* which means processing in that country. The usual tourist tendency is to switch to these unfamiliar films only when the imported supply has run short; then the films must be sent to the foreign processor who in turn will mail them to the given address. However, if you are going to be in one country for a few weeks and taking a lot of pictures, try a couple of the foreign films right off; find out about how long processing takes, and have the slides or prints mailed to your address abroad. In this way you can see which films you prefer, can avoid a long wait for pictures after your trip, and may even be able to retake some pictures that didn't turn out as well as they might have.

INTERNATIONAL REGULATIONS. How many cameras may be taken into another country varies: better check on this if you plan to travel with more than one. Some countries allow a "reasonable number," some only one, some two if they are of different sizes or types. Some countries may interpret "reasonable number" rather freely in favor of the tourist; however, equipment in excess of allowance is subject to some kind of bond or in some instances, to payment of duty. Some countries require you to enter and leave with the same number of cameras, to circumvent unlawful sales.

Restrictions regarding rolls of film vary, too: sometimes it is a "reasonable number," sometimes it may be 6, 10, 12, or another specific number of rolls. Whatever the regulations, they are that country's laws and must be observed. Moreover, officials generally tend to respond favorably to a polite and cooperative attitude; argument and arrogance, on the other hand, can only discredit your intentions and your country.

16

Portraiture

"PORTRAIT" has a rather formal connotation for many people, partially because of its association with the paintings of old masters and partially because of the "pictorial representations" of many professional photographic studios. By contrast the word "snapshot" seems extremely informal and unplanned, and a "study" of a person perhaps lies somewhere in between. Nevertheless, any picture that successfully conveys some facet of the subject's personality may be correctly considered a portrait, whether taken with professional equipment under studio lamps or with a box camera in sunlight.

Portraiture styles and techniques are as diversified as the human beings involved. A portrait may be a close-up of a face or a head-and-shoulders view; it may be a three-quarters or full-length figure; it may be pensive or gay, with props or with none. The principal difference between making a portrait indoors and outdoors is that greater control of lighting is possible with lamps than with sky light.

With amateur equipment, which is the concern of this text, there are a few basic pointers and pitfalls to note. After considering the broadest of these, this chapter will cover (1) relatively formal portraits indoors, and (2) relatively informal portraits outdoors.

BASIC CONSIDERATIONS

Cameras. As a rule, the best camera for taking successful pictures is the one with which you are familiar. Especially in making portraits, operation of the camera should be practically automatic so that you can give your attention almost wholly to the subject. While professional portraitists generally use an 8 x 10 studio camera and possess a dazzling array of lighting equipment, these are not requisites for good portraiture.

Reflex types of cameras with groundglass viewing screens have the advantage of letting you compose your portrait in the viewer, with the image upright (instead of upside down as in a studio camera). A small portrait-viewer attachment which is available for many miniature cameras permits you to look down at an image of your subject while the camera is positioned on a tripod below eye level.

Photographers who specialize in portraiture frequently prefer to work with a 4 x 5 press camera and sheet film, or with a 2¼ x 2¼ (or larger) twin-lens reflex, as the larger negative size is more practical for cropping and retouching and requires less enlargement than 35mm films.

A telephoto lens of 85mm to 135mm focal length, preferably 105mm, is advantageous to have if your 35mm camera accepts interchangeable lenses and if you are working outdoors or in a fairly large room. Such a lens, with its correspondingly narrower angle of view, allows you to get a large frame-filling image without bringing the camera abnormally close to the subject. This, in turn, makes possible a substantial decrease in depth of field, which reduces the likelihood of undesirable background emphasis or too much foreground. Another advantage of a greater than normal focal length is that a more pleasing perspective can be maintained—i.e., you can avoid the distortion caused by placing a camera extremely close. A too close placement, besides cutting down on working area you may need indoors for arranging the lights and the pose, usually results in making the subject uncomfortable and self-conscious.

All of this points up the observation in Chapter 2 that no one camera (or focal length) is best for every kind of photography. The 2¼ twin-lens reflex, even with its parallax problem, is a good size for informal portraiture. A majority of amateurs with one 35mm camera quite logically prefer the all-round versatility of the so-called normal focal length of 44mm to 58mm, with the 50mm average lens the continuing favorite. Even within this relatively narrow normal range for cameras using 35mm films, there are differences which could be important to you, depending on your aims and preferences. A 44mm or 45mm lens tends toward a wide angle, covering slightly more picture area and resulting in a freer composition having greater apparent distance between foreground and background. A 55mm or 58mm lens, standard for single-lens reflexes, tends toward a narrow angle and an apparent condensing of the picture area for a tighter composition.

Avoiding Distortion with an Average Lens. Particularly with a 50mm lens, it is important to keep the entire subject more or less *on one plane*—that is, the face, hands, shoulders, and legs should all be approximately the same distance from the camera. A common error, for example, is to permit a person's hand to pose on a plane nearer the lens than the plane of the face on which you are focusing, thus causing the hand to appear disproportionately large, much as the right hand does in Figure 81. When photographing a full- or half-length figure close up, of course, it is sometimes difficult to have all parts of the subject seem equidistant from the lens; therefore, the face will often be in sharper focus than the rest of the figure.

Distortion can be further controlled by posing the subject at an angle to the camera rather than facing it squarely. This is especially important if you are focusing down to the minimum distance of your lens or using a supplementary "portrait lens" for an even closer focus. Placing an average small camera farther away from the subject—say, eight or ten feet—will improve a head-and-shoulders perspective but give you a smaller image than you may want. To obtain a closeup portrait effect from such a shot, you can have only the center portion of the negative enlarged and printed, a procedure which is more satisfactory with film sizes larger than 35mm. With a standard small-camera lens, it is not advisable to attempt to fill the negative with a head only; you should include about a third of the figure as a minimum image before cropping.

PORTRAITS INDOORS

Lights. Photoflood lamps are favored for indoor portraits because of their convenience and flexibility. However, any light source, including natural window light or table lamps, can be used effectively with practice and judgment. The success of a portrait does not depend on the type of lighting but on your use of it, as well as on your handling of camera and subject. Ordinary photofloods or high-wattage tungsten bulbs need a metal reflector; reflector-type floodlamps and spots can be used in any convenient holder with an adjustable neck.

A single photoflood used with ingenuity can prove quite adequate for home portraits. It can be supplemented by the existing light, by flash, or by a simple subject reflector, such as a large sheet of white cardboard, for filling in the heavy shadows. When two photofloods are used, one serves as a modeling light and the second as a fill-in light.

Accessories. Photographic supply stores offer a variety of lamp-stands and other accessories, none of which you need to start taking portraits. If you do wish to buy a basic *lampstand,* select one that adjusts in height as well as in direction; most come with *barndoors,* which are hinged metal flaps for better control of light distribution—including shielding the camera lens from the light. These barndoor brackets are also available for attaching to reflector photofloods. Be sure that your *extension cords* are the right length for moving lamps easily anywhere in your working area. If you plan on flash as a fill-in, check beforehand on *bulbs and batteries.*

Besides the lighting fixtures mentioned, a *tripod* is recommended for home portraits, also a simple *cable release* as further insurance toward camera steadiness. A long cable release with a switch allows you to stand near the subject and away from the camera while the photograph is actually being taken. See that your tripod is not surrounded by such a clutter of fixtures and extension cords that it will be in danger of being knocked over while you are posing and lighting your subject. On the whole, it is best to begin with minimum equipment and add to it as your own personal techniques and requirements evolve.

Indoor Backgrounds. Simplicity should be the keynote of all backgrounds. Particularly in portraiture, nothing should detract from the subject. Plain walls are usually the most available and satisfactory backgrounds; otherwise it is advisable to have some sort of plain material which can be tacked up behind the posing bench. Except for special effects, such a backdrop should be sufficiently light in color to be reflective. Keep the background really back, allowing five or six feet between bench and wall if space permits; if you don't, the subject will merge with the background and your portrait will have no illusion of depth.

For the relatively formal portraits under discussion here, a bench or stool is preferable to a chair. There are several reasons for this recommendation: First, a lightweight bench or box—whatever back-less seat of a comfortable height is available—can be placed where you want it in relation to background and illumination. This will make your working space more flexible and will eliminate the problem of how to incorporate (or exclude) the back of a chair in your composition. More importantly, your subject will sit straighter, and therefore clothing will fit more smoothly; jackets and other collared garments especially tend to bunch at the neckline if the person leans back. A further reason is that any slump will be more pronounced in the finished picture. Finally, when the subject is fairly erect, you will find it easier to arrange the pose on a single plane and at the most advantageous angle.

Films. Unless you have had a good deal of experience, by all means begin your portrait practice with black and white, choosing a slow or medium-speed film for fine grain. This gives you not only great latitude and enlargement possibilties, but also an opportunity to experiment more freely with a variety of poses and lighting arrangements in order to determine what effects you can achieve with your equipment. For color portraits indoors choose a fairly slow fine-grain film in the type balanced for artificial (tungsten) light (e.g., Kodachrome Type A); it is generally not practical to convert daylight color films to tungsten use by means of a filter. Color portraits are likely to be more successful in natural daylight.

Basic Lighting Setups. Ideally, portrait lighting should simulate the natural conditions of sunlight or of a well-lighted room. Therefore the best preliminary study is to observe the highlight and shadow patterns on people's faces, indoors and out, under any and all types of lighting. Because we do not normally see faces lighted from below, shadows cast upward on a face produce an unnatural effect which offends an innate sense of rightness. Good lighting can show the subject to advantage, with pleasing modeling that lends depth and expressiveness to the features. Inept lighting can distort features, even to the extent of making the subject unrecognizable in the photograph.

The basic suggestions and diagrams in these pages should be considered takeoff points, not rules. They will give you some idea of where to place your lights, but the correctness of the placement can be ascertained only by studying the effect of the illumination on the subject's face. Lighting should blend with the mood or personality you wish to portray: for instance, softened lighting to suggest femininity, and less diffuse lighting for a more forceful impression.

Main Light. To acquire a confident control of portrait lighting, start with a single modeling light, preferably a No. 1 photoflood. With the lamp about four feet from the subject and above eye level, observe its effect on the subject's face as you move the light very gradually to one side and then the other. The distance between subject and lamp will depend on the lens you are using, how close your camera can be brought in, and also on the intensity of the light. Keep it in an arc, at a uniform distance from the subject, as indicated in the diagram in Figure 123. Notice carefully the highlights

Fig. 123.—Study effect on face as you move light in an arc about the subject.

and shadows on checks, forehead, nose, and chin as you shift the lamp position, for it is these highlights and shadows that reveal a face's characteristic curves, which give modeling, dimension, and expression to a portrait.

Light Position for Broad or Narrow Faces. As you move the modeling light in a semicircle, watch how it seems to alter the shape of the face. When the lamp is close to the camera, as in Figure 124, the front or flat lighting appears to broaden the face. When the lamp is at the end of the arc, as in Figure 125, the side lighting appears to narrow the face. As a rule, therefore, it is advisable to use flat front lighting on a long thin face, and a modified side lighting on a round wide face.

If the side lighting is extreme and without fill-in light, it can produce a hatchet-like division of half brightness and half deep shadow. Front lighting, especially the type referred to as "butterfly" lighting, is frequently preferred for feminine subjects; the main light is raised just enough to produce a butterfly-shaped shadow about midway between nose and mouth. The reason this lighting style is rarely used for men is that it would highlight both ears and make them protrude. If a setup of more than one light is arranged so

Fig. 124.—Flat lighting tends to make a face appear broad.

Fig. 125.—Side lighting tends to make a face appear slender.

that a central panel of the face is brightly lighted and both sides somewhat shadowed, this has a narrowing effect on a broad face.

Normal Light Position. For most faces the main light should be placed more or less halfway between the front and side extremes of the arc, about 45 degrees to one side of the subject, in approximately the triangular lamp-camera-subject arrangement shown in Figure 126. When the subject is facing the camera, the modeling light is

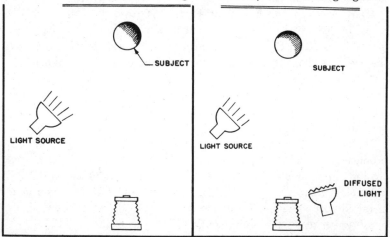

Fig. 126.—Normal light position for average subjects.

Fig. 127.—Normal two-lamp lighting arrangement.

placed on whichever side seems to present the more photogenic appearance, leaving the other side of the face somewhat in shadow.

Height of Main Light. The modeling light should not be allowed to cast a shadow from the nose or brow across the eyes of the subject. A standard practice is to elevate or lower the lamp until it forms a triangle-shaped highlight below the eye and adjacent to the nose shadow on the cheek away from the light. On some faces this key highlight may be more of a rounded U-shape than a triangle. This effect is normally produced with the light coming down at an angle of about 45 degrees. The side of the face away from the light will be in shadow except for the triangular patch of highlight which should extend no lower than the base of the nose. This type of lighting, approximately 45 degrees to one side and 45 degrees above the subject, is frequently referred to as "Rembrandt" lighting.

Adjusting for Eyeglasses. If your subject wears glasses, attend to the problem of reflection before considering lighting adjustments or the rest of the pose. Place your lamp or lamps in the basic setup you plan to use; then, when your subject is seated, look at the image on the focusing screen or viewer for the spot of light you are almost certain to find on the glasses. Watch the image, and ask the subject to move his head very slowly until the light spot disappears; it may be necessary also to move the modeling light slightly to extinguish the eyeglass light. There are many types of glasses and optical corrections, just as there are many types of photographic lenses; consequently the characteristic spots of light on glasses will vary and must be coped with individually.

Position of Second Light. When using a basic two-lamp setup, place the fill-in light close to the lens axis, on the side of the camera opposite the modeling light, as indicated in Figure 127. If you have a small camera at a closeup limit of three to four feet (or even closer with a "portrait" attachment), your fill-in light will be somewhat back of the camera position. It should be diffused light, about eye level, and always farther from the subject than the modeling light— usually about one and one-half times the distance. For example, if the modeling light is four to five feet from the subject, the second light should be six to eight feet away.

Diffusion of fill-in light follows common sense and can be achieved in numerous ways. Lower wattage, greater distance, and a screen of cheesecloth or thin plain material are some of the ways to reduce the relative intensity of the secondary light. Natural window light or a portable subject reflector can serve the same purpose as a second lamp, which is to balance the main light by subduing too dark shadows. The mean ratio of brightness between highlights and shadows is generally accepted as about 3:1.

Using Three Lights. The modeling light and the fill-in are primarily to show the subject's face to best advantage. A third light (photoflood, flash, or other illumination) can be used for background, for accent, or for raising the general light level. If you wish to illuminate a background with a natural effect, the distance between a third lamp and the background should be about the same as the distance between the main light and the subject. If a third lamp is too close, the background will seem unnaturally light; if too far away, the background will seem too dark in relation to the main subject on which your exposure is based.

A third lamp is sometimes used as a backlight, especially to accent the hair of a woman or child. The light may be placed at an angle directly behind and above the head—anywhere that seems to achieve the effect you want as long as it does not strike the lens or interfere with the basic lighting of the face. Often it is directed at the background from a low placement behind the posing bench.

Caution. The three most common errors on first attempts at indoor portraiture are (1) placing the main light too close, thus causing glare, discomfort, and excessive contrast; (2) placing the second light at the same distance (and intensity) as the main light, resulting in a harsh cross lighting, which tends to eliminate shadows entirely or to produce two undesirable shadows close to each side of the nose; and (3) using too many lights. The simplest arrangement is usually the most successful.

Posing the Subject. If you are a beginner, practice on a willing friend or on a model arranged for by a group; but let even the most informal practice include an awareness of being considerate and agreeable. Try to keep the subject in a relaxed mood and interested in something other than the mechanics of having a picture taken— unless you have a professional model—and refrain from making excessive demands. See that there is a reasonably convenient mirror for the subject's use. Sometimes a photographer can loosen a rigid pose or thaw a frozen expression by letting the person think that the camera is being clicked, then taking the actual picture quickly before the pose itself is changed. Rather than asking the subject to "smile" or assume a specific expression, try casual conversation. If you talk easily about the weather, a news item, any little topic that comes to mind, the person will inwardly "look" at that topic and his face will reflect some degree of interest instead of the blank or tense look which results from having his attention only on the business of picture taking.

WHICH SIDE? One side of a face is nearly always more photogenic than the other, and the better side should be turned toward the modeling light. Unless the subject has definite opinions about this, it is the photographer's responsibility to determine which side is more flattering.

BASIC BODY-AND-HEAD POSITION. Start by having the seated subject turn away from the camera, then turn *just the head* back toward the camera. This kind of pose gives an impression of motion and is generally more graceful than a head-on position which not only tends to be static and awkward but to make the ears too prominent. In most poses it is desirable to have one ear wholly or partially out of the picture; however, be sure that a partial ear is recognizable as such.

Regardless of the head angle, the eyes should normally look straight ahead so as not to show too much of the whites and so they will appear natural. Since the eyes are the primary focal point of a portrait, whether looking at the camera or at an angle to it, special care should be taken to see that the posing and lighting does not distort them. Hands and arms should be kept quite close to the body: even when not showing in the picture, they affect the balance of head and shoulders. When hands are part of a portrait, as they frequently are, keep them back on the facial plane to minimize distortion; usually it is best to have just the edge of a hand toward the camera. (Note Figure 81 again.) If a portrait is to include the legs and feet, have whichever leg is nearer the camera crossed over the other; this will avoid having a foot and knee—and possibly a shoe sole pointing at the lens and appearing exaggerated. *Any part of the body that is nearer the camera than the part being focused on will appear unduly large.*

Effect of Camera Angle. Although an "average" or "normal" subject is purely hypothetical, we must assume such a classification to refer to a face of oval shape, with medium-size head, neck, nose, chin. On this predication it is suggested that the camera lens be approximately at eye level and the lights placed as already indicated. From this norm the interrelated positions of subject, lights, and camera can be altered to achieve a particular effect.

A high camera angle—that is, above eye level—will tend to shorten a too long neck, play down a double chin, and play up the hair. A low camera angle tends to improve a very short neck and can often camouflage a long nose. But a low camera angle is difficult to work with, and it usually requires elevating the modeling light so that the nostrils blend into the shadow area. Sometimes it is used for deliberate "horror" portraits such as are seen on book jackets of mystery stories. A high camera angle can sometimes impart a "highbrow" feeling by emphasizing the forehead. A low camera angle may add a feeling of "glamour" or sex appeal by emphasizing the mouth. It is important to note which features are most in need of suppression or accent; for example, you would not normally choose a high camera angle or elevated modeling light for a subject with thinning hair. To repeat: successful portraits cannot be created by rules or diagrams.

Makeup and Minor Blemishes. Freckles can be quite appealing on a youngster, but adults are inclined to consider them something to be hidden or subdued, like scars or wrinkles. All these can be softened to some extent by diffused lighting (or a special soft-focus lens, which is under-corrected). Although professional makeup is used extensively to glamorize movie stars, heavy cosmetics are not recommended for amateurs. Generally speaking, darker areas tend to recede, while lighter skin tones receive more emphasis; but unless expertly applied, makeup should be simple and natural looking. Distracting blemishes, which would be exaggerated in enlargements, are usually corrected by retouching.

Clothing. The principles of makeup also apply to what the subject wears. Dark colors tend to recede and light colors to stand out. To minimize stoutness or a larger than average body, the subject should wear dark clothes and avoid large patterns. A dark background can further reduce apparent size by softening the contrast between subject and background. A person who is too thin will appear somewhat plumper in light colors and patterned fabrics against a plain dark background.

Focus and Composition. Since eyes are a person's most expressive feature and the point to which a viewer's attention is instinctively drawn, they are generally considered the main interest of a portrait composition. The critical focus in a close-up, therefore, should be on the eyes even if other parts of the portrait are slightly less sharp. Allowing each eye to catch a tiny bright reflection from the lighting will impart a sparkle and liveliness to the expression as a whole. This "catch light" should not be confused with the distracting spots of light reflected by eyeglasses.

The fundamentals of composition discussed in Chapter 12 are

applicable to portraits. While it is desirable to fill the picture frame, try not to have the negative so crowded that it cannot be cropped. The side toward which the head turns is the direction of the "action" and should have more space beside it than the other side. See that the pose seems to support the head in such a way that arms and shoulders will not "fall out" of the picture. Usually the arm nearer the camera should be pulled back slightly and the farther arm brought slightly forward; arms should always be sufficiently close to the body to block out slits of background. It is important to learn to watch for all these things easily and confidently, almost automatically, if you are to keep your subject comfortable and relaxed once the pose has been decided upon.

Exposure. A shutter speed of not longer than 1/25 of a second, and preferably 1/60, should be used for portraits. Besides the possibility of unnoticeable camera movement, even with a tripod and cable release, there is the physical fact that a live face is never completely motionless. Although the person may be sitting very quietly, eyelids blink and facial expressions change with subtle yet surprising rapidity. The blurring caused by some almost imperceptible change of expression may be so slight as to be detected only after the negative has been printed or enlarged.

The aperture you choose for a portrait will be determined by the intensity of the lighting, the index of the film, and the f/stops of your camera. You will recall that when a lens is wide open, only one distance is sharply in focus, and that there is practically no depth of field; also, reducing the distance between camera and subject reduces the depth of field. Since you generally take portraits close up, with a fairly fine-grain film, and do not want the background to be in focus, you will probably work near your camera's maximum aperture (lowest f/number) for most takes. If your equipment permits a choice, the exposure setting should be as close as possible to the critical aperture (see page 60) of your lens, with a shutter speed sufficiently short to prevent blurring.

Exposure for a combination of artificial and natural light is always based on the *main light,* whether from a photoflood or a window. It is possible to use photoflood lighting without a meter by following the directions which come with the lamps. A meter is a much surer guide, however, even though your own evaluations are what count most in the long run.

Meter Readings. A reflected-light reading of the triangular highlight on the shadow side of the face is a standard way to determine the amount of exposure (shutter speed plus aperture) required for a portrait. In any case, the measurement should be based on a facial highlight; for color portraits, a white or gray card held near the face is used. Such a reading, which is of light reflected *from* the face, should be taken at a closeup range of 6 to 12 inches. Be sure that you do not cast a shadow on the area being read, since this could result in overexposure.

Some photographers prefer an incident-light reading, which also should be taken at a close point. Since it measures light reflected *to* the face, an incident reading should be taken with the meter held close to the subject and directed toward the light source. Remember that the baffles of different meters can vary slightly, as can the whitenesses of cards; therefore it is a good idea to keep the same white or gray card on hand and to make a record of the distances at which you place it for a series of test exposures. With regular practice in doing this, it is possible to learn to move your modeling light and fill-in closer and farther to correspond to the exposure you prefer to use for a particular film and subject.

OUTDOOR PORTRAITS

Although the photographer has greater control of artificial lighting than of daylight, taking portraits outdoors offers many compensating advantages. When nature supplies the background, a subject usually appears more natural. Pleasant weather generally induces a pleasant, more relaxed mood; and color films, by and large, produce more satisfying results when knowingly used in natural lighting. Moreover, most amateur photographers enjoy combining the multiple pleasures of a trip or other outing with outdoor portraiture.

Sun as Main Light. Visualize the basic lighting arrangements described in the preceding pages and think of the sun as your modeling light. Indisputably you cannot move it about, nor decide how diffuse it shall be on a given day. But you *can* decide where to pose your subject in relation to this main light. Whether or not you try closeup portraits outdoors before attempting indoor portraiture, it is essential to develop a habit of observing the effects of various kinds of daylight on faces; the fundamentals of good lighting remain valid anywhere.

How Much Sunlight? One of the first things to learn—or unlearn —is *not* to pose a portrait subject in direct sunlight if this can be avoided. Hazy sunlight or open shade is generally much more satisfactory, and shadows are regarded as less objectionable than squints.

Under a hazy sun the sky is slightly overcast with thin clouds. Open shade assumes a sizable area of clear sky above and ahead of the subject but no sunlight striking the person's face directly; it should not be confused with ordinary shade, such as under heavy foliage or a porch roof. Open shade is somewhat more diffused than haze. For example, say you are using a color film rated at 32 and have calculated your exposure in hazy sunlight as 1/60 second at $f/8$; for the same film and time of day your correct exposure in open shade would probably be 1/60 at about $f/4$. If the light is much less, it is not open shade.

In open shade or haze, the light is a trifle bluer than when it is being warmed by direct sunshine. For daylight color films, therefore, it is usually desirable to use a no-factor filter, like the Wratten Skylight type, to reduce the blueness. The same holds true for water, snow, or any other condition that may be imparting a bluish cast to the light.

With an adjustable camera, normal exposure should be as near as possible to the critical aperture of your lens, as explained in the foregoing pages. Outdoors you are less likely to be using a tripod or to have a subject sitting perfectly still; consequently you may need a briefer shutter time than you might choose indoors.

Softness vs. Strength. If you are taking an informal portrait where you cannot find a suitable spot in open shade or hazy sunlight, your next best bet may be back lighting, with some sort of reflected light in front as fill-in. This is a favorite with many experts, particularly for feminine subjects; expose for the face and allow the background to go overexposed as well as unsharp for an effect of softness and also for a good separation of subject from background. If you wish to give a masculine subject strong shadows, try cross lighting with sky light on one side and a reflector or flash fill-in on the other; see that the lighting is far enough to the side to prevent the twin nose shadows which often occur when cross lighting is used carelessly.

Midday sunlight during the months when the sun is directly overhead should not be used for portraits, as this top lighting casts dense shadows under brows, noses, and lips. The best time is midmorning or midafternoon, when the sun slants down at somewhere near a 45-degree angle. If you place the subject so that this slanting sunlight produces approximately a 45-degree side lighting, you can get the key patch of triangular highlight on the shadow side of the face—

just as with a photoflood. Similarly, you can use flat front lighting or extreme 90-degree side lighting to alter the apparent shape of a face in sunshine, just as you can in artificial light.

Fill-in Light. Portrait lighting outdoors benefits from secondary illumination, such as flash or some type of reflector, even though this may not be as necessary as it is indoors. Since the fill light should always be appreciably less intense than the main light, you will need very little filling in of shadows if the main light is already diffused, as in haze or open shade.

Watch for natural reflectors outdoors. Often the side of a white house or nearby monument, for example, can reflect as much fill light as the shadow areas of your composition need. In open shade, an open newspaper strategically placed on the side away from the main light will sometimes do a remarkably good reflecting job. If you can find open shade near a beach or water, try to pose your subject to take advantage of indirect sunlight on one side and the reflected light on the other.

Portable Reflectors. A large sheet of white cardboard (about 30 to 40 inches) will furnish good fill-in illumination outdoors as well as indoors if someone—or some*thing*—will hold it where you want it. For more convenient carrying, a hinged reflector, like a miniature folding screen, can be built of two or three smaller panels of thin plywood, with one side painted white and the other covered with crinkled silver-color foil. Foils are too harshly reflective for most portraits, and any foil less neutral than silver will affect the results if you are using color film; however, with some experience and experiments, you can aim deliberately for different color effects, such as a warmer tone with gold foil.

Flash as Fill-in Light. The principle of fill-in flash and calculation of flash-to-subject distance has been explained in some detail on page 131. Remember that if you are using on-camera flash at a closeup position, the lamp should be diffused by covering it with one to three thicknesses of a white handkerchief, depending on the distance; extreme close-ups, such as under four feet, should have three thicknesses for black and white or color.

Remember also to use blue flashlamps, or the blue section of a plastic diffuser, with daylight color films. Too much distance or other diffusion will nullify the flash effect; on the other hand, too intense a flash will destroy the naturalness of the daylight and produce even more unsatisfactory results.

Fill-in flash can be a very helpful tool to a photographer, outdoors or indoors. But its value depends on the skill and judgment which come only with practice.

Backgrounds. There is no more important aspect of outdoor portraiture than your choice of background; simplicity is paramount. You may be looking only at the person you are photographing, but bear in mind that the lens is looking at everything within its range. Particularly with an average small camera, which has a short focal length and relatively great depth of field, it is important to keep the background as unobtrusive as possible and to be sure that such objects as posts, branches, and door frames do not seem to be growing out of the subject's head.

Selective focusing on the face from a reasonably close camera position will help cut out extraneous scenery and reduce depth of field. Some of the loveliest backgrounds are the most available if you simply angle your camera so that the subject is against a blue sky, green grass, or blended fall foliage. Deep shade can prove a very satisfactory dark background if the subject is in sunlight and the background is out of focus. Be sure that your subject is not placed where adjacent shrubbery or overhead leaves will reflect on the face and give it a greenish tinge.

Posing. Outdoor posing can be comparatively casual, or should seem casual enough to put the subject at ease. However, careful attention to details, especially the background, will be worthwhile. Some sort of seat, or something to lean against or touch, may contribute to a pleasantly relaxed pose; and a conversational distance (neither close enough for whispering nor far enough for shouting) will also make the subject more comfortable. When you have decided on the general camera position, ask the person to turn the body slightly away, then turn the head slowly back toward the camera—just as you would indoors. See that the hands and other parts of the body are on approximately the same plane as the face. If an informal portrait is to include a "prop" of some sort, such as a book, a kitten, or a tennis racquet, you may need a bit more than minimum depth.

People are by far the most popular of all photographic subjects, no doubt because they are essentially the world's most interesting components. Studying photographs of them in newspapers and magazines can be instructive; but learning really to see them makes a more fascinating hobby.

17

Ultra Close-ups of Small Objects

CONCENTRATION on the main interest is perhaps the basic reason why extreme close-ups fascinate practically everyone who takes or looks at pictures; the distracting elements must be eliminated, which in itself helps to strengthen a photograph. While it is true that a sizable percentage of the most admired examples, such as those in magazines and exhibits, are made by skilled technicians with expensive equipment, many amateurs turn out praiseworthy photographs of miniature subjects with standard lenses and very inexpensive attachments. The scientific term for large pictures of small objects is *macrophotography*.

Flowers and insects are favorite material for closeup fans, who generally find them more satisfying than tabletops or other indoor still lifes. One of the most interesting indoor projects is making title slides, which is practical photographic exercise with a built-in purpose. Ordinary copying can also be done with the closeup lenses and other simple accessories discussed in this chapter. The same equipment is often used for amateur portraits or closeup snapshots of people, but it is well to keep in mind that an average head-and-shoulders is considerably larger than an average blossom or bug, trinket or trophy, and that distortion is less acceptable in a photograph of a face than in one of a flower. The only way really to know this, of course, is to experiment freely and study the results closely.

BASIC CONSIDERATIONS

Cameras. An optical system that permits the photographer to view the composition through the taking lens is best for extreme close-ups, since the problem of parallax becomes more critical as depth of field becomes shallower. The single-lens reflex is, therefore, first choice of amateurs whose chief interest is in nature studies or other close photography.

A completely removable lens, standard with SLR, is also a feature of some rangefinder cameras; this is a highly desirable design if you intend taking many ultra close-ups because it permits the use of relatively inexpensive extension tubes as well as more costly semi-professional items. Some rangefinder cameras have a removable front lens component; this type will not accommodate extension tubes. Lens interchangeability is essential, of course, for separate telephoto elements and for such highly specialized accessories as a reflex bellows housing for converting a small precision camera with a focal-plane shutter into a kind of miniature view camera.

Noninterchangeable rangefinders with between-the-lens shutters, however, and even very simple box cameras can accommodate ordinary "closeup lenses" which look like filters and fit right over the camera lens. For twin-lens reflex cameras it is possible to buy a pair of matched closeup lenses; in some sets the upper (viewing) lens has a prism factor for parallax correction.

Closeup Lenses. These little accessories are not for use by themselves but are supplementary meniscus lenses whose purpose is to modify the distances at which the camera lens can produce a sharp image. They require no increase in exposure.

Closeup lenses for amateur photography come in three powers, measured in diopters, $+3$ being the strongest, and they can be used singly or in pairs. When two closeup lenses of different powers are used together, the stronger (higher number) should be next to the camera lens. Sometimes referred to as *portrait lenses,* they are widely available to fit different makes of cameras; trade names vary—like "Portra," "Proxar," "Auto-up," "Close-up No. 1"—and a table of working distances is customarily supplied by the manufacturer.

Some of these devices for 35mm rangefinder cameras with non-removable lenses are designed to extend the focusing range as well as the distance at which the lens will record sharply; such units have, in addition to the closeup attachment which mounts on the taking lens, a correction lens which mounts on the viewfinder and makes it possible to refocus down to about 10 inches. When this extra attachment is corrected for parallax as well as for focusing, the fact should be specifically indicated by the maker.

Size of Field. Most amateur cameras can focus down to about $3\frac{1}{2}$ feet, at which working distance the normal lens of a 35mm camera covers an area, or lens field, of about 27 x 18 inches. By adding a closeup lens of $+1$ strength, the working distances can be reduced to a range of approximately 40 to 20 inches; and a pair of $+3$ attachments can bring this down to around 6 inches, which would cover a field not much more than 4½ x 3 inches. A 2¼ x 2¼ twin-lens camera with a +3 set of closeup lenses can focus down to around 10 inches to photograph a field approximately 6 inches square. Various printed dialguides of valuable data concerning filters and depth-of-field scales also contain closeup-lens tables for computing the dimensions of the field at different working distances.

Focusing for Sharpness. Because depth of field is practically nonexistent in extreme close-ups, there is no margin for error; focusing should be accurate to the fraction of an inch recommended for a specific closeup lens. You may have a single-lens reflex camera which shows the image as recorded, or a rangefinder type with the correction attachment referred to in the preceding paragraphs; but if your camera is a simple one without these devices, you will need some kind of measuring and framing aids along with the closeup lenses.

Working distances should be measured from the front of the closeup lens to the front of the object being photographed. If the camera is on a tripod, a yardstick can be used to position it at a specified distance from the point of focus. For a camera held at less than arm's length from the target, a casual but fairly workable solution is to tape to the camera a piece of string knotted at 14 inches or 10½ inches or whatever distance you plan to work from. With such elementary computers, you will have to estimate the picture size roughly, which is not very satisfactory for ultra-close work. Or you can use a focal frame similar to that in Figure 144.

Extension Tubes and Bellows. For large images at medium-close working distances, there are small rigid metal tubes, fixed or focusing types, designed to hold a camera's removable lens at one end. The tube's smaller end is threaded to screw into the camera body or to be combined with other pieces of the set to form a longer tube. By holding the camera lens farther from the film plane, these tubes allow you to come in closer to a small subject in order to obtain large images at comparatively convenient working distances. Bellows extensions, which are bulkier, more versatile, and more expensive than the rigid tubes, are used by advanced photographers who do a lot of closeup work. These units vary greatly and generally fit cameras with focal-plane shutters.

Basic exposure is subject to change with extension tubes or bellows, since they actually alter the lens-to-film distance. Thus the light-transmitting capacity of a lens aperture diminishes in relation to the length of the tube, necessitating a longer exposure for a given ƒ/stop than the basic lens position requires. This obviously includes a reduction in the maximum "speed" of the lens. Tables of these exposure factors, or times by which exposure must be increased, come with the equipment.

Parallax Compensation. With cameras other than the single-lens reflex, which relays the composition to the film just as you see it in the groundglass, parallax is a tricky problem at close working distances. Some of the best 35mm rangefinder cameras are "fully corrected for parallax" by means of an automatic feature that causes the frame outline to move within the finder as the focus is changed. The "correction" of some other models consists of fixed markings showing, within the regular frame outline, the top boundary for a single closeup distance. Most cameras need to be tilted toward the viewfinder to minimize parallax.

Tilting the camera slightly up for horizontal formats, or to the side for vertical ones, is usually adequate parallax compensation at medium distances, but exact correction by tilting is virtually impossible within the range of closeup lenses. However, the recommended tilt at which to aim is: for a +1 closeup lens, up by about one-eighth of the picture; for a +2 lens, by about one-sixth of the picture; and for a +3, by about one-quarter of the picture.

Camera Steadiness. A rigid camera support is also essential for close-ups, which are usually taken at relatively slow shutter speeds or at time exposures. When using telephoto equipment or a combination of extension tubes, the camera may become front-heavy; this makes it more susceptible to jarring and to vibration from traffic or tramping about, especially during long exposures. Tripod legs should be extended no farther than needed, as longer legs make it less steady; another aid to steadiness is a weight hung from the center of the tripod head.

The blur of an out-of-focus background, resulting from focusing sharply on the main point of interest, is generally desirable. But an action blur, caused by subject motion, or the overall blur caused by camera motion, is a fatal flaw in ultra-closeup photographs.

Backgrounds. Because an extreme close-up is focused concisely on the main idea, in a small area, background simplicity is fairly easy to achieve. In sunlight, backgrounds tend to look after themselves by going softly out of focus. Indoors, a piece of unpatterned material, or the dull-finish paper sold in more than a hundred colors by various artists' supply stores, can be tacked behind the photographic subject when you are shooting by flood or available light. With flash,

Fig. 128 (left).—Close-up of spiderweb in damp dawn makes interesting pattern in black-and-white.

Fig. 129 (opposite).—Ultra close-ups of flowers and insects are best with natural out-of-focus backgrounds. (Courtesy of the Newspaper National Snapshot Awards)

only the foreground subject usually receives sufficient light to record an image on the film.

In the very broad closeup categories discussed in the next pages, a few specific suggestions for backgrounds are included. Generally speaking, however, for black-and-white photographs the background color should be one that will reproduce as a light gray tone for dark objects and one that will reproduce as a darker gray for light objects. Color photographs are more successful, on the whole, when the background choice is a relatively flat tone which complements without too sharp a contrast the colors of the subject.

FLOWERS AND OTHER NATURE CLOSE–UPS

Nature close-ups comprise an area in which color films are used almost exclusively. Nevertheless some insects, fungi, ferns, seashells, and other small subjects with distinctive shapes and patterns can be very effective in black and white, as in Figure 128. Working distances will depend not only on your equipment but on the size of your subject. Some tiny specimens can scarcely be seen without a magnifying glass, while a large flower or a cluster of blooms may fill the picture frame at a distance of two feet or more.

Exposure. Very fine-grain color films, being relatively slow, often require a shutter time too long for hand-held steadiness; in these instances a sturdy tripod and cable release are indispensable. If you do not have a tripod and your camera offers a good range of settings, select a shutter speed no longer than 1/25 second and the corresponding ƒ/stop. If the day or the location is fairly breezy, it is better to shoot at 1/60 and to circumvent subject motion by careful timing.

If a flower, for example, is swaying noticeably, try to trip your shutter between breezes. The base of a swaying stalk can be weighted without injury by means of medical clamps called "hemostats." These clamps, or the flexible plant ties used by gardeners, are useful also for holding back leaves and small branches when you wish to isolate a single plant or blossom.

Another handy little accessory is a mirror, preferably a shaving or makeup mirror which is mounted on a base and can be tilted easily. It can serve as a fill-in light by reflecting daylight into dark shadows where a bulky reflector might be impractical, and it is particularly good for lighting plants or insects in deep shade such as might be encountered under logs or overhanging rocks.

Flower Backgrounds Outdoors. Selective focus at a wide aperture with its consequent thin depth of field, usually takes care of backgrounds in close-ups, as in Figure 129. But watch out for sharp little spots of color, particularly yellows and whites; even when considerably diffused and out of focus, bright spots or specular highlights can mar an otherwise pleasing effect. When your floral subject is in a crowded or busy area, especially in a sunny garden or yard, an artificial backdrop may be needed. If so, a plain sheet of dull-finish art paper can be used, preferably in a light sky blue or subdued foliage color; don't choose an intense color which might overpower the main subject. A less artificial effect can sometimes be achieved by attaching a fern or other appropriate bit of foliage right behind the flower.

Live Objects. Insects and other wildlife or small pets, such as kittens and canaries, cannot normally be photographed at shutter settings as slow as you would choose for flowers or still life. Although you may need a comparatively fast shutter time for living things, it is important to *move yourself and your equipment slowly* and smoothly in order to avoid frightening and perhaps losing your subject. Most pets and other animals react in alarm to flash; it is usually better to try for available light with reflector and fill-in and, possibly, to use a faster film. Since live insects are likely to scurry off before a photographer can get set, artificial insects appear in some slides.

Experienced photographers who specialize in apparent close-ups of wildlife frequently employ various remote-control devices for releasing the shutter while watching through binoculars the area on which the camera is focused; or they may have an even more complicated setup in which the subject itself trips the shutter. This is mentioned only so that you will not expect the impossible in amateur photography with an average small camera.

TABLETOPS

Although the term is sometimes loosely applied to still-life photographs, *tabletop* is a photographic coinage intended to refer to pictures of small-scale objects which incorporate some sort of theme—in other words, an "idea" carried out in miniature still life. For example, if you place a set of toy soldiers on a table and photograph it, you get a picture of some toy soldiers; if you place an African violet on a table and take its picture, you get a flower portrait. But if you arrange the toy soldiers and a couple of tanks in some authentic battle formation on mud-colored fabric, you may get a successful tabletop. And if you place an African violet on some textured paper and arrange a doll of suitable size with a miniature watering can in realistic relation to it, you may get a pleasing tabletop.

Within the framework of the basic definition, anything goes in tabletop photography. It is dependent upon your imagination, resourcefulness, and good taste, without which the results can be pretty awful or just plain dull. When you are not sure about a picture, follow this rule: if in doubt, toss it out.

Backgrounds. A piece of fabric, a sofa, draperies, or a rug can serve as background for tabletops, title slides, and similar close-ups. More often used, however, are the colored papers mentioned earlier —i.e., textured water-color paper or a roll of seamless display paper (sometimes available in half-width). Part of the background material is customarily attached to a large piece of heavy cardboard, so that it can be propped vertically against a wall or furniture, and the balance of the paper or fabric brought forward on a table or other horizontal surface. When you have arranged the composition on this flat surface, check your viewfinder to be certain that all elements are well within the background boundaries.

Lighting Very Small Objects. The basic lighting arrangements detailed in the preceding chapter on portraiture are applicable to many inanimate objects; but for photographing really tiny objects only a few inches away, you should have slightly different equipment in order to achieve modeling, texture, or special effects. One reason for this is that the exposure generally calls for the maximum possible illumination. Another is that standard floodlamps placed very near a tiny object are likely to light it too evenly and flatly; furthermore, if the object is perishable, like a flower or fruit, the heat from the floods will be excessive. A more appropriate lamp is a 150-watt miniature spot, which confines the light to a comparatively small area. To the spot can be added a *snoot,* a metal tube designed to funnel the light into a narrow beam. One or more reflectors can further intensify this main light. For fill-in lighting, the mirror previously suggested for small objects in deep shade can furnish sharply focused secondary light. For simply softening shadows, an ordinary white cardboard reflector can be used as in other types of photographs.

TITLE SLIDES

If you plan some showings of color slides for more than small family gatherings, it may enhance your act to include some courtesy slides, like "Good Evening" and "The End," and some transitional slides, such as an airplane takeoff or an area-map close-up for a vacation series.

Titles can be nonverbal—for example, a picture of a confetti-showered car or of a jolly Santa speaks for itself in introducing a pictorial record of wedding or Christmas festivities. And whether you make a few titles occasionally, perhaps to finish a roll of film, or make a larger supply at one time, it is a good idea to keep an interchangeable assortment on hand for putting a slide show together.

Title slides can be made in daylight as well as by artificial light with the basic equipment already described. Sometimes a background of sky or grass or treebark will blend more harmoniously with other outdoor pictures than will a floodlit colored paper. And words written in sand will last a lifetime if photographed for your title collection.

Lettering. Words to be placed against the background can be clipped from magazines or brochures, and can be handwritten or typewritten. They can be the title of a book included in a suitable arrangement, or they can be composed from game letters like scrabble. Words can be finger-painted on a 16 x 24 sheet of clear glass, with white paper back of the glass for maximum brilliance.

Some stationery and camera stores carry one or more types of ready-to-use letters: individual die-cut letters on gummed colored paper; self-adhesive letters to stick onto the background or, if you wish to reuse them, onto clear cellophane; colored plastic letters that can be placed above any printed matter; small three-dimensional display letters with white matte surfaces. Color tapes from $\frac{1}{16}$ to $\frac{1}{2}$ inch in width can be used to underline words and for decoration.

Props for title slides, like those for tabletops, can be anything you consider suitable; cutout figures and shapes, travel folders and post-cards, jewelry and trinkets are favorites. Watch out for glare from any highly reflective surfaces like silver or polished metal.

Lettering Within an Existing Slide. If you wish to add a title to the sky or other light section of a color slide, you can do so by sandwiching a slightly underexposed black-and-white negative with the original slide. Place white letters against a dull black ground, leaving plenty of black space below. Before exposing the film, carefully compare the image in your viewfinder with the existing color slide to be sure that the title is well inside the sky area. Enlargements from these black-and-white negatives can serve as covers for albums of print pictures.

Lighting. For texture and a feeling of depth, use strong side lighting, keeping any fill-in light far enough away so that it does not create double shadows in your composition. If the composition includes a postcard or other picture-within-a-picture, see that the shadows created by your lighting fall in the same direction as those in the postcard.

Title slides, to be effective, should have original arrangements of props, with letters neatly mounted and properly lighted. Perhaps even more important is their mood and message, which should be fitted to the subject matter *and* to the audience with whom you are communicating through the slides.

COPYING

Copying is an aspect of closeup photography and, as such, can be done with the same accessories and equipment. It is also, like portraiture, a highly specialized profession in which specific copying cameras and extensive commercial setups are employed.

The camera preferred by the layman for copy work is the single-lens reflex, for the advantages already noted. Besides eliminating the parallax problem, the SLR's groundglass focusing reveals any lighting glare which may need correcting and also simplifies measurement of the image size. For serious copying work, microphotography, magnification, or slide copying, there are elaborate attachments, adapters, and various extension bellows designed for individual small cameras. When using any of this special equipment, you should carefully follow the instructions in the booklets provided with the equipment.

For ordinary copying, a focal length approximately the diagonal of the film size (see page 37) is satisfactory. If at the lens' minimum focusing distance the original to be copied fills most of the viewer, no lens attachments are needed.

Terminology. *Copying* refers to photographic reproduction of flat, or two-dimensional, subject matter. The material to be copied is called the *original,* or the *copy.* Copy as a noun refers also to the photograph obtained by copying: the *reproduction*. Subject matter that has only two tones, such as printing or line drawings, is a *line original*. Any material having several gray tones, such as a photograph or wash drawing, is a *continuous-tone original*. A photomechanical reproduction, in a pattern of tiny dots, of a continuous-tone original is called a *halftone*.

Basic Copying Setup. Any camera can be used for copying, provided there is some means of holding the subject matter parallel to the film plane and perpendicular to the lens axis. This may be a horizontal or a vertical setup, depending on available equipment, working space, and condition of the original. The standard *horizontal setup* includes a copying stand to which the camera is mounted, a horizontal board with graph lines for measuring and squaring the original, and clips to hold the original in place. A camera mount without its own board can be used with any sturdy table and special clamps. Some enlargers provide special equipment for converting the enlarger bellows into a copying camera.

Most *vertical setups* need less working space and are usually less subject to vibration. They require some kind of easel or focal frame to hold the original upright and a sturdy tripod for the camera. In either a vertical or horizontal setup, a small bubble level is useful for determining whether camera and all parts of the setup are perfectly level.

Lighting Equipment. Any light source, like any camera, *can* be used for copying, but it must furnish even lighting. Daylight is generally too variable to be practical; however, it may be used successfully if the original is directly facing the window. Ordinary flash is not recommended because it does not permit a preview of the lighted original.

The most practical lights are photofloods or household lamps of 60 to 150 watts; they should be identical pairs and used in twin reflectors sufficiently large so that from the camera position no part of the bulb is visible. Lampstands which are easy to move and tilt are convenient for copying and for other artificial-light photography.

Low-wattage lamps are often preferred to photofloods for copying. Although they necessitate longer exposures than floods, the entire copying setup—including the original to be photographed—should be rigid enough to make this no problem. A lower intensity is more comfortable to work with and easier on the subject matter if it happens to be something like an old document or print which could be faded or otherwise damaged by too intense illumination.

Even Lighting Setup. Uniformity of illumination is usually achieved by placing the twin lamps on opposite sides of the copy holder, at an angle of 45 degrees to it, as indicated in diagram "A" of Figure 130. When you are using a camera with a lens of longer

Fig. 130.—Lighting arrangements for copying.

than normal focal length, the angle of lighting can be narrowed, as shown in diagram "B." Reduction of the angle of lighting is sometimes a means of counteracting problem reflections in an original.

When the original to be copied has rough surfaces (like wrinkles in an old document) which cause misplaced highlights, adjust or diffuse the lights to eliminate any glare. If you wish to emphasize rough surfaces (for example, the brush strokes of an oil painting or the texture of a fabric), experiment with a modified cross lighting.

Filters. For clean black-and-white copies of colored subjects, a filter is often advisable, and the principles explained in Chapters 9 and 10 apply to copying as well as to general photography. A brief summary will remind you that a filter lightens its own color (yellow being red + green), and darkens its complementaries:

Filter Color	Lightens	Darkens
YELLOW	reds, greens	blues
RED	reds	blues, greens
GREEN	greens	blues, reds
BLUE	blues	reds, greens

Be sure to check on the filter factor, as accurate exposure is vital to successful copying.

A green filter is needed for most panchromatic films used in tungsten light. Blueprints are customarily copied with a red filter, which holds back the blue-green, making the white lines stand out sharply. A blue filter, less usual in general photography, is often used to copy prints or photographs that have become yellowed or slightly brown. To "erase" transparent stains, such as ink, use a darker filter of the same color as the stain.

Films. The finest-grain films should be chosen for most line copying, since sharp contrast is generally desired. For a continuous-tone original, where excessive contrast would be undesirable, it is better to use a medium-speed film such as you would choose for ordinary snapshots. As an example, for copying a photograph in which your aim is to preserve highlight and shadow detail with several in-between tones, a medium-speed film will give the nearest to normal reproduction. High-speed films produce still lower contrast and are liable to overexposure and loss of detail in the light areas. Of the popular Kodak black-and-white films, for instance, you would pick Panatomic-X for high-contrast line copying, Plus-X for continuous-tone copying, and avoid the very fast Tri-X.

The purpose of most copying is to make black-and-white records, whether the original is in color or not. The basic principles of balanced lighting and fine-grain films apply to copying with color films, but you should not expect exact duplication of the colors being copied; this is a problem even with the most advanced commercial reproduction equipment.

Warning. There are laws regarding the copying of many subjects, such as stamps, money, citizenship papers, and innumerable other documents as well as any copyrighted subject matter. If you are in doubt, check before you click.

18

```
┌─────────────────────────────────────────────┐
   Night Pictures and Trick Shots
└─────────────────────────────────────────────┘
```

UNDER COLORFUL city lights or brilliant country stars, amateur photographers find challenging opportunities for a hobby within a hobby. Since so many after-dark pictures are taken at longer than a second, some general suggestions regarding time exposures are included in this chapter. Not included are suggestions for sunset and moonlight landscapes (see Chapter 13), nor recommendations concerning night photography indoors (see Chapters 11 and 17). Since time exposures and a tripod-held camera are also utilized in many trick shots, including multiple exposures which combine night and day lighting, a few of the fairly common tricks you may have seen, or attempted yourself, are also described.

BASIC CONSIDERATIONS

Cameras and Accessories. Any adjustable camera with a setting for bulb or time and a maximum aperture of $f/3.5$ or larger is suitable for taking pictures at night. Simple cameras with no settings for time exposures are likely to be unsatisfactory, except for occasional snapshots in very bright areas such as under a theater marquee; however, today's high-speed films permit preset cameras to record some subjects that a few years ago would have been possible only with time exposures.

If you expect to take long exposures, you will probably want a tripod and cable release. But a tripod, even a fairly heavy model, is no guarantee of absolute steadiness, especially out of doors where there may be gusts of wind, numerous passersby, and darting dogs. Many photographers, refusing to be encumbered by extra gear, either look about for a ledge, post, step, car door, windowsill, or other tripod substitute, or brace the camera firmly against a wall.

A lens shade is even more important at night than in daytime to minimize glare. And if flash is to be used, it is best to have some provision for using it off the camera. A piece of black cardboard, or some article such as a dark hat with a black lining, should be carried to serve as a mask when you have occasion to interrupt a time exposure; for example, to block out headlights of a passing car, simply hold the mask in front of the lens for a moment without touching the camera. A small pocket flashlight may be needed to make out camera settings and meter readings.

Films. Fast panchromatic or high-speed color films are usually preferred by amateurs for night photography in order to reduce the exposure time and thus eliminate the necessity of carrying a tripod. A daylight-type color film recommended previously for sunsets and moonlight will give more normal sky colors during twilight hours but will render street and building lights rather strongly red and yellow. A color film of the type balanced for artificial light may render early evening skies more blue than normal, but it will probably reproduce the colors of a lighted night scene more nearly as they appear to you. In short, daylight films will render the colors of a night scene some-what "warmer" than will artificial-light films. But either can create interesting effects, and you should not pass up a good picture pos-sibility just because you have the "wrong" film in your camera.

Time Exposures. Markings for exposures longer than one second are usually indicated by a letter at the slow end of the shutter speed index. When set at that letter, the shutter is no longer controlled by its timing mechanism but is controlled manually. If the marking is a "T" for *time,* you press the shutter release in the usual way to open it; at this "T" setting the shutter will remain open until pressed a second time to terminate the exposure.

On cameras that have a setting "B" for *bulb,* or *brief* time, or an "L" for *long* exposure, either of these markings indicates that when the shutter button is pressed and held, the shutter will remain open until the button is released. Beginners occasionally confuse "bulb" with "flashbulb"—the bulb setting does *not* mean flash.

A cable release is a practical necessity for time exposures because it is almost impossible not to jar the camera slightly while pressing or holding the shutter button on a tripod-held camera. Always press the plunger of the cable release gently but firmly, and remember to hold the cable in a slack curve; pulling it taut will jar the camera, especially if you are holding a bulb exposure.

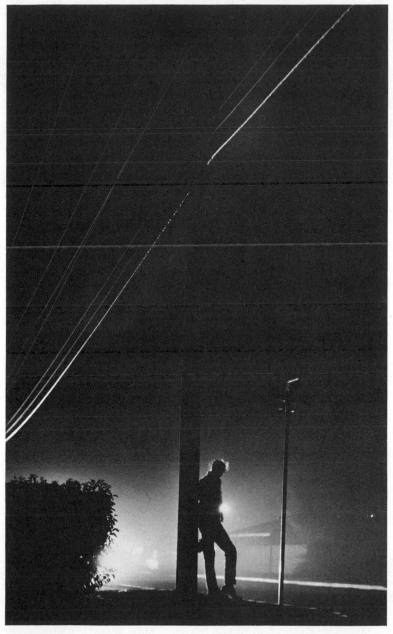

Fig. 131.—Time exposures are usually needed to capture mood or activity at night. (Courtesy of Scholastic High School Photo Awards)

Flash by Night. If you plan to use fill-in flash for a scene needing more than existing light, try to place the flashgun at an angle that will simulate a high street lamp, a low window light, or some other natural source of illumination. This can be done, of course, only with an off-camera flash arrangement. A statue, a person, or other foreground object in a night scene can be lighted with flash.

Night photographers usually prefer *open flash* (see page 125), firing the flashlamp sometime during a time exposure. If there are people in the picture, it is preferable to fire the flash near the end of the exposure; this is because people are inclined to turn toward the flash or otherwise move when it goes off. During long exposures of at least a minute or two, and if there is not much existing light from windows or street lamps, it is possible to use the painting-with-flash technique outlined on page 126. If the situation—and your temperament, experience, and equipment—warrants doing this, you would choose the aperture giving the desired depth of field and proceed as indoors.

Estimating Exposure at Night. The principal problem in night photography is to determine how long the exposure should be; in some instances this is bound to be a wild guess. The variables are far more diverse and unpredictable than by daylight, and the brightness range of most night scenes is too great for any film to reproduce accurately at any exposure. Exposure meters are generally less effective in dim light than in normal illumination, but when there is sufficient light to activate the needle, read your meter in the usual way. Many newer meters have a switch for low-light readings.

The exposure suggestions which follow are simply starting points, to be modified according to your estimate of specific conditions and the film you are using. If you wish to be reasonably sure of some picture, take at least three shots. After shooting at what you have decided on as the best exposure, bracket this with another at 4 times estimated exposure and a third at 1/4 the exposure. A narrower bracket, such as two times and one-half the exposure, is not likely to produce appreciable differences at night. For a double bracket, on a must-have-now-or-never picture, take two extra shots, one at 8 times and another at 1/8 the key exposure.

Basic Exposure Guides. First of all, there is no *one* correct exposure for pictures at night; at practically any exposure you select, you are bound to get something. Since modern color films offer a wide choice of speeds, the starting-point recommendations in the list which is to follow are based on medium-fast types with speeds a bit above or below Kodachrome-X (ASA 64). If you are using a slower color film (ASA 25 to 50), double the recommended basic exposure; if you are using a high-speed color film (over ASA 125), cut it in half. For very fast black-and-white film, like Tri-X, reduce exposure by still another stop.

As explained earlier (see pages 42 and 82), each f/stop, going up the scale, transmits half as much light as the preceding aperture. This principle works in the same way for exposures on time or bulb settings by halving (or doubling) the number of seconds. For example, to decrease a 16-second exposure by three stops, cut 16 to 8 for one stop, 8 to 4 for two stops, and 4 to 2 seconds for the fast black-and-white film.

The reason that films of varying ASA indexes or speed values are grouped together for night pictures is that when either illumination or length of exposure is not "normal" the law of reciprocity fails, and thus the exposure estimate can be only approximate.

Reciprocity Failure. Do not be daunted by this formidable little phrase. You may hear it, and you may wish to have some idea why precise exposure guides are not possible except when conditions are more or less average. Basically the law of reciprocity predicates that decreases in light intensity can be compensated for by corresponding increases in exposure. This theory works fine until the exposures become extremely long or extremely short, which occurs when levels of illumination are very low or very intense. If the light is average, you can expect a doubling of the exposure to double the density of the negative; but if the illumination of a scene is so low that you need a time exposure of ten seconds, for example, this does not mean that the negative density will be ten times what it would be at one second. Hence the unpredictability of results in night photography.

RECOMMENDED EXPOSURES

The following guides are based on medium-fast color films (e.g., Kodachrome-X); double the basic guide for slower films and halve it for high-speed films.

Brightly Lighted Streets. One of the calculated risks of photographing night scenes is that unexpected pedestrians or cars can show up during a long exposure and ruin the picture. By studying the flow of traffic for a while, you can often see a pattern of stopping and starting which will allow you to take your picture when there

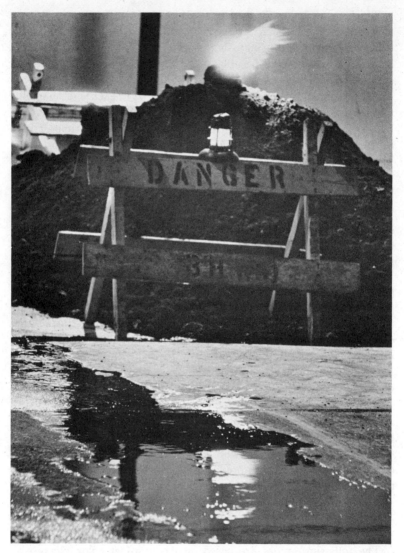

Fig. 132.—Water in foreground of a picture reflects city or roadside lights. (Courtesy of Scholastic High School Photo Awards)

is the least motion, perhaps when people and vehicles are waiting for a traffic signal to change. If the scene is quiet except for an occasional car or pedestrian, you can cover your lens with a black mask during the movement, and uncover to continue the exposure. Basic recommendation: *2 seconds at f/5.6 or 4 seconds at f/8.*

Neon and Electric Signs. An exposure of *1/2 second at f/11* or, if you are bracing your camera without a tripod, *1/25 second at f/3.5* will record the lighted sign but not much detail outside the display itself. You can get more detail in the area around the sign by increasing the exposure, but then the display lights will be overexposed.

Rain and Fog. Wet pavements often make streets more interesting, keep more pedestrians out of the way, and reflect about as much light as supplementary flash. If you are exposing for highlights, rain will increase their number; and reflections can double the amount of color you get. Fog lends mood to a picture, adds halos to street lamps, and imparts an illusion of depth by swallowing up distant areas and emphasizing near ones. Be sure to protect your camera from rain and excessive dampness by keeping it covered when not in use and by photographing from under some shelter, such as an awning, doorway, or umbrella. Depending on the brightness of street signs, use *4 seconds to 1/2 second at f/8*.

Water Reflections. City lights reflected in a pool or fountain, like those sometimes found in a city square, plaza, or small park—or even a large puddle—can add color and interest. Try to compose your picture so that the reflections serve, in the same way as flash, to brighten the foreground. Use the same exposure as for bright streets: *2 seconds at f/5.6 or 4 seconds at f/8*.

Store Windows. Some window displays are bright enough to be photographed at *1/30 second at f/2* or *f/2.8* with high-speed color film (which requires no exposure increase for glass). The majority of store windows do not have that much illumination and need, on average for the medium-speed color film being used here as basic, an exposure of *1 or 2 seconds at f/8*. Reflections, which are the biggest problem, can often be controlled by finding the right angle for your camera, and by standing two or three feet away from the glass. It is rarely advisable, and usually impossible, to photograph windows head-on. Professional photographs of window displays are generally taken very late when traffic is at a minimum and sometimes with assistants holding a large black curtain behind the camera. Observant amateurs can occasionally turn a problem into a pictorial advantage by making reflections part of the composition.

Floodlit Buildings and Monuments. Practice will soon tell you how much exposure is needed for monuments and other public buildings in floodlight. A lot depends on the light or dark color of the structure itself, as well as on the intensity of the floodlighting, which often varies considerably. Here again, a hand-held exposure may be

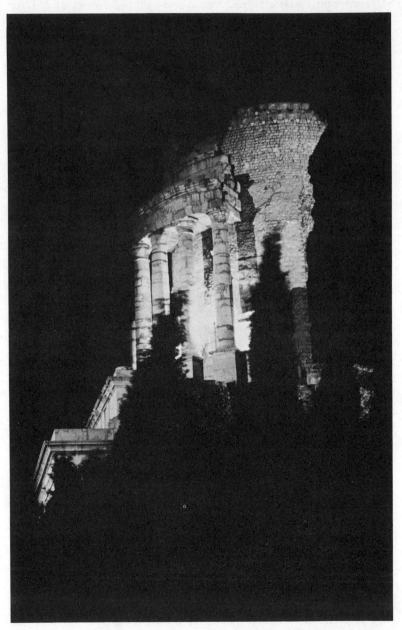

Fig. 133.—Intensity of floodlighting affects amount of exposure needed for monuments at night. (Courtesy of Scholastic High School Photo Awards)

possible with fast film and a fast lens. An average basic recommendation otherwise is from *8 seconds to 16 seconds at f/8*.

The color of the floodlighting makes quite a difference in exposure. For instance, in photographing an outdoor spectacle like Niagara Falls, a basic recommendation for white floodlighting would be about 30 seconds at *f/5.6*. Fairly bright colored lighting would require from 10 to 40 seconds at *f/2.8*, and deep colors about 60 seconds at the same aperture.

Fireworks and Carnivals. Spectacular color photographs of distant fireworks are usually achieved by aiming the camera up toward the display area, leaving the shutter open while three or four bursts explode, then closing the shutter. Time for this is generally about *8 seconds at f/8*. This multiple-exposure technique can be used for a lighted ride, like a Ferris wheel; obviously it will not stop the action, but the whirls of color can create interesting patterns. For very bright fireworks nearby, you might try a hand-held exposure of *1/8 second at f/5.6 or f/4*. If your camera does not have an automatic film advance, or does otherwise permit multiple exposures, you can take several fireworks shots on the same frame at even less exposure per shot.

Campfires. A basic recommendation for recording the flames of the campfire itself would be *1/10 second at f/4.5 or 1/30 second at f/2.8*.

Fig. 134.—Flames of fires at night can be recorded at hand-held shutter speed with fast films. (Courtesy of Scholastic High School Photo Awards)

If you are more interested in catching the faces of a group at the campfire, at the expense of blurring the flames, try *1/2 second at f/11;* a supplementary flash on the far side of the campfire will help reveal features.

Burning Buildings and Bonfires. Here you would in all probability be trying first for flames and then for faces. Since flames have a good deal of "action" you would choose the shorter time of *1/30 second at f/2.8.*

Christmas Trees and House Lighting. For outdoor trees or doorways decorated with colored lights try a basic exposure of *8 seconds at f/8.* For close-ups of lighted Christmas trees indoors where you can use supplementary flash, *1 second at f/11* should be adequate exposure.

Theaters. For a few atmosphere shots outside a theater where marquee lights are illuminating the scene, you will probably be able to take a meter reading. If that is not convenient, you can generally get fairly good results with a wide-open lens and a shutter speed that will catch movement as well as color. Try *1/60 at f/3.5* or the equivalent exposure for 1/125 if you have a faster lens.

For spotlighted acts inside, whether a stage show, ice show, or circus, you can use *1/30 at f/2.8*—if you have an unobstructed view and if pictures are permitted.

Effect of Distance on Exposure. Some increase over basic exposure is generally recommended for night scenes at relatively great distances. For example, a picture of the New York skyline taken from New Jersey or from a Staten Island ferry should have more exposure than a city scene taken on a New York street. If you will review the foregoing suggestions, you will note that the most frequently recommended aperture is *f/8;* in fact, *4 seconds at f/8* might be considered an average "basic basic" exposure for night photography in general.

Calendar Considerations. Darkness arrives at different hours in different months, and city scenes have different aspects and moods at various times of the year. On a summer evening you may find more strolling and less bustling, but in winter there will be more dazzle and more lighted office buildings. Buildings silhouetted against the sky will show up best if photographed after sunset but before it is really dark. During December this twilight zone comes early, before closing time of most offices, making it possible to get many lighted windows in your night scenes at the end of the year.

But December need not confine you to business sections or Christmas lights. In residential areas a snowy night scene can evoke a variety of moods or emotions. Street lamps reflecting on white-blanketed shrubbery or ice-coated trees, dark shapes cast on snow-covered walks, silhouettes of a homebound couple or a late shoveler, friendly lights in a living-room window offer right-at-home opportunities for the amateur with a seeing eye and a ready camera.

MULTIPLE EXPOSURES

When you see a photograph that looks like a lighted city scene against an early sunset sky, a woman conversing with herself, a person recoiling before a ghost, or a man balancing a girl in the palm of his hand, you know that things are not what they seem. But what are they? The apparently single photograph usually turns out to be more than one exposure on the same negative; sometimes it turns out to be two negatives sandwiched together.

Many modern cameras have a lever to advance the film and cock the shutter in one easy operation—a device designed not only for speed but also to prevent unintentional double exposures. Check your camera booklet to ascertain if and how your film-advance mechanism works to permit double exposures.

Atmosphere à la Carte. Unusual effects can be obtained by combining daylight and evening exposures on a single negative. As an example, suppose that while you are vacationing in a large city you observe from your hotel window that the view takes on a special magic as lights and more lights come on after dusk. To capture this scene, place your camera on a tripod or other support where it can remain focused on the view for a few hours. Make a daylight underexposure of the general scene, using about two stops below normal. When the after-dark scene is the way you want to photograph it, make a time exposure on the same negative. In a similar manner a double-exposure photograph of a lighted city scene silhouetted against a sunset sky can be obtained: take a picture of the sky at a slight underexposure; keep your tripod unmoved until the lights appear; then take a second exposure against the darker sky.

With planning, practice, and patience, you can use this technique to record three or four exposures as one picture. This is done by building up the composition with progressive underexposures, putting the background and secondary elements in first and superimposing the main interest on them. Similar effects can be achieved by sandwiching negatives or color slides together.

Double Take. The first secret of shots such as that of a woman conversing with herself or that of a man beating himself at chess is a black background which, by itself, does not affect the film during exposure. For a hand-held camera, you can have your subject chalk-mark the black ground to correspond to the frame corners in your viewfinder before your two-way conversationalist steps into the picture. Pose her talking on one side of the picture area and make an exposure but don't advance the film; then pose her listening on the facing side and make another exposure on the same negative.

If your plan calls for something in the center of the picture, like an unfinished chess game on a table, the central object will be exposed twice. This usually does not matter, provided you have your camera on a firm tripod so the chess game is in exactly the same position during both exposures, but try to keep the setup simple. Pose your subject on one side of the table puzzling over a beleaguered bishop, make the first exposure, then pose the same man on the opposite side with the complacent expression of a player about to capture an opponent's queen.

These half-and-half photographs are sometimes made by masking one side of the lens for the first exposure, then shifting mask and subject to the opposite side for the second exposure. However, unless you get the mask exactly the right size, there will probably be a vertical line in the center of the picture where the exposures did not quite meet or overlapped slightly.

Exposing a Ghost. This time not only should your camera be stationary for two exposures, but your subject should be ready, willing, and able to remain fixed during both takes. Seat him in a reading chair with a lamp and arrange the ghost character opposite the live character. Place an open magazine or newspaper as if it had just fallen from the hands of the suddenly affrighted subject. When the setup and pose are as you want them, take one shot very under-exposed (about one-fourth normal), tell your subject to "Hold it" while the ghost exits and you reset your camera to normal exposure, then take another picture on the same negative.

Or you can do it the other way around, using one actor instead of two. Photograph a pseudo-terrified boy against the black background, and don't advance the film. Now boy exits, to be set up as the spook with something light behind him instead of the black background. This and a half-normal second exposure should make the subject somewhat translucent, like a proper ghost.

Offbeat Balance. A very simple version of man balancing girl in palm of hand can be done outdoors in a single exposure by posing the man as close as your equipment permits, and posing the girl far back until it appears in your viewfinder as if she were standing on the outstretched palm. Focus about halfway into the double subject and make the exposure.

The balancing act is easier if you have a groundglass viewfinder, on which you can mark the hand position, and the camera on a tripod for an accurate double exposure. Pose the man with his hand stretched out to one side in the foreground of your finder, mark the hand on the groundglass, and expose against a black background. Now move your camera back until you get a small image of the girl standing on the hand line and make a second exposure on the same negative.

Paste-ups. While not strictly a multiple exposure, a composite photograph can be made of multiple elements—in the standard way illustrations and text are pasted up to be reproduced as an advertising page. Amateur photographers, with less serious intent, sometimes use this method for trick pictures by rubber-cementing a cutout from one photograph onto another, or several cutouts onto a white cardboard. The result may be simply a pair of odd-scale figures, like the balancing act, or a pretty girl looking into a mirror which startlingly reflects a cutout crone; or it can be a more original and fanciful concoction of your own making.

PHOTOGRAMS

Look, No Camera! Photogram techniques are based on the fact that light can produce an image without a lens. (See description of the pinhole principle on page 31.) By arranging small objects on sensitized paper, exposing the composition to light, and developing the print by standard methods, you can produce a black-and-white photograph known as a *photogram*. (Do not confuse with "Photogrammetry" which is defined in Appendix B.)

Any objects that will fit the photographic paper size may be used. Tiny objects strewed in some pleasing pattern are the most popular "subjects"—for example, grain kernels, cereals, marbles, beads, buttons, tacks, nuts, petals, pods, pebbles, toys, jewelry. Even with no objects at all, a photogram can be made by "painting" (see page 121) a design with the light.

Exposure. Because the sensitized paper should be used by safelight (see Chapter 19), it is advisable to experiment with your designs first on plain paper. Theoretically, sunlight can be used for photograms, but such a method makes it very difficult to protect the photographic paper before exposure.

Place the composition to be photographed under an ordinary light bulb, and turn the lamp on for a few seconds—much as you would for making a contact print with a printing frame. Wattage and distance will largely determine the length of exposure, which is not critical and is generally done by test.

Shadow or Substance. The customary goal of photograms is a print showing opaque objects as sharp black shapes on a white ground, so overexposure is no problem. However, you may wish to render a particular design in pale shadowy silhouette, which is done by underexposure. Or you can try for middle tones by using translucent rather than opaque objects. A pattern within a pattern, like the vein structure of a leaf or the motif of a thin fabric, can be reproduced by experimenting with the length of exposure.

Photograms offer interesting and useful practice in composition and printing to the amateur photographer, even one who does not plan to do any darkroom work—the fundamentals of which are described in the following chapter.

19

Darkroom Fundamentals

PHOTOGRAPHIC CHEMISTRY as known today dates back to 1839 when an unprosperous French painter named Daguerre, after years of experimenting, happened upon the discovery of a latent image which could be developed and fixed. Although modern scientists agree that the silver halides in a photographic emulsion form an invisible image when correctly exposed to light, there are still many theories as to exactly *how* the latent-image reaction occurs. But occur it does, allowing the affected halides to be reduced to metallic silver and subsequently to be reproduced as a photograph.

DEVELOPMENT THEORY

The Developing Solution. To convert a latent image into a photographic image, a developer is compounded of several chemicals having specific functions. These generally include (1) a reducer, (2) a solvent, (3) an accelerator, (4) a preservative, and (5) a restrainer. The most important ingredient is the *reducing agent* which combines with oxygen to react on the silver halides and thus reduce, or separate, the silver.

The water in which the dry chemicals are dissolved acts as a *solvent,* softening and swelling the gelatin of the emulsion to permit the solution to penetrate. To energize the reducing agent, an *accelerator,* or activator, is usually added. Since a reducer and an accelerator oxidize in solution, a *restrainer* is added to make the solution selective. Overoxidation speeds deterioration of the solution, causing it to leave rusty stains in the emulsion; so a *preservative* is added to lessen staining and to prolong the life of the developer.

Combinations of reducing agents are used to form an all-around balanced developer, usually one that has soft action and good detail ability for medium-contrast work.

Rinse Bath. When the film is removed from the developing solution, it must be rinsed before being placed in the fixing bath; otherwise the surplus developer would continue to react on the emulsion. Even a very small amount of developer in the fixer, or of fixer in the developer, can cause stains. Rinsing can be by plain water or by a chemical *stop bath,* also called *shortstop.*

A water rinse is normally sufficient to remove excess developer and to prevent contamination of the fixing bath. In printing, water rinsing sometimes precedes an acid stop bath. Plain water rinsing will probably necessitate more frequent replenishing of the fixing solution. An acid stop bath, on the other hand, not only neutralizes the alkaline developer but also lengthens the useful life of the acid fixing bath.

The Fixing Bath. Photographic emulsions, when removed from the developer and rinsed, still contain some light-sensitive silver halides unaffected by the reducer. To prevent eventual darkening and discoloration, these residual halides must be eliminated from the negative by a fixing bath. To do a good job, a fixer must dissolve the excess silver without affecting the image and must form soluble compounds which can be removed. The chemical most commonly used is sodium thiosulfate, which has another name, hyposulfite, from which comes the familiar abbreviation "hypo."

Because strong acids in quantity can cause the fixer to decompose, a preservative, usually sodium sulfite, is added to the hypo solution. An *anti-stain neutralizer,* usually acetic acid, added to the fixing bath stops the alkaline developer's activity more completely than a rinse can and prevents staining. Without a *hardener,* swelling and softening of the gelatin during development would leave the emulsion vulnerable to scratches and other defects; so a hardening agent is added to the fixing formula.

Rapid Fixers. Increasing the amount of ordinary hypo in a standard solution will *not* increase the rate of fixation; in fact, it can decrease it. When speed is vital—as in printing news, medical, or tactical photographs—a concentrated solution of other hypo forms can be used to fix film in about three minutes and paper in about half that time. These special chemicals are unstable in powder form, so they are sold in concentrated solutions costing slightly more than ordinary fixers.

Exhaustion Symptoms. The manufacturer's directions will explain how much film or printing paper a specific amount of solution, such as one quart, can be expected to fix satisfactorily under average conditions when temperature and other recommendations are adhered to. Fresh solutions, which are characterized by the sharp odor of acetic acid, a grippy feel, and very temporary bubbles, will clear film in about five minutes and fix it in about ten; older solutions take slightly longer. If the fixing time runs very much longer, the bath should be replaced. Among the symptoms of an exhausted fixing bath are a sulphur odor, a slippery feel, a milky look or other discoloration, and persistent bubbles.

Replenishing Solutions. Because the chemicals in developing and fixing baths are used up at different rates, a special solution called a *replenisher* is usually added according to directions. If a developing solution has a self-replenishment recommendation, then more of the regular developer or fixer can be added instead of a special replenisher.

WHERE AND HOW TO WORK

Makeshift Darkrooms. Any lighttight space can serve as an occasional darkroom. To be efficient, however, it should have running water, electricity, and a reasonable amount of ventilation. If there is no running water, solutions can be mixed, and negatives and prints washed, outside of the darkroom. But the disadvantage of this, besides the inconvenience, is that without water at hand there is less control of temperatures during the actual processing.

Kitchens and bathrooms, therefore, are the favored choice. A counter top or table beside the kitchen sink or a piece of plywood across the top of the bathtub provides work space. Processing chemicals stain, so floors, walls, and counters should be protected by oilcloth or newspapers.

If you are mixing solutions and washing prints outside the darkroom—and especially if you are sharing the setup—it is very convenient to have a changing bag for loading rollfilm tanks for developing. A *changing bag* is a large lighttight pouch with two thicknesses of black cloth double-zippered along one side and snugly sleeved on the opposite side. The camera and tank are placed inside the bag, which should be on a table or other convenient working surface. The bag is then zipped shut and the hands inserted in its sleeves. When the hands, working blindly inside the bag, have transferred the exposed film to the tank and replaced the tank's lightproof lid, the remaining development steps can be completed in a normally lighted room.

Darkness Check. In kitchens or bathrooms you will probably need some black twill or felt for the windows. To check any darkroom for light leakage, simply remain in the closed area for four or five minutes; then if you cannot see your hand, or a sheet of white paper on the ·work table, the room can be considered adequately dark. A common source of leaking light is the crack beneath the darkroom door; a dark towel or a length of weatherstripping will usually be sufficient to make the doorway lighttight.

Permanent Darkrooms. Makeshift darkrooms require a lot of setting up and putting away, so if you can snare a corner for your very own, that will be more satisfactory. Home darkrooms are often constructed in basements or utility rooms, where water and electricity are readily available; any excessive dampness or seasonal temperature extremes should be avoided or controlled. All you need for a one-man operation is a space approximately five or six feet square. When space is no problem, amateur darkrooms average at least 8 x 10 feet. Sometimes a camera club or a group of friends undertake to share the expense, maintenance, and housekeeping of a darkroom. Darkroom walls should be painted white, and work surfaces should be about three feet high. For new darkrooms there are stainless-steel sinks especially designed to resist processing chemicals. There are a number of books about darkrooms which include directions for building them and suggestions for working arrangements.

Basic Equipment. Besides the appropriate chemicals and paper, these are most of the needed items for black-and-white developing and printing:

Trays, three, preferably large enough for 8 x 10 sheets
Graduate, or pitcher, for measuring liquids
Thermometer, accurate, for liquids
Tongs, two
Stirrers, two
Spring clips
Funnel
Timer
Safelight
Rollfilm Tank
Printer and/or Enlarger

Since metallic substances, except stainless steel, are generally prone to contaminate photographic chemicals, it is best to acquire the items in a photographic store after conferring, if possible, with friends who have used some of them. Smaller trays can help economize on developer and shortstop solutions, but fixing solutions, which can be saved for reuse, perform better in larger trays. A fourth tray, fairly large, is handy for washing and for holding several prints about to be washed. You will also want to have on hand a heavy apron, towels, absorbent cotton, and possibly rubber gloves—although some photographers use neither tongs nor gloves. You should remember, though, that the different solutions contaminate each other and must be kept separate.

Economical kits of various sizes are available from photographic dealers. They may contain all or part of the foregoing list, along with developing or printing chemicals, or both. You may expect a kit to include general instructions as well as directions for the individual products.

Emergency Substitutes. If you are short on trays, nonmetallic cooking or serving dishes can be used. A safelight substitute can be either a 15-watt bulb in a desk lamp, with red cellophane or plastic used as a filter, or a yellow "bug light." If you need to make a contact print without a printer, you can use a piece of window glass on a flat board or table; put the negative and paper, emulsion sides face to face, inside the board-glass sandwich and expose as with a printing frame.

Basic Darkroom Cautions and Tips. A few important darkroom habits should be learned so thoroughly that they become automatic.

Read the directions. This injunction cannot be overemphasized.

Keep trays, tanks, and other equipment *clean* to avoid contaminating the solutions.

Rinse funnel, graduate, and other equipment in cool water promptly after each measuring and pouring of liquids.

Pour chemicals *away* from you to keep any spillage from skin and clothing.

Hold funnel slightly *above* bottle neck to admit air and lessen spilling.

Mix chemicals *gently*, pour *slowly*, to keep air bubbles from forming.

Use gentle, *uniform* motions when agitating trays or tanks.

Observe carefully all *time and temperature* recommendations.

Label all storage bottles and *make notations of each use* on the label to avoid using exhausted solutions.

If you are sharing a darkroom, *do not open the door* to go in or out without asking if it is all right to do so.

Agitation. If a negative or print is placed in a developing or fixing solution and left there without any movement, the solution in direct contact with the emulsion, especially with the highlight areas, will soon lose its power. Agitation of the tray or tank is therefore necessary to bring fresh solution continuously to the emulsion.

A key word in photographic processing directions, *agitation* is sometimes qualified by "intermittent" or "constant" or "gentle" or "uniform." Constant agitation often applies to mechanical methods not usual for home processing. Intermittent agitation is recommended for most amateur work. For *tray* development, this generally means a gentle rocking of the tray for about five seconds every minute or half-minute. For *tank* development, it means a gentle twisting or slight shaking of the tank almost constantly for the first minute or two, then for about five seconds every one or two minutes of the remaining time. Lack of agitation can cause underdevelopment; excessive or vehement agitation can cause frothing and relative overdevelopment of some areas.

Advantages of Lab-developed Negatives. Some amateur darkroom hobbyists choose to do only printing or enlarging. The basic reason back of this is that it is easier to work from good negatives developed by a photo lab than from poor negatives that may not have turned out as well as they might. If you are interested mainly in enlarging, you may prefer to bypass both developing and contact printing.

DEVELOPING FILM

Developing is done by one of two general methods: tray or tank. The traditional tray method should be part of your photographic knowledge, even though you may have occasion to use it not for developing but only for printing. A major objection to tray development is that it subjects the film to continuous handling which can easily cause damage. Furthermore, tray development of panchromatic film in total darkness is quite difficult and not advisable at all if development time runs to more than ten minutes. However, this method is convenient for an occasional short strip of roll film or a small number of sheet films. Both sheet films and film packs are usually developed in professional tanks which facilitate the handling of films in quantity.

When choosing chemicals, most amateurs prefer to use one of the many convenient and economical prepared developers to mixing their own formulas. Ready-mixed liquids, and mixed powders ready to be dissolved in water, come in practically any quantity desired; they are accurate, clean, space-saving. On the packages, bottles, or cans, you will find detailed directions which should be read carefully and followed exactly. Unless you are using the materials with professional frequency and proficiency, the manufacturer's instructions should be referred to each time the product is used. Any reference to "cool" water usually means about 68° F.

Small Tank Development. A rollfilm tank is generally used for developing 35mm and roll films. It is not only convenient but is the only practical way to handle these sizes. Small tanks, when correctly

Fig. 135.—Components of a rollfilm developing tank.

used, are economical of solutions and spill less than trays; they are easier on the film because it need not be handled while in solution; and they help keep chemical stains from hands and clothing. Only one step requires total darkness when using a rollfilm tank: inserting the exposed film into the tank.

Rollfilm tanks are essentially simple equipment similar to that in Figure 135. The round metal or plastic tank has a lid containing lightproof pouring holes which allow liquids to be added or removed while the lid remains tightly in place. To support the film, there is a reel (as illustrated), or a plastic apron, onto which the film is wound. Popular tank models have adjustable reels (or aprons of different widths) which accommodate different sizes of film; or two rolls of 35mm can be developed at one time on a double reel.

Loading the Film. Rehearse tank loading in daylight with a practice strip of developed film before attempting to load the exposed film you wish to develop. Another practice step, in the interests of economy and efficiency, is to measure the amount of liquid needed to cover the film size you are processing. Note also the time you take to pour the liquid into and out of the tank, in case you want to adjust the development time later on. Be sure that the reel is perfectly dry before loading; otherwise the film may stick. Have scissors handy to snip film leaders; you should also have a small prying tool in case the end of the cassette does not come off with the usual sharp tap on a hard surface.

In a darkroom or changing bag, remove the end of the metal cassette and snip the film leader to start 35mm film at its full width onto the reel; after reeling, remove the sticker from the end of the film. For roll films, remove the paper backing before loading (or as you load) the film on the reel or apron. When the film is in place, insert the reel in the tank, replace the lightproof tank lid, and continue the processing in normal light.

Single-solution Tank Processing. Relatively recent on the amateur market are *monobath* formulas which combine developer, shortstop, and fixer in one solution. This all-in-one method does not permit control over the processing but, like a preset camera, it is easy to use and a boon to beginners. Townco #1 (originally Unibath) is currently the correct formula for standard black-and-white films exposed at recommended ASA ratings. Use is based on these simple steps:

(1) Read directions on bottle.

(2) Insert film into lightproof tank. This is the only step requiring total darkness.

(3) Fill tank with cool water, shake gently, pour off water.

(4) Pour developer into tank.

(5) Set timer for six minutes (check directions), which is full development—no danger of overdevelopment.

(6) Agitate tank gently at about half-minute intervals.

(7) Pour developer into graduate.

(8) Wash film for five minutes or longer by removing lid and placing tank with film under cool running water, with intermittent agitation.

(9) Hang film to dry.

(10) Pour developer into stock bottle; note on label amount of film processed.

Conventional Tank Processing. Film should be developed according to the time and temperature recommended by the manufacturer of the products used. Some developing solutions allow a substantial temperature latitude and are easier to use than others; ask your dealer about current products. The basic steps for *time and temperature* development are these:

(1) Read directions on bottle or package.
(2) Load film into lightproof tank in total darkness.
(3) Fill tank with cool water, shake gently, pour off all water.
(4) Pour developing solution into tank and . . .
(5) . . . start the timer as you start pouring.
(6) Agitate gently at about half-minute intervals.
(7) At the end of development time, pour solution into graduate for transfer to stock bottle.
(8) Pour solution of *shortstop* into tank for recommended time OR fill tank with clear *cool water* for about three minutes. Agitate regularly, then discard stop bath.
(9) Pour the hypo or fixer into the tank, timing according to directions.
(10) At end of fixing time, pour solution into graduate.
(11) Remove tank lid and, with film on reel, fill tank with cool water and empty it two or three times; then place tank with reeled film under cool running water, with intermittent agitation, for at least twenty minutes.
(12) Hang film to dry.

During the fixing interval, add the recommended amount of *development replenisher* to stock bottle and transfer used developer from graduate to bottle. Rinse the graduate and funnel. During the washing interval, add the recommended amount of *fixing replenisher* to another stock bottle and transfer used fixer to bottle.

Additional optional steps may be added to the foregoing list of basic steps as recommended by the manufacturer. A popular one is the use of a *hypo neutralizer* solution to shorten the washing times listed in these pages for negatives or prints.

Tray Development. Amateur films are seldom developed by this old-fashioned method which requires a proper darkroom and, for panchromatic films, a dark green safelight with a 25-watt maximum by which to work. Besides, it is very difficult to manipulate a yard or more of 35mm in a tray. Trays for development, or for printing, are customarily arranged from left to right. From your left the trays would contain (1) developing solution, (2) acid stop bath or water rinse, and (3) fixing solution. If the sink or tub is not right beside your work table, you should have an additional tray of clear water to receive negatives (or prints) for washing.

After trays and materials are ready, and all lights extinguished except the single safelight, remove the film from its cartridge or paper backing. Then follow the conventional time-and-temperature steps just described for tanks. For a predevelopment rinse, hold the strip at each end (hold single films by the edges), emulsion side down, and dip it through clear water in a tray or sink. (Emulsion is the duller surface, on the inside of rolled film.) Holding a strip of film in a U-curve, emulsion side up, draw it smoothly back and forth through the developing solution for the specified time. Single pictures or short strips should be immersed in the solution and the tray should be rocked gently at half-minute intervals. After the negative has been run through the stop bath and the fixer solution in the same manner, transfer it to clear water for washing and turn on the room lights.

Development by inspection refers to safelight examination of the negative while it is being fixed. This requires considerable experience since the film looks dark and different in the dim green light. If you do try it, hold the negative at least a foot away from the safelight, keep your inspections down to a few seconds, and use only reflected light: that is, do *not* hold the negative up to the safelight and look through it.

Washing Films. All negatives should be washed in cool *running* water for about half an hour. Roll films can be washed right in the tank or in a tray. Single negatives (or prints) can be washed in a large tray with a siphon attachment on the sink, or in the sink itself. Always keep the water running in a gentle stream, just enough to maintain circulation in tank, tray, or sink. Check at intervals to be sure the temperature remains fairly near 68° F.

Drying Roll Films. After the negatives have been washed, hang them where there is good circulation of air—not in a closet or unventilated area. For 35mm and other roll films, an easy way is to attach one end of the film to a clothes hanger with a spring clip. Hang it up (the shower rod is a favorite rack), and attach another clip or some paper clips to the bottom of the strip to keep it from curling. Single larger negatives should also be hung by film clips and the negatives handled carefully by the edges.

Surplus moisture, which might spot the negative, should be removed. A simple method is to take two swabs of absorbent cotton, as large as the film width, and squeeze them out in cool water. Then with one swab on each side of the film, wipe *slowly* down from top to bottom. If you hold the two swabs of cotton at the outer edges of the film strip, there will be no pressure on the emulsion. Viscose sponges are easy and popular for drying; however, chemicals and grit tend to cling to them and may damage subsequent negatives.

Do not turn the film around while it is drying, as this can adversely affect the emulsion. Leave it alone. You will note that negatives curl slightly along the edges while still wet; don't worry, for they flatten out as they become dry.

Drying time, usually a half hour to two hours, depends on room temperature, humidity, and circulation of air. There are various rapid-dry solutions to use on film before washing when time is a problem; some can cut normal drying time by more than half.

Filing Dry Negatives. Roll films are usually cut into single pictures or pairs and kept flat in transparent glassine envelopes. Some photographers (and some processors) cut 35mm films into strips of 4, 5, or 6 frames and keep them flat in glassine "sleeves"; others prefer to leave the film uncut and keep it rolled. Some processing labs that return negatives uncut (by request or regularly) keep them rolled in a gentle oval with a strip of protective paper, *not* tightly curled, and this is how you should keep uncut negatives.

To cut or not to cut depends on your own preference and on what you are going to use the negatives for. Uncut 35mm cannot be fitted into a standard contact printer; but if you are going to use the negatives only for enlarging, you may find complete rolls more satisfactory than short strips. Since enlargers vary a great deal, the choice may be governed by the available equipment. Some record of date, subject matter, and technical data should be noted on the filing envelopes of negatives you wish to keep.

PRINTING

Photographic printing is the process of transmitting light through a *negative* to form a corresponding *positive* image. The basic steps for transforming a negative image into a positive print are the same as those for transforming an exposed film into a negative: (1) exposure, (2) development, (3) stop bath, (4) fixing, and (5) washing.

Printing Papers. Although printing papers look quite different from films, both have light-sensitive emulsions, that of papers being extremely thin with far less concentration of silver halides than in negative emulsions. Sensitivity of the emulsion varies; enlarging papers, for instance, are generally more sensitive than contact papers because the light reaching them must pass through a lens and be spread over a relatively large area. Photographic papers are considerably less sensitive than film and, while a crack of light under a door might not fog them, they should always be handled carefully and guarded from unintentional exposure. Keep papers in their protective packages, or well covered, withdrawing a sheet in darkness as required and promptly closing the package.

Papers come in a wide choice of weight, texture, contrast, and tone. Single weights are used for most contact prints, double weights for enlargements, and extra-thin papers for printed matter to be folded. Glossy textures are chosen for retaining maximum detail, and semimatte textures for subduing detail and grain. Papers vary in degree of contrast: low-contrast papers counteract excessive contrast in a negative; high-contrast papers help to bring out the most in a flat negative. Average negatives are usually made on medium- or normal-contrast papers; these are numbered 1, 2, 3, for low, normal, and high-contrast types. Photographers who do not like to buy different kinds of expensive enlarging papers often prefer to use one variable-contrast type with filters. These filters come in sets of graduated densities and can be placed in the enlarger as needed to increase or decrease the contrast quality of the paper. The tone of papers may be warm for brownish blacks or cool for bluish blacks.

Preparations for Printing. Arrange the three trays containing solutions of developer, stop bath, and fixer as for tray development. If you have a sink or a wash tray, it should be next to the fixer. Place the printer or enlarger at the left of the trays and the covered-up printing paper on some perfectly dry surface at the left of the printer. Place the timer where you can see and reach it easily. Place one pair of your print tongs between developer and stop bath, the other between stop bath and fixer. When not in actual use, the tongs should remain between those trays to avoid any mixup which would contaminate the solutions. This then is the basic arrangement:

PAPER on dry surface	PRINTER or ENLARGER	TIMER	Tray 1 DEVELOPER	Tongs	Tray 2 STOP BATH	Tongs	Tray 3 FIXER	WASHING

If you use fingers instead of tongs, keep your left hand for the developer and your right hand for the fixer. Remember also that clean negatives are essential to good prints, especially in projection printing which enlarges specks as well as image. To remove loose dirt or lint, dust the negative gently with a camelhair brush.

Printing Methods. There are two general classifications of photographic printing: contact and projection. The basic procedure to be outlined for contact printing applies also to projection printing, except that for projection an enlarger instead of a printing box is used and larger trays may be needed to accommodate the blownup prints.

In *contact printing* the emulsion side of the negative is in direct contact with the emulsion of the paper to produce a positive image the same size as the negative image. This contact is effected by some kind of printer, either a printing box or a printing frame.

In *projection printing,* usually referred to as *enlarging,* there is a space between negative and paper and a lens to project an enlarged or reduced image onto the sensitized paper. This is effected by an enlarger whose lens projects an image down onto an easel (rather than horizontally onto a screen as a slide projector does).

CONTACT PRINTING.

The Printer. A standard printing box is basically a metal housing with a plate glass roof, the appropriate light bulb inside, and an electric cord. There is usually a red safelight to aid in positioning

Fig. 136.—A contact printer (left) and a printing frame (right).

the four masking strips on the glass. A hinged pressure pad attached to the case clamps down to bring paper and negative into firm, uniform contact; this contact may switch on the light for exposure, or there may be a manual switch. The white borders of finished prints are made by the masking strips; if your printer does not have metal strips, you can buy masking material to place on the edges of the paper. A homemade printing box can be built of wood, with some kind of hinged and felted pressure pad to clamp negative and paper onto a sheet of glass above a light bulb.

Another type of printer is a printing frame, which is essentially like a picture frame but has a hinged back with spring clips to hold the inserted negative and paper in contact. This is appreciably less expensive than a metal printing box but, because it must be used in open light, the printing frame is at best inconvenient and prob- lematical.

Exposure. When your equipment has been lined up, examine the negatives for density and try to keep similar densities together. Several small negatives or short strips of 35mm can be printed on a single contact sheet. Place the negatives on the printing-box glass *emulsion side up*. Place the paper *emulsion side down* on the nega- tives, close the pressure pad, and time the exposure. The length of exposure needed for a good print will depend on density of negative, type of paper, bulb wattage, and distance of exposed contact from the light. If a printing frame is used for contacts, the size of the light bulb used for exposure depends on the paper's degree of sensitivity, its distance from the bulb, and the length of exposure. A normal negative held in a printing frame about a foot from a 40-watt bulb should require an exposure of five or six seconds, but the correct timing can be determined only by experiment. The bulb in a printing box can be changed according to your needs as they become apparent.

Test strips can be made by cutting a sheet of printing paper into narrow strips (about an inch wide) and giving them a series of different exposures; you might, for example, decide to try 2, 4, 6, and 8 seconds. None of these may be right; but test strips will provide a key to the correct time, and practice will teach you to estimate the density of a negative. Try to place test strips over a section of the negative that represents the tonal range of highlights and shadows. On the back of each strip, or on a separate pad, note in pencil the exposure times of the test. If the test print turns out too light, it needs a longer exposure; if too dark, it needs a shorter exposure. Correction should be made by re-timing the exposure, not by changing the recommended development time.

Print Development. Lift the hinged top of the printer to terminate an exposure and promptly slip the test strip or contact sheet into the developer, emulsion side down. Hold the print by its edge, slide it gently into the solution, and wipe any solution from your hand. Agitate by a slight rocking of the tray and pat the back of the print with the first tongs to keep it from floating on the surface. After about half a minute turn it face up to see how the image is coming along, then turn it face down for the balance of development or leave it face up if well covered by solution. Full development time will probably be one and one-half to two minutes. At the end of development time, use the first tongs to transfer the print to the stop bath for about five seconds and replace the tongs.

Print Fixing. With the second tongs transfer the print from stop bath to fixer, draining excess liquid from the print momentarily during each transfer and sliding it into the solution gently. To prevent stains which might be caused by air reaching the emulsion of a floating print, keep prints face down in the hypo, turning them up for periodic inspection. After two or three minutes of immersion, the prints can be inspected by room lighting, unless other development is going on. Normal fixing time is about five to ten minutes, depending on the type of fixer, after which they are ready for washing.

Group Processing. After processing a few tests to check results, you can make several prints at one time. Do not attempt a greater number than you can keep track of, as each print should be put into the developer separately and at regular intervals. Agitation during development should include rotating the prints by transferring the bottom one to the top of the pile and seeing that they do not stick together. Transfer each print to the stop bath in the same order in which it reached the developer so that each print gets its full developing time. After ten to twenty seconds in the stop bath, transfer the prints to the hypo, sliding each in turn under the others to insure its getting fresh solution. Edging the prints in sideways helps prevent air bubbles from forming under the emulsion. Agitate the fixing prints frequently and keep them separated. After a couple of minutes in the hypo they can be inspected by room lighting, and they can be transferred one by one as fixed to a large tray of clear water until all are ready for a thorough washing.

Washing Prints. Because paper absorbs more of the processing solutions than film does, prints need more extensive washing than negatives to avoid fading and discolorations. The simplest way is to place the prints under cool running water for at least thirty minutes and preferably an hour, moving them about in the washing tray or sink at intervals. An alternative is to change the water in the rinse tray every five minutes for at least one hour; this method is easier with two rinse trays, to keep the prints in one while putting fresh water in the other.

Drying Prints. Special photographic blotters are generally used to dry prints, but a clean absorbent cloth such as lintfree sheeting may be substituted. (There are also blotter books which are convenient for carrying wet prints home from an outside darkroom.) First, drain as much water as possible from the washed prints before laying them on the blotter face down. Blot to remove excess water, then roll up the prints in the blotter for drying, or leave each one between the sheets of a blotter book. If you have the space free to do so, leave the prints flat between blotters with some large books or magazines on them while they dry. Prints tend to curl when drying, but they can be flattened later. Electric dryers are often used for club groups or schools; the blotted prints are placed face up, with a taut cover of heavy fabric which shows wet patches as prints are drying. Do not allow prints to become bone dry; remove them while the cover is still slightly damp.

Ferrotyping Glossy Prints. The high gloss characteristic of prints returned by photofinishers results from compression in the emulsion gelatin during drying. In the step referred to as *ferrotyping* the wet print is placed face down on a polished metal plate, usually called a "ferrotype tin," squeegeed or rolled into firm contact, and left to dry until it peels off by itself. Use only printing papers designated as suitable for ferrotyping; wash the tin occasionally in warm water with mild soap to prevent sticking, and store it carefully to avoid scratches.

Enlarging.

Since it is designed to project an image instead of receiving one, an enlarger is fundamentally a camera in reverse; it transmits a cone of light, expanding toward the paper rather than contracting toward a pinpoint focus. A unit housing the lens, lamp, and negative carrier is attached to a rigid vertical standard; a base with a masking easel holds the paper to receive the projected image. The advantages of projection printing over contact printing, besides the enlarged print sizes, are the opportunities for special effects, for localized controls, and for composition improvements.

Enlargers. The system by which the light is spread uniformly over a negative, with no uneven hot spots, may be either condenser or diffusion; there are innumerable combinations of the two systems

Fig. 137.—Components of diffusion and condenser enlargers.

among today's enlargers. Ask about the different kinds available, about the lens quality and focusing mechanisms, as you would in choosing a camera, to decide on the one that will suit your purse and purposes.

Condenser enlargers, in principle, have no diffusion between negative carrier and projection lamp. Optically the most efficient, this type can produce brilliant images with great contrast; unmodified, however, such sharpness can be a disadvantage since it shows up minor negative imperfections which might otherwise pass unnoticed in the print. Their chief usefulness, consequently, is in technical work.

Diffusion enlargers have ground or opal glass plates between negative carrier and lamp in a housing shaped to increase the diffusion. The result is a softened image, minimizing grain and negative defects, and most nearly matching contact-print quality. Because of the lessened light intensity, diffusion enlargers generally require longer exposure times than condenser types.

Most of the popular enlargers are a combination of the two types. Some offer considerable versatility by providing interchangeable clear and opal bulbs as well as removable diffusion plates.

Enlarger lenses do not have automatic shutters, since exposures are timed in seconds; a light switch controls the time. "Click stops" to count off when stopping down the lens make it unnecessary to read the aperture markings by safelight. Most enlargers have adjustable easels with masking strips to regulate the print borders. Lens-to-easel distance governs the image size: the farther the enlarger head is from the paper, the larger the image will be.

Enlarging Procedure. Arrange the printing setup in the manner outlined for contact printing and be sure your trays are large enough; also mix larger quantities of the solutions. Handle negatives carefully by the edges and see that they and your equipment are clean.

Place the negative in the carrier, emulsion side down toward the lens and shiny side up toward the lamp house. Place a sheet of plain white paper (or the back of a finished print) on the easel and set the masking guides for the desired print size. Open the lens to maximum aperture (lowest f/number), turn off room lights, and switch on the enlarger lamp. Start focusing with the enlarger head farthest from the easel, bringing it gradually toward the paper and adjusting the distance until the image is exactly the right size. Adjust the focusing knob until you get the sharpest image obtainable, concentrating on eyes or some important detail.

This is the time for cropping and compositional corrections. Now you can determine whether a horizontal or vertical format is better, can eliminate superfluous background, and can straighten a horizon line or a tree or a building by moving the easel and adjusting the masking strips. When you are satisfied with sharpness and general composition, stop down the lens to its most effective aperture, usually f/8, and turn off the enlarger lamp. By safelight replace the sheet of plain paper with a sheet of enlarging paper, emulsion side up, and proceed with a test print.

Test strips for enlarging differ from those for contact printing in that a series of four or five exposures can be made on a single strip;

Fig. 138.—Printing paper, emulsion side up, slides under masking strips of easel.

Fig. 139.—Use cardboard to cover part of printing paper when exposing successive test strips.

an 8 x 10 sheet may be cut into ten or twelve strips. A standard method is to expose the strip, section by section in four to six steps, giving the same exposure time to each; some prefer to start off with 2-second exposures, some with 5 seconds, some with 10 seconds. As an example, you might decide to make five tests at 5 seconds: cover four-fifths of the strip with the cardboard and expose the remaining fifth for 5 seconds; move the cardboard so it covers only three-fifths and expose another 5 seconds. When you have done this five times, the first section will have received a total exposure of 25 seconds and the last section only 5 seconds. Develop the test strip for the full recommended time. After it has been in the hypo for a couple of minutes, turn on the room lights and inspect the strip. If none of the exposures looks right, make another test strip. In adjusting your exposure time, try to avoid extremely short exposures, which are impractical both for accurate timing and for the manipulations to be described, and overlong exposures which subject the negative (and the operator) to excessive heat. When one of the exposures, or halfway between two exposures, seems about right, go ahead with a straight print.

The *straight print* is a full-size enlargement exposed according to your evaluation of the test strip. Develop, rinse, and fix the exposed sheet of enlarging paper. If you are doubtful about your choice of paper, you can treat the straight print as an additional test. Rinse it in clear water, flatten it face down in an empty tray or on a blotter to sponge off surplus water, and inspect the print minutely under white light. You may then wish to make one or two additional straight prints on papers of different contrast or texture. Wash for full time and place enlargements face down on a photographic blotter for drying.

Printing Control Techniques. Examination of a straight print generally suggests some improvements which can be effected by further manipulations during exposure. Besides cropping and straightening, there are several commonly used methods.

Dodging refers to holding back some of the enlarger light from certain areas of the image which need to be lighter in relation to the shadows. The dodging tool may be simply a cardboard disk, usually about the size of a half-dollar, attached to a rigid wire about a foot long, or one of the mounted plastic disks available in stores. A favorite—certainly the most convenient—dodging tool is a hand. It is used to shade an area to be lightened—something like a parasol against the burning sun. Hold the tool a few inches above the paper and keep it moving slightly to prevent its forming a sharp shadow line.

Burning-in, or *printing-in,* is dodging in reverse: to darken certain areas of the image by giving them more exposure than the other areas, use a large piece of dark cardboard with a half-dollar hole. During part of the exposure, hold the cardboard over the image so

Fig. 140.—Dodging holds back exposure from area that needs to be lightened.

Fig. 141.—Burning-in gives more exposure to area that needs to be darkened.

that the hole is above the area to be darkened while the cardboard shades the rest of the image. Again, use a constant gentle motion to blend the areas.

If you want to darken a large irregular section of a picture, you can focus the image on a cardboard (instead of on plain white paper) and pencil the shape to be cut out before starting the actual enlargement.

Vignetting is a combination cropping-and-shading technique for printing only the main feature of an image; it is used mostly to abstract a single portrait from a group or a busy background. A cardboard with a cutout corresponding to the area to be retained is handled in a manner similar to that described for burning-in.

Diffusing in printing is a softening of the image in much the same way that harsh illumination is diffused for photographing. Various informal diffusers serve quite satisfactorily, such as crumpled tissue paper or a handful of cheesecloth or other netting, which are moved about between enlarger and image during exposure. However, there are special diffusion disks of glass, designed to be held next to the lens during approximately half of the exposure time.

There are a number of other more advanced methods for altering the contrast, tone, or general quality of an unsatisfactory print or negative, some of which are identified in Appendix B. But far better than a closetful of remedies is the healthy photographic habit of exercising care and judgment about taking the picture in the first place.

20

┌───┐
│ **Showing Your Prints and Slides** │
└───┘

THERE ARE a number of ways in which black-and-white or color prints can be enjoyed besides putting them in albums. They can be mounted on display mats, put in picture frames, reproduced as greeting cards or announcements, used for bookplates or screens. Color slides can be shown to advantage in projection, either by putting together your own private slide show or submitting individual slides to club competitions. Prints, either black-and-white or color, can be made from slides to fill in album collections but, of course, this is more expensive than taking photographs for prints.

DISPLAYING PRINTS

Albums. Picture albums have grown up with photography and no longer does one have *a* family album containing a chronological and intermittent record of domestic events. Modern albums are colorful and various as to bindings, sizes, and formats—as you can see in photo and stationery stores. Although you can still find gummed corners to paste a print down on a plain page, most commonly used are transparent acetate pages which hold pictures where you place them, flipover acetate envelopes for different print sizes, and other quick and versatile variations on the scrapbook theme.

Albums of pictures can be edited like slide shows or home movies to present travel stories in book form, high spots of school years, and interesting phases of family life in separate albums of suitable size. Any editing can advantageously include omissions: arrange albums of your better pictures while they are fresh and of immediate interest, keeping the weeded-out ones in labeled envelopes for later discard or change of mind. Dates, places, and names can be penciled lightly on the backs of prints until they go into albums. Consider a black-and-white enlargement, protected by clear plastic, for a personal and provocative album cover.

Dry Mounting. An enlargement for display can be mounted flat on a single mounting board or mat. This is usually white, sometimes black or gray, and may even be colored if the color frame enhances your picture. Besides the enlargement and mat, you will need a cutting board (or equivalent), a welding iron, dry-mount tissue, and plain paper; then proceed step by step:

(1) Trim print accurately to size wanted on a cutting board (or use razor-and-straightedge substitute). Then cut most important edge first. The border is seldom left on, unless it is part of the pattern.

(2) Try the cropped print on mounting board to determine overall mat size. A standard board is 16 x 20, which is generally appropriate for an 11 x 14 enlargement; for an 8 x 10 print you will probably want to cut the mat down to about 12 x 15, and reduce it proportionately for small prints. It is conventional but not at all mandatory to have the bottom of the mat slightly larger than the top, and the sides about equal to the top. After deciding on placement of the print, lightly pencil in the position of the top corners.

(3) Heat a photo-welding iron, which is thermostatically controlled, or put a household iron on the lowest heat setting. Cut a sheet of dry-mount tissue the exact size of the print, or the least bit smaller. The tissue is sticky on both sides and has some separating sheets in the package. With warm iron tack the tissue to the back of the print, using single firm pressures at the center, corners, edges. Do not use back-and-forth ironing strokes.

(4) Now place the print in position on the mount. Over the print place a piece of fairly heavy plain paper and press down with iron. Go over the print, especially corners and edges, with hard downward pressures until it is welded to the mat. Place a heavy book on both print and paper for a few minutes.

Enlargements for portfolios are usually dry-mounted without a mat border. In cutting the mounting board to print size, it is best to err on the skimpy side, to be sure that the enlargement covers the mount completely.

Cutout Mounts. Enlargements may also be mounted in double boards with a frame cutout in the top mat. When buying double mounts, be sure to specify your print size and whether the print is horizontal or vertical. Indicate also whether you prefer a wider base, as some stores sell centered cutouts for horizontal or vertical use. Cutout mounts cost slightly more than single mounts but they can be reused for different enlargements.

For cutout mounting you will need only a small roll of double-stick scotch tape, about ½-inch wide. On the back of the print, place a strip of sticky tape (about 3 inches for an 8 x 10 print) along each of the four sides, place the print in position on the underneath mat, and press down so that the print adheres to the mat. Or you can mark where the print is to be placed, put the four strips of double-stick tape on the bottom board, then place the print on the tapes. Leave a heavy book on it for a few minutes.

Amateur black-and-white prints for exhibition are usually 8 x 10 enlargements with matte finish, but individual exhibits often accept various sizes. A title and the photographer's name are generally written lightly in pencil on the mat just underneath the print, the title flush with the left edge and the name flush with the right edge. Your address and any technical data should be on the back of the mount. If the exhibit accepts flush-mounted prints, the title may be on a separate card as well as on the back of the mount.

VIEWING SLIDES

Color transparencies returned from the processor are usually masked in cardboard mounts and may be viewed in three ways: by using normal light, a viewer, or a projector. The simplest and least satisfactory way is to hold a slide up to a lamp or window. This method not only gives no magnification, but the illumination passing through the transparency also distorts the color quality of the picture. To minimize this disadvantage, aim an adjustable desk lamp at a sheet of white paper, then look at the slide by the light reflected up to it from the paper. If you like, you can hold the slide in one hand and a magnifying glass in the other. Even if you have a projector, this is a good way to preview and sort slides.

Thumb Spotting. While you are having a first look at a new batch of slides is the best time to "spot" them, perhaps roughly, for later viewing. The term refers to a corner mark which indicates how the slide should go into a projector, and there is a standard procedure: hold the slide toward the lighted white paper so that you are looking at the scene as you photographed it. Now with a red pencil make a large dot or a quick circle in the *lower left corner* of the mount. This is the way the slide goes into a hand viewer; when the slide goes upside down into a projector, the red dot will be in the upper right corner under your right thumb.

Even if you are going to discard quite a number of slides, a quick mark in the lower left corner will cut down on subsequent handling until more positive spots are put on the slides you decide to keep. A thumb spot does not have to be red, but it should be large enough for a projectionist to see easily in dim light. Self-stick spots are available in some stores.

Hand Viewers. There are many types of small viewers which vary in size, degree of magnification, and price. Some are pocket-size folding viewers without illumination; some operate on batteries or electrical connection, or both. A majority of models are designed to accept only the 2 x 2 mounts of 35 mm and super slides. The pocket-size viewers, which must be held up to a lamp or bright window, are very convenient if you are carrying a few slides to show someone; otherwise it is more satisfactory to have an illuminated viewer.

Basically, an illuminated viewer is a plastic case with a magnifying glass and a tiny lamp, between which is a slot for the slide. The slight fingertip pressure that illuminates the slide can bend the cardboard if it does not go in straight. Some viewers need to be held fairly close, others are large enough to be positioned on a table for three or four persons to look at simultaneously. Whatever the type, the viewer should be used in fairly low room light, and the slide should be inserted carefully.

Slide Projectors. For showing color slides or home movies, a projector is a kind of enlarger which throws a greatly magnified and illuminated image on a viewing screen. Projection is much the best way to appreciate the brilliance and quality of color transparencies. The focal length of lenses for slide projectors is considerably longer than for movies, an average being about five inches. The projector lamp for slides is also larger, usually 500 watts. Follow specific recommendations for projector-to-screen distances.

The carrier in which the transparency is advanced and withdrawn in front of the lens is called a *slide changer*. Some are operated manually, some automatically; some accept only single slides, some a tray of thirty or more slides. All standard projectors accept 35mm or slightly larger transparencies which fit the usual 2-inch mounts; some projectors are equipped also with changers to accommodate larger mounts of rollfilm transparencies, like the 2¼ size of popular twin-lens reflex cameras.

Cropping and Remounting. The size of 35mm transparencies limits to some degree their cropping possibilities. For informal viewing, a slide that needs only straight-line masking—eliminating some dull foreground or sky, for example—can often be cropped with black photographic tape. See that the new mask remains parallel to the edge of the mount so that the projected picture will not appear tilted. Notice, too, whether the masking would result in unmatched square or rounded corners, which would be undesirable.

Cropping is usually done by removing transparencies from the processor's mounts, and inserting them in new mounts which are available in various sizes, shapes, and materials. It is necessary to have some kind of light box on which the slide can be studied carefully in different masks to be sure that the intended revision will improve the composition as a whole. By this method a tilting tree or slanting horizon can sometimes be straightened in a smaller mask, or a scene dramatized in a narrow panel. The dramatic impact of a larger slide can be achieved by cropping a rollfilm transparency and putting it in a 2-inch mount with a very narrow mask. When you have cropped and positioned your transparency, tape one edge of it to the inside of the new mount, and press the self-sealing edges of the mount together smoothly.

Glass mounts are preferred for slides which are to be shown often or submitted to numerous competitions. They protect transparencies from dust, fingermarks, and scratches, and from buckling, or "popping," in the heat of a projector lamp. Various makes of thin 2-inch glass covers and pressure tapes for binding them together are available. There are also metal frames which hold glass covers without taping, as well as other metal and plastic types. The process is a basically simple one, done differently by different people; but because slides and glasses must be spotlessly clean, and taped borders smooth, it is well to practice a few times before subjecting your best slides to possible mishandling.

Glass covers are also preferred for sandwiching two or even three slides into a single picture called a *montage;* in fact, it is difficult to keep a montage flat and in focus without glasses. This technique is frequently used to add clouds to an otherwise drab sky, to insert a full moon in a night scene, or to place a figure in an empty foreground. Abstract patterns are often superimposed on the transparency according to the whim and ingenuity of the photographer.

NEWTON RINGS. This is the term commonly given to the color spots that· occasionally appear on remounted slides, sometimes along with condensation spots. The problem is caused by contact of the smooth glass surface with the smooth film base. Remounting important slides in glass fairly soon after they are returned in cardboard mounts and before any "popping" has set in can help avoid Newton rings. Another suggestion is to attach only one side of the slide to the mask when remounting, leaving the opposite side free so that there will be some expansion leeway. Always store slides in a relatively dry place away from dampness and humidity.

COLOR MODIFICATION. Gelatin filter sheets in different colors, referred to as *gels,* are also available from some photo supply companies and are used to counteract an overall color cast or create a special effect. Clean colored cellophane can be substituted, if necessary. If a transparency is too blue, or too much on the orange side, for instance, a compensating gel may correct or improve this. Hold the slide over a light box and study the effect different gels have on it; if one pleases you, sandwich that filter into the mount.

As a rule, the color quality of slides is not impaired by frequent brief projection. However, because prolonged projection with lamps of maximum wattage may in time cause some deterioration, it is advisable to keep single projections under one minute. Many photographers like to coat new slides with Permafilm to protect them from marring and other damage. It is also possible to change color areas of a slide completely by retouching with quite simple materials. However, the process itself is not so simple, nor feasible to attempt from written directions; it should be learned from a workshop or private demonstration by an experienced amateur.

Cleaning Slides. Cleanliness is always a requisite for good slides, as specks or smudges are magnified along with the subject itself. Use a fine camelhair brush to remove dust and lint and a recommended film cleaner sparingly if necessary. Handle slides carefully by the edges of the mount, and keep them protected between showings. Individual glassine envelopes are sometimes used to protect slides which are handled frequently.

If the surface lacquer of a transparency has noticeable scratches and must be refinished, the marred lacquer should be removed first. Ask a reliable darkroom-supply dealer for specific instructions, or write Eastman Kodak Company, Rochester 4, New York, for their pamphlet about the care of color films.

Labeling Slides. Slides to be submitted to competitions or photographic markets should have a thumb spot, a title, and your name as minimum information. Labeling is less uniform than spotting and can be on any part of the mount. An acceptable method is to print the title (or subject) across the top of the mount the way it goes in the projector—that is, with the spot in the upper right corner. Your name (and address) can go across the bottom or on the back of the mount, and any technical data and the date can go on the sides. Small printed return-address stickers make convenient and neat nameplates.

Careful labeling and cross-referencing of your slide collection is especially important when putting together a number of shows for different audiences. Interchangeable courtesy titles and transitional slides (see page 230) can be numbered and indexed according to locales, seasons, subjects—whatever is practical for your own purposes. Photographers who have occasion to plan frequent shows from a large collection sometimes key their slides with numbers or letters in different colors. Some photographers collect sunsets or doorways or bridges or interesting characters, and a private indexing system should be worked out to make the collection flexible.

Showing Slides. The general suggestions in the following chapter about appropriate music, discriminating commentary, and a fitting regard for individual audiences apply to slide shows as well as to home movies. Consider whether you are showing as-is slides to family, submitting single slides to competitions, or putting together a travelogue or other pictorial essay to be viewed by a group.

Primary slide editing is a matter of sorting, omitting, and rearranging; it requires no special equipment and deserves to be done critically. Are you including a slide out of sentimental attachment or because it was a difficult shot, or will it really contribute to the audience's enjoyment and understanding of your story?

Slide shows can be given a change of pace by interspersing relevant close-ups with general and atmosphere pictures, as in movies, and by varying the color emphasis. Follow predominantly red subjects with green ones, for instance, or mainly blue subjects with yellow ones. Try to keep related subjects in some logical sequence, whether or not it is the order in which the pictures were taken, but avoid dwelling overlong on one theme or on different views of the same scene; it is preferable to come back to it if necessary. Travel shows should generally have sufficient commentary to let the audience know rather than guess where the scene is; even very famous landmarks are numerous enough to be confusing, so they usually need a brief mention. In fact, you might find some of the following suggestions regarding home movies pertinent to your slide shows.

21

```
┌─────────────────────────┐
│     Home Movies         │
└─────────────────────────┘
```

PICTURES in motion benefit from observance of the principles that apply to photography generally: in composition, backgrounds, lighting, types of films and filters, angle and speed of action, camera steadiness, and selection of suitable subject matter. Most important, to restate a primary instruction, study the operating manual provided by the manufacturer of your particular equipment. Some basic problems which apply to making a motion picture, but not to making other pictures, will be discussed in this chapter.

PRELIMINARY CONSIDERATIONS

"Motion" and "Still" Pictures. It is easy to see why the fundamentals of good photography pertain to home movies when you realize that "motion pictures" are actually "still pictures," caught on a series of frames much smaller than those of films for other cameras, and shown in motion. If you were to photograph a sequence of so-called still pictures with a small camera using 35mm film and could project those pictures with excessive rapidity, you would see a "movie."

The reverse is also true: individual frames of movie film can be printed as "still" pictures; however, the extreme magnification such a tiny negative requires does not make this too practical for 8mm movie makers. Moreover, a lack of sharpness that would be unnoticeable in a speeding "movie" could be glaringly evident in a "still" print.

If you do wish to have a print made from an 8mm or 16mm negative, give the photofinisher a strip of several frames, with a thread or string tied in the sprocket holes beside the picture to be printed. Do not cut out a single frame, which would be impossible to manipulate in an enlarger.

Persistence of Vision. The principle on which the illusion of
motion in a picture sequence is based is the power of the optic-
nervous system to retain an image after the eye has closed or the
image has been otherwise occluded. For example, if you are looking
at a brightly lighted object which is suddenly blacked-out so that
the image is no longer visible, your eye-brain mechanism will continue to retain that image for a fraction of a second. The normal
limit of a person's image-retaining power is considered to be 1/50
of a second and is termed the *persistence of vision*.

Without this natural follow-through, the eyes would see merely a
rapid succession of still pictures. But because of persistence of vision,
the individual images of a movie strip are carried through the black
intervals which actually separate the frames, making possible the
visual illusion of motion pictures.

Essential Equipment. For motion pictures, unlike color slides, a
projector and screen are as necessary as camera and film. Many
photographers who concentrate on color slides do not own slide projectors; there are various hand viewers which illuminate and slightly
magnify a slide, and holding slides up to a room lamp is often adequate previewing when they are to be shown to clubs or other groups.
But a series of 8mm pictures intended to be seen in motion cannot
be viewed by such casual means. Consequently it is important for a
movie photographer to understand not only the operation of his
camera which records the action but also of his projector which
returns the action to a viewing screen.

Some editing is also essential to most movies. Color slides for
projection can be "edited" simply by tossing out some and shuffling
the order of others. But motion-picture footage usually needs to be
cut and spliced and arranged in understandable sequence if it is to
be an acceptable movie. Therefore some editing equipment, even if
it is only scissors and splicing cement, is a must for makers of
home movies.

CAMERA BASICS

Most cameras for home movies are characterized by a slim vertical
shape in contrast to the horizontal form of most small still cameras.
(See Figure 9.) This is due to the direction in which the film travels
within the camera (or projector). It is quite possible, of course, that
home-movie equipment may undergo radical changes sooner or later
at the hands of designers and manufacturers.

Essential Camera Parts. One of the photographic fundamentals is that all cameras, as stated on page 6, have four primary components: lighttight housing, lens, shutter, and a film carrier at the focal plane. Except for the shutter, these parts have a basic similarity in movie or still cameras.

The *shutter* most usual in movie cameras is a focal-plane type—not a curtain, as in still cameras, but a rotary disk from which a segment has been cut to create a light cycle and a dark cycle. During the light cycle the film is exposed, and during the dark cycle the film is advanced. Home-movie cameras have "camera speeds" instead of the "shutter settings" of still cameras.

Operating Principle. In addition to having a different shutter, movie cameras require a *film-drive* mechanism to advance the ribbon of film continuously from the supply spool, or reel, to the takeup spool which holds the exposed footage. The film drive is usually powered by a spring motor, although some models feature a battery-driven motor which eliminates winding. Winding is normally done after each scene to forestall a rundown motor in the middle of a subsequent scene; how much footage a full winding is good for will be indicated in your camera instruction booklet. The film drive's sprocket teeth, or claws, engage the perforations along the film's edge for taking and for projecting motion pictures.

A movie-camera mechanism also has a stop-and-go feature, referred to as *intermittent action*. It repeatedly pulls the film down one frame at a time, then disengages the sprocket holes at the *film gate,* a small pressure plate back of the lens. During actual exposure the individual frame of film is held in place by the gate; during the actual advance of the film, pressure is released each time the claws re-engage the sprocket holes.

Types of Cameras. Home-movie cameras are generally classified by film size, 8mm or 16mm; by type of film load, roll or magazine; and by type of lens mount, which can be fixed-focus, interchangeable, turret, or the variable zoom. In addition, there is an ever increasing number of models featuring developments typical of the age of automation, such as the electric eye and self-threading mechanisms. As in other photographic equipment, any specific "improvements" are subject to change (and obsolescence) without notice.

8MM AND 16MM. The majority of all strictly amateur movies are made with 8mm equipment for showing to home-size audiences on screens up to five feet wide and normally about 40 inches wide. A "home-movie camera" usually refers to the 8mm size which is compact, lightweight, and less expensive than the 16mm size. Since each frame of 16mm film is approximately four times as large as 8mm, the 16mm equipment is considerably bulkier, heavier, and more expensive. It is used to produce a bigger and brighter image on relatively large screens for clubs, auditoriums, and lecture halls, and for professional use.

A strip of 16mm film has perforations along each edge, similar to 35mm film for still cameras. For 8mm cameras the 16mm film has additional perforations and a double row of frames, as in the illustration on this page; it goes through the camera twice, and during processing is slit into the narrow ribbon of film, perforated along one edge only, that goes through the projector.

FILM LOADS. Most home-movie cameras are *roll loading* and the film is fed through the camera to be received by an empty takeup spool. Such cameras are also referred to as *spool* types—appropriately enough, since the loading is rather like threading a sewing machine,

16mm Film   Double 8mm Film (before slitting)   8mm Film (after slitting)

Fig. 142.—Sizes of film for home-movie cameras.

installing the thread at prescribed points to assure smooth feeding without breaking. The film leader anchors into a notch of the takeup spool and is then positioned in the film gate and other guides specified by the camera booklet.

Because a roll of 8mm film is to be run through the camera twice, it is necessary to make sure that the correct side of the empty spool is facing up to receive either the new or the half-exposed film. When the first half (25 feet) has been exposed, the filled spool is removed, turned over, and reloaded. To assist the forgetful, there is usually a HALF EXP punched into that end of the film.

Occasionally some confusion arises as to whether a roll of film is an unused one or an exposed roll that should have gone to the processor. About the only way you, or the photofinisher, can make a good guess in this event is to examine the film leader: if it looks new and smooth, it probably has not been exposed; if the leader shows any definite creasing, the film probably has been exposed. Eastman

Kodak suggests that you save the paper band from each roll of new film as you open it; then, as soon as you have removed the completely exposed roll from the camera, you wrap the band around the film and write your name and address on the paper. By forming this practical habit, you will never be in doubt: a plain paper band will indicate an unused roll of film; a band with your name on it will identify an exposed roll.

Magazine loading cameras offer easier handling, faster loading, and more flexibility. The preloaded magazine is placed in the camera's film chamber and is ready to roll with very little threading. Since the magazine is a lighttight container which protects the film until processing, it allows you to change from one kind of film to another for indoor and outdoor shooting while either load is only partially exposed. When alternating 8mm film loads, it is important to mark on each magazine the exact footage already exposed so that the camera's footage counter can be reset at that number when the partly used magazine is reinserted. A disadvantage of magazine film is that the container, which goes to the processor, adds to the cost of the film package.

The continual quest for simplified loading has included an 8mm camera design (by Carena) for automatic loading by means of a swivel-mounted spring guide which slides the film leader into the core of the takeup spool. A dual-run mechanism (by Sekonic) pivots the entire film chamber at midreel, thus eliminating the need to remove the magazine and turn it over. More recently Eastman Kodak, pioneer in 8mm magazines, introduced a lighttight drop-in cassette for one of its movie cameras. This *drop-in* loading provided by several cameras does away with threading and incorporates a pressure plate to hold the film securely in contact with the gate of the camera. Unlike plant-loaded magazines, the cassette is user-loaded and reusable and so does not add to the cost of each film. Also, for an initial expenditure of extra cassettes, the user can preload several standard rolls of 8mm film for continuous shooting.

Lenses. The same basic difference as that explained in Chapter 2 between preset and adjustable still cameras holds true for fixed and focusing lenses. In movie cameras, too, there are simple "box" types with *fixed-focus* lenses that predetermine the acceptable range of sharpness, like the so-called universal focus of fifteen feet (page 65). Such settings are generally quite satisfactory for long and medium shots, but not for real close-ups.

If the lens has *adjustable focusing,* it can be set for camera-to-subject distances, to focus sharply on the major interest of individual scenes. (Review the effect of aperture on depth of field in Chapter 5.) Some cameras have one lens with a threaded mount for interchanging with telephoto and wide-angle lenses. Some models have one nonremovable lens which will accept a lens converter to hold supplementary lenses designed to alter the focal length.

LENS TURRETS. Turret cameras have two or three lens mounts on a kind of wheel, called a *turret,* which rotates to bring the lens you wish to use into position. These mounts may hold nonremovable lenses or lens converters for complete interchangeability.

VARIABLE SINGLE LENSES. A more convenient method of gaining the result of interchangeable lenses is with a *zoom* lens, a type whose focal length can be varied continuously for wide-angle, telephoto, or normal effects. This permits you to film a sequence without having to back away or move in closer. Viewfinders on most zoom cameras adjust to indicate how much is being included in the picture as the lens is moved back and forth. Zoom lenses are available on some still cameras, but their principal use is for movies.

STANDARD FOCAL LENGTHS. A normal lens on a 16mm camera has a focal length (see page 37) of 25mm, which is about one inch, and an 8mm camera lens has approximately half that focal length: 12mm or 13mm, as marked on your camera. However, the normal lenses of some 8mm cameras have a focal length of only 10mm, to take in a wider picture area.

APERTURES. Lenses for home-movie cameras have the same scale of f/stops—often indicated by the number without the f/—as still cameras. Standard full stops are: 22, 16, 11, 8, 5.6, 4, 2.8, 2, 1.4. On some cameras the largest aperture may vary from standard full-stop numbers—for example, 1.9 or 2.3 or 2.7—as explained on page 43. The sharpness range of all lenses extends to infinity; it is the near limit that changes. How this near limit varies for 8mm fixed-focus lenses is shown in this table of approximate distances (in feet) at different apertures:

Aperture	1.9–2	2.3–2.8	4	5.6	8	11	16
Distance	10	8½	6	4½	3½	2½	2

Camera Speeds. The speed at which a camera or projector is operated is identified in *frames per second,* abbreviated *fps,* and indicates how many individual pictures, or frames, reach the film or screen during each second of operation. Standard speed for the 8mm cameras used by most home-movie makers is 16 fps. This covers scenics and the everyday activities usually essayed by amateurs and casual photographers. For a normal effect—that is, reproduction of the subject matter as it looked when taken—the projection speed should be the same as the taking speed.

For professional photography with a 16mm camera, or for panning with a smaller camera, the standard speed is 24 fps. Other speeds are used for catching faster action than average and for special effects.

Variations in subject action on the screen should be effected by changing the camera speed, not by varying the projector speed.

SLOW-MOTION PICTURES. With cameras that offer a choice of operating speeds, a smooth slow-motion effect can be achieved by photographing action at faster-than-standard speeds. A sports action taken at 32 fps, for example, and projected at the standard rate of 16 frames, will seem to be occurring at an unnaturally slow pace. This is due mainly to the fact that you are seeing more than the normal number of individual pictures per second. In other words, if you take two minutes to expose a roll of 8mm film at 32 fps, it will take four minutes to project it at 16 fps; therefore the screened action will appear to be in relatively slow motion.

An even faster taking speed, such as 48 or 64, will further decrease the apparent pace, and is especially useful for checking on sports form, like a golf swing or a ski jump. In complex laboratories and test centers camera speeds may run to thousands of frames per second for studying at measurable slow motion such "action" as the fall of liquids or the flight of aerial objects. The opposite of slow motion has very limited use and can cause an annoying flicker problem.

FLICKERS. When shooting at slower-than-standard camera speeds, amateurs sometimes encounter a problem reminiscent of Hollywood's earliest productions, colloquially called "flickers." This can occur when motion is photographed at 12 or 8 frames (as in the days of hand-cranked cameras) and projected at 16 fps. What happens is that the decreased taking speed causes an increased time lag between frames, which is visible when projected at the standard speed. Such a sequence is likely to flicker on the screen in the jerkily speeded style of an old Keystone-cops routine—and indeed, entertaining comic effects can be obtained this way, if that is what you want. Otherwise, slower speeds than 16 fps are not advisable for continuous-run shooting.

SINGLE-FRAME EXPOSURES. Most cameras provide for single-frame as well as continuous-run operation. If you set the single-frame release according to your instruction booklet and the speed indicator at the recommended fps you can make one-at-a-time pictures for movie titles. This operation also makes it possible to employ techniques similar to those described in the chapter on close-ups for photographing objects you might like to splice into your edited film.

Animation, which refers to the apparent action of subjects not capable of live motion, is also accomplished by separate exposures of one or two frames. The subject might be a series of cartoon drawings, like Mickey Mouse, or it could be some inanimate object which you move slightly between each exposure. If you wish to indicate your itinerary of a trip abroad, for instance, you might place a toy plane on a map at New York or your home city, shoot a second or two, then place the plane on a picture of clouds for another exposure, then on another map, moving it step by step so that it appears to be flying to London, Rome, Tokyo, or wherever the motion pictures to be shown were photographed.

Exposure Compensation. Camera speeds different from the standard operating speed on which normal exposure is based will require some exposure compensation. Since a slow-motion film shot at a fast 32 fps allows each frame only half as much light as when taken at a standard 16 fps, the picture may turn out rather dim. To avoid underexposure, use the next largest lens aperture: if a recommended lens setting is $f/8$ at 16 fps, you would use $f/5.6$ to photograph the same subject at 32 fps. Open up a full stop more for 64 fps and additional half-stops for the intermediate speeds of 24 fps or 48 fps. Conversely, the lens should be stopped down to avoid overexposure at slow speeds.

PROJECTOR BASICS

Any projector, like an enlarger (see page 264), is fundamentally a camera in reverse: instead of receiving an image through a cone of light contracted to a pinpoint within the camera, a projector lens is designed to send an image out through an expanding cone of light. To create apparent motion on a screen, this beam of light is interrupted by the shutter action to produce a light cycle of individual pictures all separated by an alternating dark cycle. At standard projection speeds the transmitted images are well within the persistence-of-vision norm, and thus the subjects appear to be in motion.

Essential Projector Parts. Besides the lens and shutter, a projector body must have places for the feed reel of exposed and processed film and for the takeup reel which receives the film during projection. (See Figure 143.) There must be a power mechanism to transport the film past the aperture through which the successive images

Fig. 143.—A home-movie projector.

reach the screen. The projector must also contain a lamp, along with switches, controls, and cord necessary to the operation of the light source, and a blower for cooling the machine.

All 8mm projectors accommodate at least 200 feet of film, and 16mm projectors at least 400 feet; either size reel when filled adds up to a 15- or 16-minute movie. While it is quite possible to project your footage "as is" in the 50-foot lengths of 8mm film returned by the processor, this is hardly the way to show your pictures to advantage. Changing film after every four minutes is hard on both audience and projectionist, and it is a rare film indeed that does not cry out for a bit of editing. Some kind of splicer for joining the ends of cut lengths of film into one long strip, and at least one large reel onto which you can rewind your spliced film, should therefore be considered part of your essential equipment.

Modern Projector Features. Variations and refinements in the different makes of projectors are about as numerous and fast-changing as those in cameras, and no operating instructions could encompass all types. In fact, detailed explanations here for threading and operating could very easily confuse rather than enlighten: it is necessary to study the manufacturer's manual carefully, to refer to the step-by-step instructions during practice runs, and to ask a dealer or other qualified representative to demonstrate any points that may not be entirely clear.

Some of the ways in which projectors vary are in the quality of the lens and the relative convenience of different self-threading mechanisms. Some projectors feature automatic stopping in the event of film breakage; and some have smoother control of forward, still, and reverse projection. The automation principle is even carried into such niceties as the turning off of room lamps when the projector lamp is turned on and their automatically re-lighting when the projector lamp is turned off.

Sound Accompaniments. Another variation stems from the increasing availability of sound projectors—a far cry from the earliest home movies which were usually accompanied by the halting commentary of the movie makers and the noisy whirr of the projection machinery. Since then there have been countless developments in stereo records, magnetic tapes and recorders, film striping, and projectors complete with built-in speakers and the equipment for adding your own synchronized words and music.

Musical records can supply a pleasing background for your movie if you can find unobtrusive ones of really appropriate mood. Records or any taped musical accompaniment should be far enough from the projector, perhaps in another room, not to compete with your movie for the audience's attention. Avoid vocal numbers and popular tunes, lest you find your audience singing rather than viewing.

Tape recorders are widely used to coordinate your own sound accompaniment with a specific movie. What you record on the tape can help maintain continuity in your film or build contrast when the mood changes, or it can interpret a mood. For example, your screen may show a young couple strolling along a deserted beach: you can select some light romantic music to indicate their contentment or you can choose music which will communicate a desperate loneliness.

Film Stripes. If you own a sound projector, you can have a magnetic track added to old or new films. This exceedingly narrow coating, measured in thousandths of an inch, must go between the sprocket holes and the edge of the film itself, and is called a *stripe*. Your music or commentary is recorded while you project the striped film, then played back by projecting the film again. Like magnetic tapes, a sound track can be "erased" if you wish to make changes in it.

Although it can be put in simple terms, this is a rather complex business. For one thing, sound-on-film impulses register many frames ahead of the corresponding image, so compensating footage must be inserted or "looped" into the film. This is particularly tricky when attempting lip synchronization during a post-recording of sound for your film. It is not really for beginners.

Image Size and Brightness. Three factors affect the satisfactory reproduction of pictures on a home-movie screen: wattage of the projector lamp, focal length of the projector lens, and screen distance from the projector.

PROJECTOR LAMP. The brighter the lamp in a projector, the brighter and farther it will throw an image. However, there is a safe and sane wattage, normally 150 watts for 8mm projectors, and the manufacturer's recommendation should be observed. Brighter lamps than the recommended maximum may be more than the cooling fan can cope with, subjecting both film and equipment to possible damage.

EFFECT OF FOCAL LENGTH. The projector-to-screen distance required for a satisfactory image depends on the focal length of the lens; shorter lenses will fill the screen at shorter distances than longer lenses. Some 8mm projectors have substandard focal lengths for showing movies in quite small rooms. If the projector has a zoom lens, variable from 10mm to 25mm, for example, it can adapt focal length to the distance and screen you wish to use.

SCREEN DISTANCE FROM PROJECTOR. An increase in the projector-to-screen distance will increase the image size but decrease its brilliance. You can experiment with this by moving your projector back or forward, but the instruction booklet of your projector should be consulted for the effective distance at which its lens should be used. Here are some typical picture widths at varying room-size distances for 8mm projectors of 1-inch and ¾-inch focal lengths:

Projector-screen distance in feet	8	10	12	16	20	25
Image width 1-inch lens	1'6"	1'10"	2'3"	3'0"	3'9"	4'8"
Image width ¾-inch lens	2'0"	2'6"	3'0"	4'0"	5'0"	

Projection Screens. Screens for viewing home movies or color slides are classified according to degree of surface brilliance and generally should be suited to the size of the room and the long-and-narrow or shallow-and-wide arrangement of viewers' seats. Sparkly beaded screens give the best and brightest image when the audience is close to the projection axis—to the center aisle, as it were; from a side-aisle seat the image is less satisfactory.

If your audience is to sit in a rather spread-out formation, it is preferable to choose a matte screen with a less brilliant surface. There is also an in-between lenticular screen whose surface yields a brighter image than matte screens but less bright than beaded screens.

A reasonably good screen can be made by covering a section of wallboard or heavy mounting board with flat white paint and hanging it on a wall. A wall itself as a screen substitute is almost certain to distort the color quality of the image. Other makeshifts, like white sheets or window shades, are not really opaque, so the projected light will pass through them with some loss of brightness.

Well—now that you have camera, projector, screen, and sound possibilities, how about making a movie?

MOVIE MAKING

Home movies can be free-style footage just for the family, like still pictures of the snapshot variety, or they can be more like exhibition prints and slides, the result of planning, patience, and practice. If you are a beginner, don't accumulate all the accessories and gadgets on the market at once: costly equipment is not a guarantee of good pictures. By the time you have familiarized yourself with camera and projector, you will have a better idea of which additional tools will be most helpful to you in making better movies.

The everyday home activities that suggest themselves for action effects in still pictures (see Chapter 14) make good starting subjects for the movie camera: children at their busy games, a day at the zoo, boy on bike headed for a spill, preparations for a wedding or vacation, a birthday party, or a backyard cookout. Instead of trying to stop motion at its peak, to catch a fleeting smile, or to pan with the cycling boy, you should photograph the more or less complete motion as it occurs.

The Story. A motion picture should tell a story naturally, with logical continuity; it should show genuine activity—people doing something, things happening—not static scenery. Study the possibilities, watch for filming opportunities but don't force them; avoid the "Smile please" or "Look at the birdie" business: it results in artificiality whether the pictures are still photographs or home movies.

The word *continuity* is longer than *story* but really refers to the same idea—in a longer way, since it may imply more extensive planning and a shooting script to detail the order of scenes. Home movies are usually more casual and can be reorganized by editing. However, it is preferable to do your editing in the camera as far as practicable; this means shooting scenes in the right order so that the film will be presentable with a minimum of post-processing work on your part.

Subject Distances. How far away your subject is from the camera determines whether you call your shots close, medium, or long. When you close in on a subject at about 6 feet or less, the shot is considered a *close-up;* if the subject is an adult, this would include head and shoulders. A *medium shot* is considered to be subject matter filmed at distances between 6 and 25 feet, which can include standing adults or jumping children. A scene filmed at more than 25 feet is referred to as a *long shot* and is often used to set the stage for the activity to follow.

A movie sequence, which is a series of related scenes, might begin with a long shot to establish a locale or a mood, then move to some medium shots to show what action is happening, and finally close in on the climax or main interest of the sequence. Shots do not have to be in any fixed order, but they should be varied and should include fairly frequent close-ups. If there is a rule, it is simply to shoot from the distance that gets in the pertinent subject matter and gives you a good composition.

Scene Length. An average scene is about 10 seconds, but this does not mean that all scenes should be that length. To avoid monotony, scene lengths should be varied, like subject distances, and the subject matter itself should be your guide as to whether it needs 3 or 8 seconds' worth of film, or perhaps 12 or 20 seconds. With practice you will often know approximately how many seconds you have ticked off without even looking at the footage indicator—the way a doctor can count pulse beats without actually timing them.

Action on the screen is seldom as long as the actual happening. There is a tendency at first to shoot too much in each scene, to get in every detail. By studying your results and motion pictures generally—as one would with still pictures—you can learn to condense less important scenes and emphasize key ones.

Handling the Camera. Holding the camera close to your eye will not only help keep it steady but will also show you more accurately the area your lens is taking in; otherwise the subject may turn out smaller and more distant than you expect. You may need to tilt the camera slightly upward for parallax correction, as explained on page 58. Panning (see page 168) is not an appropriate technique for amateur movies; let the movement be in the scene you are shooting, not in you or your camera. Some cameras come equipped with, or will accept, a "pistol grip," which is a shaped handle for the base of the camera and an aid to steadiness. (See Figure 9.)

Experienced home-movie makers often use a tripod for camera steadiness and for better planning of shots. A tripod-held camera allows you to study the scene more carefully, choose a different angle before shooting, check on your lighting and exposure, and even to set the self-timer so you can slip into the scene yourself. It also restrains any panning impulses. A tripod is almost essential for steadiness when using a telephoto lens or a zoom lens at its longest focal position.

The impulse to zoom wildly needs restraint, too. Like panning rapidly or unevenly, zooming in and out on scene after scene can result in footage too dizzying to inflict on even your most lenient friends. Zoom sparingly and purposefully, the way you would use separate lenses of different focal lengths, to gain an effect of going in close or backing off for a wider view.

Lighting. The principles of good lighting explained at length in Chapters 7 and 8 pertain to motion pictures as well as stills. Learn to recognize basic light conditions outdoors and the direction of the light, using a light meter as a guide. Because motion is involved, it is generally impractical to use portable reflectors, although you may be able to take advantage of natural reflectors. For shapely clouds and haze penetration, the no-factor "skylight" filter may be used.

Before filming indoors, review the section on photofloods in Chapter 11 and the arrangements of artificial lighting for portraits in Chapter 16. Instead of flashholders, movie cameras accept an accessory known as a *light bar* holding 2 to 4 small reflector photofloods which may vary in size from 200 to 375 watts each. Like flash, the bar can be used on or off camera, for bounce or fill-in lighting; unlike flash, it requires an electrical connection, so its usefulness is more or less restricted to indoor shooting. On the whole, you will get more pleasing and interesting pictures without a light bar.

Newer and more versatile than light bars are the battery-powered rechargeable lightweight lamps for movie cameras. For filming in natural light on a shaded porch or backyard patio where you have electrical outlets, you can increase the illumination by setting up some blue photoflood lamps. This technique overcomes some of the lack of mobility which a light bar imposes, but be careful not to overload the circuit (see page 120).

Filters for Indoor-Outdoor Color Film. A technique that permits shifting between indoor and outdoor lighting without changing magazines or cassettes is to use a film balanced for artificial light (like Type A Kodachrome), adding a No. 85 daylight filter when shooting in natural light. Some newer movie cameras have a built-in filter, to convert indoor-outdoor film by pressing a button which slides the filter in front of the lens or away from the lens.

For 8mm cameras color film is used almost exclusively; in fact, at this writing, the popular domestic film manufacturers do not produce an 8mm film in black and white. However, black-and-white duplicates of 8mm color film can be ordered through some dealers.

Camera-setting Reminders. (1) Focus affects picture sharpness at different distances. Close-ups have a shallower field of sharpness than long shots. Preset cameras have a fixed focus and should be used at distances of six feet or more. (2) Lens aperture is the main control over the amount of light reaching film. The lowest f/number is the largest opening, and the highest f/number is the smallest opening. Too much light (overexposure) causes washed-out colors; too little light (underexposure) causes dark pictures. (3) Camera speed governs whether the filmed motion will appear normal or slowed-down or extra fast. Speeds other than normal affect the amount of light reaching the film: faster camera speeds admit less light, and slower speeds more light. Some 8mm preset cameras have a fixed speed.

MOVIE SHOWMANSHIP

The activities you photographed are returned to you from the processor in short reels: fifty feet of pictures for 8mm film. If you have photographed the activities in the order in which you intend to show them, you may run the film through your projector and decide it needs no more editing than a few splices, especially if the pictures are intended solely to please family and fond relatives. If less personal footage is to be shown to friends or club members, it should be edited into a movie of more general interest.

Splicing. Defective frames, such as overexposed, underexposed, blurred, or dull pictures which may mar your movie, can be cut out of the film and the remaining pieces joined end to end. Shortening any scenes which seem to drag will improve the pace of your movie. There are splicers to do the job quickly and neatly, either by joining the cut ends with pressure-sensitive splicing tape or by welding them with splicing cement. Tapes are newer and generally preferred, particularly for quick repairs when a film breaks during projection. Those without a commercial splicer but with time and ingenuity can find, in various home-movie books, simple do-it-yourself guides for making splicer and rewind substitutes.

Titling. The easiest titling, like editing, is done as an integral part of the movie you are filming, using the single-frame release to photograph place names, recognizable landmarks, and whatever informative signs will add to your story. For impromptu lettering you can use

Fig. 144.—A simple titler (left) and focal frame (right) for use in close-ups.

chalk on a sidewalk, lipstick on a car window, or a finger in the sand of a beach. You can make a batch of titles separately, to be spliced in, by using a titler or simple focal frame and techniques similar to those described in the section on making title slides in Chapter 17. (See Figure 144.) Some of the materials mentioned there are included in movie-titling kits available in photographic stores.

Editing Methods. Combining sections of old or new films into a ten- or fifteen-minute movie may require considerable planning and patient work. The more interested and methodical you are about editing, the more rewarding can be your finished movie. You may be able to edit your own movies satisfactorily by simply projecting them two or three times, making written or mental notations of what you wish to cut, splicing the films accordingly, and rewinding them onto a larger reel. For more extensive revisions there are complete editing kits with splicer and tapes, a pair of rewinds, and an *editor,* which is a miniature viewing screen-and-projector for conveniently studying the movie material. The kits vary in size and price, but the basic setup is similar to the diagram in Figure 145.

To use the editing setup for an all-out rearrangement of many films, have a package of small index cards handy and, as you critically view each scene, make whatever brief notations will identify

SPLICER
Fig. 145.—Components of a basic editing outfit.

the scene later, using a separate card for each scene so that you can shuffle and re-shuffle them into a final order. Nick the edge of the film you are editing at the beginning and end of a scene or sequence you wish to keep, and cut out the unwanted sections.

If you are going to all this effort, you may want to make yourself a wood T-rack to hold the strips that are to be re-examined and spliced into the movie. Make a "T" two or three feet tall and nail the bottom to a wastebasket or sturdy box. To the crossbar on top, which should be about the width of the basket, nail a row of small brads on which you can hang the pieces of inspected film.

The Commentary. Your completed movie can be shown as a silent film, accompanied simply by your occasional comments. Or you may prefer to plan a musical background, suiting it to your pictures and your equipment, as discussed earlier in this chapter.

Any narration or comments, whether spoken during projection or incorporated in a sound track, should be planned as thoughtfully as a musical accompaniment. Subordinate what is said to what is being seen, give the pictures a chance to speak for themselves, and supplement them with as few words as clarity requires. Refrain from editorializing: if an action is breathtaking and suspenseful, or a fiesta is colorful and gay, let your pictures say so.

An effective commentary should also maintain a consistent viewpoint. If you start with a third-person documentary style, don't suddenly switch to first-person phrases or shift tenses. Present-tense narration, as a rule, is preferable to saying something "was" or "happened"; try to make it seem as if the action on the screen is occurring while your audience is looking at the movie.

Show Business. As far as possible the business of setting up your show should be done before your audience arrives. The projector should be threaded and focused, the screen in place, and room lights ready to be switched off efficiently. Try to see that the projector cord is placed so that it will not be tripped over; as an extra precaution, you can wind it several times around the leg of a projector table to keep the projector from being pulled off. If you have a sound accompaniment, test it and adjust the volume. If you are showing separate reels of film and must rethread the projector during the show, don't keep the audience waiting while you rewind the first reel: do that later. Finally, don't make your show so long that the audience becomes restless—and the projector overheated.

General Maintenance. When you switch the projector lamp off at the end of the show, it is good practice to keep the motor running for three or four minutes so the cooling fan can lower the temperature of the equipment. Some projectors and movie cameras require lubricating, others are self-lubricating and could be damaged by oiling; consult your instruction booklet about this and also about cleaning the gate and lenses.

All films should be protected from excessive heat and humidity (see page 54), and exposed films should be sent out for processing without undue delay. If your movie films are worth editing and worth keeping, store the reels in proper cans and label them for future shows.

22

More Than a Hobby

PHOTOGRAPHY for most amateurs is a pleasant hobby, engaged in only occasionally by some and more whole-heartedly by others. It can, however, be also a source of limited and unpredictable income, a method of therapy, or a preliminary training ground for a professional career.

Amateur Contests. The principal "market" for photographs of the strictly amateur variety consists of the numerous contests offered periodically by newspapers, magazines, and business concerns. Some are limited to persons of school ages or to a specific theme; some are open to all amateurs. Usually very few restrictions are placed on subject matter, in order to encourage the originality that makes a prize winner. Look for details of such contests in photography and general magazines as well as local publications. Only a few entrants can win, of course, but acceptances without prize money can be a source of stimulation and gratification.

Other Amateur Markets. Amateur photographs are occasionally purchased for publication if they are interesting, timely, technically adequate, and meet the needs of the individual picture editor. Generally it is preferable to send a written inquiry, with a brief description of your material, before submitting the photographs. Calendar and postcard publishers may be interested in exceptional color pictures, particularly if they are color negatives or larger transparencies than 35mm. Don't tackle the nationally famous magazines right off, but browse through some of the hundreds of little known periodicals to see what kind of pictures they are using.

There are a number of books which catalogue the specific requirements of many photographic markets; however, it is difficult to keep such lists currently accurate, so you should double-check on the particular markets in which you might be interested. The large majority of these published requirements specify film sizes larger than 35mm—usually 4 x 5 press sizes.

Spot news pictures have been taken by amateurs who happened to be on hand at the right time—with a ready camera. If you have photographed a holdup or a fire or a crash, don't stop to develop your film: phone the picture editor of your newspaper, describe what you have, and find out whether he is interested. If he is, he will want you to rush your undeveloped film to him. Insurance companies are sometimes glad to get an eye-witness photograph of an accident. If you take such a picture, get the names and addresses of the parties involved, and write them later what pictures are available. Real-estate agents often like to be saved the bother of taking their own pictures of listed property; inquire first about their interest and any angles they would like emphasized.

When you do succeed in selling some photographs, remember that you are an amateur; be reasonable about prices, which will be very modest in most instances.

Legal Aspects. Pictures can be taken in most public places without restrictions; however, museums, libraries, private parks, theaters, and other places can forbid the use of cameras on the premises as they see fit. Taking candid snapshots of persons in streets, transportation terminals, and other public areas for your own private enjoyment does not require written consent. But selling candids for trade purposes does require a formal release; otherwise such use of the pictures may be considered an invasion of privacy.

Publications or reputable businesses to whom you might sell amateur photographs will probably give you the necessary information. If in doubt, you can consult a book entitled *Photography and the Law* written by Chernoff and Sarbin.

Photography as a Therapy. For more than twenty years photography has been adopted as a therapeutic technique in a number of hospitals, rehabilitation institutes, and youth centers through a volunteer service program in New York City; and there are similar if smaller programs in other cities. Equipment is usually donated to the program, and photographers who are willing to donate a few hours each week are trained to assist small groups, under hospital or welfare supervision, to use cameras and to learn the mysteries of developing and printing. This creative hobby has in many cases proved to be "just what the doctor ordered," giving handicapped patients a genuine interest and sense of accomplishment. You may wish to share your own photographic skills and enthusiasm by organizing such a service program in your area.

Careers in Photography. If you are a beginner now but seriously considering photography as a profession, it is worthwhile to channel much of your amateur shooting in the general direction of the photographic field in which you are primarily interested. If you look forward to training as a photojournalist, for example, practice at as many small events as possible—family outings, school sports, local awards, anything that will help you develop an alert eye and accurate timing skill. If you expect to become a portrait specialist, concentrate on people and lighting.

If you should decide to take up photography as a profession, you must learn to work with larger cameras, more complex equipment, and must either attend a commercial photography school or become apprenticed to a professional. Besides technical and general photographic instruction, large schools of photography offer a choice of courses designed to qualify students for work in advertising, illustration, fashion, publicity; industrial, scientific, and medical photography; studio and home portraiture of children and adults, bridal and social events; retouching and darkroom techniques.

Apprentice photographers are traditionally assigned to the darkroom lab, which has always been excellent basic experience for other assignments, particularly in the opportunity it affords the observant worker to profit from the photographic mistakes of others. But more and more, today's lab technician is a creative artist, imparting to the finished print some wanted quality which the camera has failed to capture.

It's Up to You. One of the characteristics of a successful photographer, amateur or professional, is a genuine enthusiasm for his work. If you really enjoy making pictures, you will keep learning from them and will acquire new techniques as needed in new phases. When there is a choice between subject matter or technique, subordinate the technical concern to the subject; go by how you feel about it rather than by how someone else claims it ought to be done.

The essence of a good photograph is that it comes alive by what you have contributed to it. In the final analysis it is you, the photographer, who must teach yourself.

WHAT'S WRONG? (A Checklist to Help Identify Some Causes of Unsatisfactory Pictures)

Blurring. If subject only is blurred, subject moved too fast for shutter speed used. If entire picture is blurred, camera moved or was not correctly focused. Check also the cleanliness of lens.

Double exposure. When two pictures are superimposed into one scrambled image, the film was not advanced after each exposure.

Lightstruck pictures. Usually caused by light rays striking the lens, especially if no lens shade was used. May also be caused by light leaks in camera, such as an improperly closed camera back.

Negative entirely blank (or *slide transparencies* densely *black*). If there is no image at all, film was not exposed. Film may have been improperly loaded, perhaps not firmly attached to takeup spool. Flash synchronization may have failed, possibly because of exhausted batteries. Lens cap may have been left on during intended exposure.

Negative too dark. Overexposure causes excessive density in the negative and a lack of detail in the print.

Negative too thin. Underexposure causes a lack of density in the negative and too light, washed-out images in the print.

Off-color pictures. May be caused by leaving a filter for black-and-white pictures on lens when switching to color film, by using a color film balanced for daylight in artificial light or vice versa, or by using an unfamiliar film with a different color balance than expected. Reddish, greenish, or faded colors, especially at ends and edges of film, may result from age or storage conditions. Check expiration date on film package, avoid excessive heat and humidity, and have exposed film processed promptly.

WHAT IS IT? (A Glossary of Common Photographic Terms)

Aberrations. Optical defects that cause a lens to record a less than perfect image.

Abrasions. Defects resembling pencil marks or scratches on an emulsion surface.

Achromatic. Term describing a lens that is relatively free from chromatic aberration.

Acid fixing bath. A hypo solution with an added acid to make an image on negative or print more or less permanent.

Actinic light. Pertains to rays capable of producing strong photo-chemical changes rather than heat; most actinic of the visible rays are blue and violet.

Adapter. Any accessory that permits a camera or lens mount to accept additional or alternative equipment.

Anastigmat. Term describing a lens that, besides being corrected for common errors, has been further corrected to focus vertical and horizontal lines with equal sharpness.

Aperture. The lens opening through which light passes to the focal plane, the size of the opening being governed by the f/stops.

ASA. Abbreviation of American Standards Association, used with a number to designate the emulsion speed of the film.

Available light. Existing and limited illumination under which photographs are taken without flash or other supplementary lighting.

Blowup. *See* Enlargement.

Bounce light. Diffuse illumination produced by directing a flash or flood lamp at a ceiling or wall instead of directly at the subject.

Burning-in. An enlarging technique for giving more exposure to certain areas of an image that need darkening.

Cable release. A thin flexible cord which attaches to the shutter release, allowing the actual exposure to be made without jarring the camera.

Cassette or **cartridge.** A lighttight metal container into which 35mm and other films are preloaded; also the twin container into which the film is advanced after each exposure.

Contrast. Usually indicates the differences in the reflective abilities of light and dark areas of a subject; it may also refer to the variations in intensities of illumination falling on a subject.

Crop. To trim or mask out unwanted portions of a picture to improve the composition.

Definition. Refers to the resolving power of a lens, which is its capacity to produce sharply defined images, and to the sharpness of the images produced.

Densitometer. A device for measuring the density of a negative to determine its printability.

Depth of field. The distance from the nearest to the farthest planes that appear acceptably sharp in the subject area on which the lens is focused.

Desensitizer. A chemical agent used to reduce the sensitivity of exposed color or high-speed film to facilitate development in somewhat brighter light than a darkroom safelight.

Developer. A chemical solution which makes visible the latent image in an exposed film.

Diaphragm. A mechanism for controlling the amount of light admitted through the lens; the f/stop being used indicates the diameter of an iris diaphragm during exposure.

DIN. Abbreviation of Deutsche Industrie Norm: a European system of designating emulsion speeds, similar to our ASA.

Distortion. An imperfect or unnatural image resulting from lens defects or from incorrect handling of the camera.

Dodging. An enlarging technique for shielding certain areas of an image in order to lighten them while other areas are being exposed.

Emulsion. The light-sensitive coating of films or photographic papers.

Enlargement or **blowup.** A print obtained by projecting an image of larger size than the original onto sensitized paper.

Exposure. Denotes the combination of shutter time and lens aperture that permits a controlled amount of light to pass through the lens and record an image on film.

Exposure meter. An instrument for measuring the light intensity of a given subject, or the intensity of the light falling upon the subject, in order to determine the best exposure.

f/numbers or **f/stops.** A system for determining and adjusting lens apertures.

Ferrotype. A print which has been given a glossy finish on a thin sheet of enameled or plated metal; also the process of glossing.

Filter factor. The number by which basic exposure must be multiplied to compensate for the reduced illumination admitted through the lens when a specific filter is used.

Flatness. Insufficient contrast between lights, darks, and midtones caused by flat lighting, overexposure, or faulty development.

Focal length. A fixed attribute of a lens: the distance from its optical center to a point at which a distant object can be sharply focused.

Focal-plane shutter. A curtain type that operates immediately in front of the film.

Focus. Refers to the point at which light rays converge to form an image, and to the adjusting of the lens to produce a sharp image.

Focusing screen. The groundglass viewfinders of certain cameras.

Fog. A hazy veil that clouds a negative or print which has been improperly developed. A fogged appearance can also result from light leakage.

Grain. Mottled appearance of a print due to noticeable enlargement of individual or clumped silver particles in an emulsion.

Guide numbers. An exposure-index system for flash, based on the combination of a specific lamp, film, shutter speed, and aperture to be used.

Halation. A kind of blurred halo, usually around a bright object, caused by the spreading of light beyond its intended boundaries.

Halftone. Middle tones between lightest and darkest areas; a photo-chemical reproduction of a subject having several tonal graduations.

Hyperfocal distance. The nearest distance at which a given lens can be focused to produce satisfactory sharpness from half that distance to infinity.

Hypo. Common term for a fixing bath; derives from sodium hyposulfite.

Infrared. Light rays beyond the red end of the visible spectrum.

Intensification. A chemical process for increasing the density of an over-thin, light negative; opposite of reduction.

Latent image. The undeveloped invisible image in an emulsion which has been exposed.

Latitude. The range within which variations in exposure or development may be made without detriment to the quality of the finished photograph.

Lens shade or **lens hood.** A detachable accessory used to shield the lens from extraneous light.

Light meter. *See* Exposure meter.

Montage or **photomontage.** A composite of two or more photographs.

Negative. Exposed sensitized film or paper on which the actual lights and darks of the subject are reversed; the opposite of positive.

Orthochromatic. A type of black-and-white film that is insensitive to reds but sensitive to other colors of the visible spectrum.

Panchromatic. A film that is sensitive to all colors of the visible spectrum.

Panning. A technique of following an action with a parallel movement of the camera.

Photogram. A shadow-pattern photograph made without a lens by exposing objects arranged on sensitized paper to light.

Photogrammetry. The science of making maps and surveys through measurements obtained from photographs, generally aerial views.

Photomontage. *See* Montage.

Positive. A print or transparency in which the colors or tones appear as seen in the subject; the opposite of negative.

Primary colors. The three components of white light: blue, green, and red.

Redevelopment. A step in the process of intensifying or toning when the negative image is bleached and then redeveloped in order to produce a specific effect.

Reduction. A chemical process for decreasing the density of an overdense, dark negative; the opposite of intensification.

Resolving power. The ability of a lens or an emulsion to reproduce sharp images or fine detail.

Reticulation. A wrinkled or leathery formation on film resulting from temperature changes or chemical action which causes the gelatin of the emulsion to expand or contract too rapidly.

Reversal negative. A negative that has been developed, re-exposed on film, bleached, and redeveloped to form a positive in which the lights and darks are reversed.

Safelight. A darkroom lamp whose low intensity and color filter does not affect sensitized materials.

Shutter. A camera's mechanical device for controlling the length of time for admitting light to the film.

Solarization. A darkroom technique for getting positive and negative effects in the same photograph, usually by exposing the negative briefly to light when it is partially developed, then continuing the development.

Spotting. A kind of retouching to remove tiny spots from a negative or print.

Super slide. A rollfilm transparency larger than 35mm which is mounted in a standard 2-inch slide mount.

Toning. Changing the overall tone of a black-and-white print by a chemical bath; a sepia toner is used for a warmer effect and a blue toner for a colder effect.

Vignette. A form of dodging in which the light is regulated to obtain an image, usually a portrait, that fades off at the margins with no sharp outlines.

INDEX